Managing by Objectives

MANAGING BY OBJECTIVES

An Operating Guide to Faster and More Profitable Results

PAUL MALI

Graduate School of Business
University of Hartford
and Paul Mali & Associates

WILEY-INTERSCIENCE, a Division of John Wiley & Sons, Inc.
New York • London • Sydney • Toronto

Library of Congress Cataloging in Publication Data:

Mali, Paul.
  Managing by objectives—a systems approach.

  Includes bibliographical references.
  1. Management. I. Title.

HD31.M284   658.4   72-1803
ISBN 0-471-56575-X

Printed in the United States of America

10 9 8 7 6 5 4 3

Dedicated to more than 15,000 managers, supervisors, and executives in more than 7500 companies scattered in more than 100 cities throughout the United States and Canada who attended my seminars on *Managing by Objectives.*

Preface

In recent years, managing by objectives has been one of the most striking developments in the managerial art of getting results in an organization. Hundreds upon hundreds of firms, from small enterprises to giant public corporations, report accomplishments of a most astonishing and profitable nature. A paper mill in Massachusetts introduced the technique and experienced a 12 percent reduction in operating costs. A national restaurant chain, using it as a management system oriented toward customer satisfaction, achieved a 22 percent improvement in sales. A hardware corporation in Connecticut used it to upgrade foreman "performance" and achieved a 15 percent improvement in productivity. An international fruit produce company, which was experiencing difficulty with low-priority projects that needed to be completed, introduced the technique in their special projects division and reduced schedule slippage by 8 weeks. An eastern seaboard shipyard used the technique for operations audit and achieved a systems "control at a glance" for reducing lag response time 30 percent. A Chicago printing firm employed the strategy to gain a clearer and more accurate appraisal of performance, which resulted in less guesswork, less subjectivity, and less reluctance on the part of the appraiser. A computer manufacturer in New York found the technique most useful for applying special motivators by levels in the managerial hierarchy. A Montreal government agency used the technique to implement job enrichment and enlargement for employee motivation. A department store chain with headquarters in Detroit used it as a unifying system for their far-flung units and experienced a 20 percent improvement in profits. A Connecticut educational system employed the technique to guide growth and expansion of multiple units and achieved student enrollment and full-time equivalency within 5 percent of projections. Other accomplishments have been as varied as work simplification, equitable compensation, better utilization of equipment, starting a new business, inventory control, and even organizational clarity.

The success of these organizations has been based primarily on the effective use of managing by objectives as a management system. This effectiveness has been due in large measure to a clear understanding of the concept of managing by objectives and of how to introduce and develop it within the enterprise.

It is clear from the vast body of information and knowledge developing around this concept that a dynamic management way of life is steadily maturing and will remain with us for some time to come. This is probably the result of several developments. First, management practitioners themselves are increasingly concerned with improving their own effectiveness. Second, initial success in using managing by objectives has spurred additional efforts toward clarification and refinement. Third, "managing at a distance" (decentralization and delegation) is now recognized as a way of managerial life. Fourth, organizations now recognize that managerial talent is the crucial component in the perpetuation and profitability of the enterprise.

Purpose and scope of this book. This book is intended to accomplish several objectives: first, to set down in one place the fundamentals, principles, and procedures for a clear understanding of the concept of managing by objectives, its benefits, and its various applications; second, to serve as a practical operating guide for those who wish to introduce and develop the concept as a management system in their organization; third, to give additional insight and alternative techniques to those individuals already practicing managing by objectives but who wish to refine their skill; fourth, to assist as a text and resource in business schools, training programs, and management seminars whose purpose is management development and skills improvement; fifth, to offer food for thought to those practitioners who are not yet convinced or committed to managing by objectives as a way of life.

The book has nine chapters. Chapters 1 and 2 provide the fundamentals and give an overview of the concept as a system strategy, offer justification for and benefits to be derived from its use, and indicate the type of organizational problems it best solves. Chapters 3 through 5 lay out specific procedures to show how to find objectives meaningful to the organization, how to specify them, and how to validate their intent with the resources of the organization. Chapter 6 deals with the manner in which commitments are shared and implemented with employees. Chapters 7 and 8 present techniques for maintaining the M.B.O. practice in an organization through control and training. Finally, Chapter 9 describes a series of improvement applications as illustrations and examples of using M.B.O. to get results.

There are several areas in this text that I consider innovative since they are not found in the literature. Formulated on the basis of my experiences, observations, and experimentations to date, these include the following: the conceptual strategy approach; feeder-objective concept; situation action model; validation processes before commitment; risk analysis in the objective-setting process; planned motivation models; and trouble-shooting charts for the practitioner.

The objectives, scope, and innovative material offered in this book should be of help to any managerial practitioner at any organizational level who has an interest in increasing the results and quality output of his group or organization. Additionally, the text should provide meaningful techniques for those nonmanagerial personnel who wish to increase their individual results in the context of their job responsibilities.

Sources for this book. The material for this book has been drawn from several sources. First, it is a synthesis of ideas, solutions, techniques, and approaches interchanged among hundreds of organizations and their practitioners who attended M.B.O. seminars that I have conducted throughout the United States and Canada over a period of years. Second, it was taken from my experiences and work assignments as a Certified Management Consultant in a variety of industries as well as government. Among these organizations are: International Business Machines; Kimberly-Clark; General Dynamics Corporation; R. R. Donnelly & Sons; United Fruit; Sun Oil Company; Benton and Bowles; Celanese Corporation; Beatrice Foods; A. C. Nielson Company; Dalton, Dalton & Little; Winkleman's Incorporated; Norfolk Naval Shipyard; U.S. Naval Weapons Systems; Bellofram Corporation; State Street Bank of Boston; Mallory Battery; Stone and Webster Engineering Co.; Pewter Pot Restaurant Chain; Glenmore Distillers; Northeast Utilities; Bolton-Emerson; Industrial Management Club Association; Groton Public Utilities; Sambo's Restaurant Chain; McGraw-Hill Publishing Co.; U.S. Naval Underwater Sound Laboratories; Emhart Corporation; and Ingersoll Rand.

Third, it was drawn from my experience as a manager while working with such companies as General Dynamics/Electric Boat Corporation, Western Electric Company, and Northeast Utilities. Fourth, it was drawn from knowledge and skills acquired as a professor of management teaching in the graduate school of business. Finally, it is the result of the influences, ideas, and experiences of colleagues, associates, and previous writers in the field of management.

Acknowledgments. I am grateful to the following people for the special encouragement and information given me for this work: William P. Sloan, Electronics Graphics Division of R. R. Donnelly and Sons; R. F. Dodd, Peter Schweitzer Division of Kimberly-Clark; Carlton E. Dixon, I.B.M.; Kevin A. Joyce, Sylvania Electric Products; Baxter Spencer, Department of the Navy, Norfolk Naval Shipyard; and William Clinton, Groton Public Utilities.

Special thanks are extended to Gemma Moran, Public Stenographer, and Marian DiFabio, University of Hartford, for secretarial and typing assistance; also to Mary S. Mali, Faith L. Mali, and Dawn S. Mali for many hours of effort and adjustments beyond the call of duty in order to see this manuscript produced. Finally, I am indebted to the many clients in Canada and the United States whose openness and confidence gave intellectual stimulus for this work.

PAUL MALI

Groton, Connecticut

Contents

CHAPTER

munications Improvement. Methods Improvement. Training Improvement. Summary. Guide Questions for the Practitioner. References and Notes.

Managing by Objectives

1. The Strategy of Managing by Objectives

Managing by Objectives Defined. How Companies Are Benefiting from Managing by Objectives. How To Manage by Objectives. M.B.O. Strategy Creates a Management System. How the M.B.O. Strategy Evaluates an Organization's Performance. Summary. Guide Questions for the Practitioner. References and Notes.

The greatest challenge offered to management is to reconcile and integrate human effort, resources, and facilities toward common goals while avoiding discord and common disasters. Several approaches to solving this problem have been tried. There are those who do it by the "hunch and seat-of-the-pants" method. There are those who emulate the management practices of their predecessors. There are those who employ management fads. There are those who use the traditional processes of management. Finally, there are those who use the managing by objectives approach.

The purpose of this first chapter is to (1) define the concept of managing by objectives, its basic idea, its principles of operation, and how it integrates human efforts toward a common goal, (2) describe how companies are using the concept and the benefits received for both the organization and the individual manager, (3) introduce a conceptual understanding of its methodology, making clear how to manage by objectives, (4) show how managing by objectives creates a management system through the concepts of strategy, tactics, and tactical-strategic interrelations, and, finally, (5) describe how the managing by objectives strategy can be used to evaluate an organization's overall performance. This first chapter sets down the fundamental ideas that are developed in greater detail later in the book.

MANAGING BY OBJECTIVES DEFINED

Managing by objectives (M.B.O.) is a strategy of planning and getting results in the direction that management wishes and needs to take while meeting the goals and satisfaction of its participants. In its simplest form, *it is blending individual plans and needs of managers toward a large-scale accomplishment within a specific period of time.* The primary purpose of such a strategy is to simplify and clarify the managerial processes operating within the firm. There are four basic ingredients to the M.B.O. concept: objectives, time strategy, total management, and individual motivation. These ingredients are explained as follows:

1. *Objectives.* Objectives are events or accomplishments planned and expected to happen. They are job or organizational results to be arrived at. An objective might be to improve sales, lower costs, create new markets, or reduce absenteeism. To achieve a net profit–net worth ratio of 6.25 percent is an example of a profit objective for a business firm. To reduce employee absenteeism from 12 to 6 percent is an example of a personnel management objective for a government agency. To increase customer inquires from 10,000 to 15,000 per year is an example of an advertising objective for an individual salesman. To reduce material waste 50 percent is an example of a cost improvement objective for a foreman in a machine shop.

2. *Time strategy.* Time strategy is the timetable for blending the activities and operations of individual managers to achieve long- and short-range sets of results. It is a deliberate coordination of resources with the calendar for signaling individual managers to propose, act, and accomplish at designated periods of time. Achieving a reduction of operating costs of 10 percent within the next three operating quarters by all departments is an example of a timetable of coordination for collecting the contribution of each individual manager. Complete development of ventilator fans, model B, within the next 6 months by all departments and vendors is another example of timetable coordination.

3. *Total management.* Total management refers to a formalized effort to involve and coordinate the contributions of each individual manager toward a common goal. A management system is created within the organization which brings together competences in the form of people and equipment for handling the organization's functions and purposes or subfunctions and subpurposes. A hospital needs an internal management system to utilize and coordinate to the fullest extent the contributions of physicians, nurses, laboratory equipment, lab technicians, operating rooms, dietitians, pharmacists, and supervisors. Similarly, an educational institution necds an internal management system to utilize and coordinate the contributions of faculty, administrators, laboratories, computer equipment, accountants, classrooms, lecture halls, and clerks. A missile manufacturer requires a similar management system to co-

ordinate metallurgists, stress analysts, computers, fluid dynamicists, electronic controls, fuel, meters, mechanical and heat transfer equipment, and control engineers. Managing by objectives creates a management system for connecting the role and contribution of each individual manager for large-scale accomplishments.

4. *Individual motivation.* Individual motivation refers to the personal involvement and participation in the objective-setting process. This involvement tends to generate a desire and willingness to achieve. Managing by objectives is a motivational strategy since individual commitments and accomplishments lead to a high degree of satisfaction. The unit restaurant manager of a large, scattered franchise chain is highly motivated when allowed to participate in all aspects of his unit operations, such as payroll, overhead, hiring, customer relations, advertising, and maintenance. A pipe-welding supervisor is motivated when allowed to participate in the many segments of the total welding job, such as pipe weld design, welding equipment acquisition, inspection, training, qualification, and weld stress analysis.

These four ingredients—objectives, time strategy, total management and individual motivation—form four basic ideas from which operating principles emerge as the foundation of managing by objectives. These principles, simply stated, are as follows:

1. *Unity of managerial action is more likely to occur when there is pursuit of a common objective.*
2. *The greater the focus and concentration on results one wants to achieve on a time scale, the greater the likelihood of achieving them.*
3. *The greater the participation in setting meaningful work with an accountability for a result, the greater the motivation for completing it.*
4. *Progress can only be measured in terms of what one is trying to make progress toward.*

In many ways the concept of managing by objectives is inseparable from other management essentials. Delegation of authority, division of labor, decision-making, performance appraisals, and policy making are but a few examples of management essentials that become involved in this concept. But the management essential that has been its historical taproot is *coordinated decentralization,* which had its inception many years ago when Alfred Sloan of General Motors sought and found a way to coordinate planning. He describes it in his organizational study:[1]

General Motors needed to find a principle of coordination without losing the advantage of decentralization . . . .

I did establish in United Motors a unity of business purpose through the principle of return on investment. An organizational concept later formulated as decentralized operations with coordinated control.

This unity of business purpose through coordinated decentralization resulted in General Motors becoming the world's largest private industrial enterprise.

The term *management by objectives* first appeared in the literature as a way of building teamwork and common effort. As Peter Drucker says, "Business performance requires each job be directed toward the objectives of the whole business."[2] Present-day practice of the concept ranges from use as an informal individual tool to use as a formalized management system. It is doubtful that any two organizations can practice managing by objectives in exactly the same manner. There are too many different variables operating in each situation. It would be disastrous to apply a firm and fixed set of procedures to all companies everywhere. Since conditions vary because of differences in types of organizations, in products and services, and in problems due to people, an eclectic approach is mandatory in making the concept operational. The practitioner needs to launch it within his organization as a "best fit" and adaptation to his unique requirements. The four basic principles stated earlier must be allowed to operate as unifying processes within the organizational scope and structure of specialization, diversification, and integration.

BENEFITS FROM MANAGING BY OBJECTIVES

The number of organizations reputed to have adopted the strategy of managing by objectives continues to grow with ever-widening claims of greater and more favorable results. The firms employing this technique number in the thousands. These organizations formulate what objectives they wish to achieve, organize resources and programs to reach these objectives, identify the barriers and obstacles to getting there, and push toward success with intense effort. With this kind of approach, results do not just happen. Rather, money, time, and effort are heavily committed to plans, programs, and actions designed to obtain these results, which often can mean the success or failure of the enterprise or the individual manager responsible. Experiencing successful results has in turn stimulated greater interest in refining and sharpening this tool to obtain even better results. Furthermore, the users of this strategy not only extol the merits of its applications for survival and growth but also claim improvements and often complete elimination of several troublesome organizational conditions. Some of the improvements and benefits reported by organizations are the following: (1) improvements in the job of managing; (2) profit attainment less a happenstance; (3) accurate performance appraisals; (4) heightened motivation to achieve; (5) management development; and (6) coordinated teamwork with organizational clarity.

Improvements in the Job of Managing

By far the most frequently mentioned benefit of managing by objectives is improvement in the job of managing itself. A high degree of clarity is brought to the normal management functions of planning and control. Managers are much more likely to achieve whatever they set out to achieve because targets are better defined.

When Honeywell[3] decided to make managing by objectives a corporate-wide philosophy for all its profit centers, it brought greater precision of thinking, planning, activating, coordinating, and controlling to its managers. The concept gave them a sense of focus and concentration. They experienced managing by objectives as a total approach to the task of management. They did not regard the concept as a program, a staff activity, or a panacea for an immediate problem; rather, it was the heart and core of *managing* the organization. One Honeywell executive reported that, formerly, managing in Honeywell was unpredictable—almost a game of chance. With the advent of managing by objectives, each manager knew just what was expected of him and how his performance was measured. Job descriptions and job specifications were clarified; instead of generalized duties performed in a number of acceptable ways, specific job results were set forth and performance levels defined. For many managers this changed the job of managing from an almost guessing, or trial and error, method to one involving precise directions, relevant activities, and needed results.

The 3M[4] Company noted the strong tendency in their operation to assume that the important goals of a unit are well known and understood. The degree to which this is or is not true often makes the difference between mediocre and outstanding accomplishments. By using the approach of managing by objectives at all levels of supervision, a clarity was brought about in the mission and results of the units. The 3M Company noted that this way of managing tended to eliminate the "political" atmosphere, that is, the need to try to guess what the boss wants and how far to go in an attempt to please him no matter what he seems to want. At the 3M Company M.B.O. also eliminated the confusion in directions that formerly ensued when there was a turnover in management at the higher levels.

Profit Attainment Less a Happenstance

The major purpose of a profit plan is to reach a predetermined profit objective through a systematic and deliberate organization of all efforts and resources in the enterprise. Hence a profit plan must include the objective, the means for reaching the objective, and provisions for making adjustments when changes occur. This basic description of profit planning fits precisely the concept of managing by objectives. The major distinction between traditional profit-planning activities and the more effective managing by objectives approach lies in personal involvement and commitment. The traditional approach is largely fiscal, with projections and budgets set by staff functions. The managing by objectives approach is motivational; profit objectives are set and agreed upon through participation and commitment of its managers.

Like all companies, United Air Lines[5] must make a profit to survive as a business and to fulfill its obligations to the public, to its stockholders and to its employees. The effort of every unit is directed toward profit making. Department and division heads down to the section level participate in setting individual performance goals and plans of actions for meeting the company's overall profit objectives. These individual performance goals are directed toward profit making with specific targets in passenger sales, cargo sales, air mail, air freight, agency sales, convention sales, reduced costs of advertising, turnover, purchasing, operations, and services.

The Otis Elevator Company,[6] which operates in the United States through the medium of ten districts or zones, conducts each of these zones as though it were a separate elevator company. Each zone operates on an individual profit-and-loss basis. Each zone is expected to set up its cost reduction objectives by the cooperative effort of all who are in the position to influence cost and expense. The president of this firm reports that through this procedure, using the managing by objectives concept, a 30 percent reduction in construction costs was realized. In the opinion of this president, the most important single obligation of managers is to determine what should be considered par for their units and then to devote their efforts to developing an organization that will reach or exceed this par.

To make profits happen, *all* efforts must be organized to meet a timed set of profit objectives. This does not mean some people or some efforts, but, literally, all people and all efforts within a prescribed period of time. This requires an involvement and commitment from people who are a part of the process.

Accurate Performance Appraisals

The process of defining qualitatively and quantitatively areas of responsibility results not only in a more comfortable feeling among personnel, but also in establishing accurate criteria for evaluation and appraisal of performance. When each member of management, down to and including first-line supervision, has a clearer understanding of what his responsibilities are, how they will be measured, and when they are to be accomplished, accountability for executing these responsibilities is intensified. Performance is judged more accurately since it is based on specific accomplishments within a period of time and not on subjective or generalized opinions. Managing by objectives provides an objective measuring instrument for linking the evaluation of actual performance against expected performance. When the concept is well developed within an organization, the practice of self-evaluations and self-accountability becomes possible. An incumbent is in the position to evaluate the results of his own performance since requirements are clear, specific, and measurable. Willingness to appraise and evaluate subordinates is improved with the concept of managing by objectives.

At the Plastic Products & Resin Division of the Monsanto Company,[7] managers had to be wheedled and cajoled into conducting performance appraisals. Many of these managers regarded this task as a staff activity rather than as a part of their own regular duties. As a result, a manager completed performance appraisal at the division only after he had done everything else for which he was accountable. With implementation of managing by objectives, a new realization developed throughout the organization—namely, that there is a direct relationship between achievement and rewards. The evaluation of performance is to justify both. Performance appraisal not only has moved closer to line activity but also has greater appeal to line managers as a measure of performance.

With the installation of managing by objectives at the Colt Heating and Ventilation Company,[8] several troublesome problems were eliminated. The concept defined their organizational structure by eliminating unclear areas of responsibility. A simplified job improvement plan was instituted, job descriptions were rewritten and clarified, and performance standards were made more relevant and specific to the organization. This reduced the amount of time spent in performance appraisals, allowing the company to devote 25 percent of its time to job review—that is, to looking back—and 75 percent to looking forward.

State Farm Insurance Companies[9] has consciously steered away from the traditional personality-factor appraisals and management-skills ratings simply because it believes these approaches tend to lead the appraisal as well as the appraiser into confusion. This confusion stems from use of indefinite terms, vagueness as to what is desired, and difficulty in assessing behavior in the directions intended. This company found that appraising men at the middle and upper levels of management was very difficult because such men possessed complex and difficult personality patterns as well as a wide variety of managerial skills. The management performance guide based on the concept of managing by objectives shifted the appraisal approach to "results-oriented," "objective-oriented," or "accomplishment-oriented." The major emphasis is on the establishment of job-centered objectives within a coming period of time.

Using the concept of managing by objectives in appraisal work has a clarifying effect on important work and ensures accountability for its completion within a period of time.

Heightened Motivation to Achieve

It is an excellent idea for a subordinate to participate and have a voice along with his superior in setting departmental or organizational objectives. It gives the subordinate an opportunity to contribute his ideas, which heightens his sense of worth, recognition, and motivation. When this opportunity is offered deliberately and systematically, motivation and enthusiasm can be intensified to even higher levels. This, in turn, tends to stimulate further participation in improvements since the individual feels and knows his ideas, efforts, and contributions may have a significant impact on the organization. The sense of participation and belonging, a recognition of worth and a feeling of accomplishment, forms a potent motivational base which the company can rely on to help it reach its goals. The more clearly a subordinate perceives how his contribution fits into the flow process of results leading to ultimate results, the more heightened will be his motivation.

At the Grand Union Company[10] motivation is encouraged through decentralizing authority and spreading responsibility. As the president put it, "Along with profit sharing as a motivating tool goes problem sharing. We have found the latter just about as important in building and maintaining the spirit of belonging."

The chairman of the board of the Bridgeport Brass Company[11] states that the biggest single factor in the success of any organization is getting the people employed in the enterprise *united* in the purpose of making it a success. At Bridgeport Brass a sense of belonging and participation in achieving common goals is encouraged by all managers on all levels.

General Electric conducted a significant study[12] on how to increase motivation in its plants. The firm's focus was on how to improve the productive motivation of workers. A pilot study was undertaken to assess several job-related factors such as cycle time, size of group, training, and repetitiveness. From this pilot study it was found that participation by employees and responsibility for their own work resulted in a high degree of productive motivation. Attitudes and motivation for getting the work out were unmistakably better for those individuals permitted to use their own discretion and their own work objectives.

Management Development

Management development is still another benefit resulting from the practice of managing by objectives. The M.B.O. strategy is a kind of self-discipline. A person must think about what he is going to do the following year. He needs to spell out the kind of activities, schedules, and resources that are required to get a particular job done. This is a great help in developing individuals as managers. Insufficient skills and development needs are easily pinpointed.

The Royal Naval Supply and Transport Service,[13] a world-wide supply and transport organization, believes the involvement factor is a strong motivation for managerial development and morale. By getting a manager to suggest ways in which performance in his area of responsibility can be improved, as well as to suggest the action he will take, the dates by which he will accomplish his task, and the standards by which his performance can be judged, the manager becomes psychologically involved in self-development.

Organization development through managing by objectives at the St. Regis Paper Company[14] was used to establish good management practice that could be used throughout the company. The *Guidelines for Managing at St. Regis* grew out of this activity and was extended to all divisions. The establishment of the guidelines was thought of as an organizational and management development program. Managing by objectives concepts are readily apparent in many of the guidelines.

Managing by objectives allows development to take place informally, naturally, and simultaneously. That is, the individual manager acquires the knowledge and skills on the job as by-products of his meeting performance requirements. This is a key need in the whole area of management development. We need more and more to shift the learning experiences from the classroom to the real world of the job where most of the problems and challenges are found. We need more and more to shift to the individual the burden of pursuing self-development and self-education. Opportunities for learning and for change, and chances for experimenting are natural ingredients in the objective-setting process.

Coordinated Teamwork with Organizational Clarity

Historically, several methods have been used to find, place, and fit individuals within the organization as members of a team. One method has been the interview process, in which team "fitness" is assessed through depth interviews to discover values, backgrounds, and interests. Another is psychological testing for identification of different traits or temperaments in order to forecast compatibility for a group or project. Still another is temporary placement within a section or group as a trial or test of behavior for a permanent placement. These methods have their virtues and their vices. They are largely behavioral and require assessment of personality, attitudes, and traits. These are difficult assessments to make.

Managing by objectives provides an alternative for getting individuals coordinated into a unity of action. This is accomplished by aligning and interlocking individual manager's plans within the enterprise without too much concern over personality assessment and trait evaluation. Essentially, this means that teamwork on each organizational level and between levels is achieved by blending individual plans and pursuits. Pursuing joint objectives is open evidence that coordination and interlocking between two or more departments, two or more individuals, or two or more functions has taken place. The evaluation of the performance of joint objectives is still further evidence that coordination and teamwork were practiced to some degree.

The General Mills Corporation[15] made what appeared to be a minor change in their approach to handling managing by objectives yet what proved to be of great importance in obtaining organizational coordination. At the top of the organization, setting specific job-related objectives seemed to come easily; at lower levels, it seemed harder to relate goals to the upper levels. It was thought the difficulty might be overcome if the objective-setting process could be tied to the manager's organizational position guide. This guide listed the accountabilities by position and level. After some juggling and experimenting, objectives were set for most accountabilities, and the General Mills Corporation experienced an organizational unity and coordinated teamwork that had not existed formerly. The spread downward and upward through the organization brought a closer and more workable control of operations.

The president of the Minneapolis-Moline Company[16] believes that building and retaining a management team requires a careful determination of where the company is heading, the establishment of areas for individual initiative, an opportunity for cross-pollination of ideas, and the development of a system of built-in checks and balances for organizational control. His policy, a managing by objectives approach, is centralized planning and control in conjunction with decentralized authority and responsibility. As a result, this firm's president views large corporations with many autonomous divisions as multiplications of well-coordinated medium-sized companies.

An organization is never really sure as to whether it is working to its maximum potential. It is never sure whether the allocated scarce resources are being utilized and coordinated where it counts most for the enterprise. Guessing is rampant! Misfits and poorly placed personnel are everywhere. Judgment becomes risky and uncertain because there is faulty and insufficient information, direction, and coordination. Managing by objectives is positively centered on blending plans of action for getting results. The implementation of the strategy tends to identify early the misfits and redundancy in the organization. This brings about definition and clarity to operating teamwork. For the company, it changes the acquisition of results from a low probability to a high expectancy.

HOW TO MANAGE BY OBJECTIVES

Getting results in an organization comes about through a deliberate effort of planning and organizing resources to meet a set of expectancies. Results do not just happen! In the past, the randomly practiced trial and error approach has been used with some success. However, panic, high costs, schedule slippage, and low morale have been by-products of this method. Managing by objectives is a plan-ahead process with a series of deliberate phases from start to finish. This section will provide an overview of the plan-ahead process of the various phases, describe briefly what the phases are, indicate the importance of time schedules, and explain why M.B.O. works as a management way of life. The description of each M.B.O. phase is dealt with only briefly in this section since later in this book the phases will be expanded to form the bases of whole chapters. In fact, the development of the entire book follows closely the sequential phases introduced in this section.

M.B.O. Is a Five-Phase Process

An organization accomplishes a total mission by breaking it up into several phases, developing operating plans for each phase, involving managers to implement each phase, and setting a time scale for each phase's completion. Managing by objectives is a five-phase process; that is to say, it is an activity carried out in a sequence of steps taken in a certain order. This is similar to a manufacturing process that takes a material through a sequence of steps, each one modifying the material in some way until it emerges as a finished product. To say M.B.O. is essentially a five-phase process is not to exclude the many additional steps required to carry out the process. These additional steps are incorporated in one or another of the following five main phases:

1. Finding the objective
2. Setting the objective
3. Validating the objective
4. Implementing the objective
5. Controlling and reporting status of the objective

To visualize these phases best, the reader should refer to the flow diagram of Figure 1-1. All phases are sequentially related to give the process a cycle of start to finish. Repetitive cycles can be generated, making the process unending. A brief explanation of each phase is as follows:

Phase 1. Finding the objective. The concept of managing by objectives begins with a deliberate and systematic identification of results needed by the organization for survival, growth, improvement, or problem solution. This identification starts with an examination of the organization as it is now constituted. All kinds of analytical situational questions are raised: Where are we? How did we get here? What is our state of affairs? Why are we deficient? What are our opportunities? Trends, projections, and indicators are examined to note situational effects on the organization. Capacity utilization and performance are measured and compared with those of other organizations. Competitive "edge" analysis is made to assess positive and negative differences. Broad areas suggesting potentially usable objectives are identified, such as product markets, improved services, new facilities, lowered costs, sales improvements, reduced turnover, work simplification, methods improvement, merger possibilities, coordinated research, productivity improvement, employee motivation, and customer satisfaction. The practitioner must give this first phase much time, analysis, and attention, since it is at this stage that drift, aimless tendencies, or incorrect directions are noted, stopped, and redirected.

Results of phase 1: list of attractive and needed potential objectives.

Phase 2. Setting the objective. The broad areas of potentially usable targets identified in phase 1 provide the basis for adopting and setting the objective. This setting process involves the management team and its resources through a form of participation until a formal statement of objective emerges. This statement proposes that a commitment is to be made by an individual, a group, a department, or the entire organization. The formal statement is written, communicated, supported by top management, interlocked with other groups, and the whole organization is accountable for its implementation. Setting the objectives is a formal process of relating the resources of the organization to the involvement of those expected to deliver the results. It is based on the principle, If you want to get maximum results from people, get them involved and accountable for these results.

Results of phase 2: formally written statement of objectives.

Phase 3. Validating the objectives. The formal statement of the objective developed in phase 2 is subjected to a validation procedure. This procedure determines the confidence an individual, department, or company may have that an objective can be reached within its stated time. Risks, assumptions, and changing requirements are checked and analyzed to see where faults or failures can occur with implementation. The validation procedure simulates in a "dry run" effects of errors or great difficulties that may emerge. It builds within the objective contingencies to avoid potential errors. *The validation procedure translates the statement of objective to a statement of commitment.* This commitment is binding since a pledge or promise is made to deliver a given set of results. The validation procedure assures that resources, facilities, materials, methods, people, and management are ready and willing to reach a desired goal. Such a procedure raises or lowers the confidence, raises or lowers the risk, raises or lowers the probability that the venture will or will not take place. It is at this point in the overall managing by objectives process that many objectives are discarded as unattainable or unworthy.

Results of phase 3: validated statement of commitment.

Phase 4. Implementing the objective. Once a validated statement of commitment has been made as a result of phase 3, a motivational system is created to implement completion of the commitment. Setting the objective in phase 2 requires motivators to be built into the objective as an inherent ingredient. Phase 4 develops job plans and activities to begin and carry out action needed for fulfilling the commitment. There must be a connection between these two phases. Phase 2 defines the target, Phase 4 is the implementation strategy for reaching the target. This will require of the practitioner a more deliberate approach in motivating, coaching, and persuading, which later in the book is described as "planned motivation."

Results of phase 4: implementation of activities to reach objective.

Phase 5.   Controlling and reporting status of objective. Phase 5 is based on the principle, stated earlier, that progress can only be measured in terms of what one is trying to make progress toward. This phase sets up all activities under a schedule in order to measure and report the current status as well as progress toward completing the objective. The controlling and reporting process senses deviations of actual progress from expected progress and reports these deviations for corrective action. The concepts of feedback (measurement of past progress) and feed forward (measurement of expected future progress) give the management team an idea of their present position in relation to where they are going.

Results of phase 5: status reporting schedule toward established targets.

These five briefly described phases partially explain the overall process of managing by objectives. Many other features, techniques, and methods must be discussed before we can claim to have given a complete description. This must wait until the five fundamental phases are expanded into full chapters.

M.B.O. Requires Time Schedules

Every practitioner knows that our entire way of economic life is pitted against time. The manager of today is racing with time. The new test for leadership is the man who can keep pace with the increasing speed of emerging complex problems and provide at the same pace and speed viable solutions to these problems.

Managing by objectives is not simply getting results but getting results within a time period. The concept is set on a "pace" theme of productivity. This means that the gain in results or output for the organization is for a given period of time. The basic principle for practicing the M.B.O. concept is:

Play the clock; never play it by ear.

Time is reliable, consistent, and regulatory. Managing by objectives sets expected results on the basis of the clock and the calendar to take advantage of this regulatory and reliable pace setter. In so doing, M.B.O. sets up a sequential pace that works against Parkinson's Law.[17] This law states that work is elastic and will fill the time set for its completion. The practitioner who sets realistic but tight time periods for jobs to be done acts against the elasticity of work, which results in greater productivity. He uses shorter periods of time to achieve the same amount of work. Time for the practitioner becomes a tool for getting greater productivity.

Obtaining results through managing by objectives within a time period is rather like playing a football game. The football goal posts are clearly in view at all times by the individual players. This is analogous to the organization's objectives. The field is marked in yardage so that a player can gauge whether he is making progress toward these goal posts. This is analogous to a breakdown of the organization's objectives to milestones of progress. The offensive team as they huddle and decide on a tactic for yardage is analogous to management planning work activities and job actions to accomplish objectives. The actual carrying of the ball and the teamwork necessary is analogous to the implementation and performance of work. The defensive team's opposing and frustrating the yardage to be gained is analogous to the constraints within and without an organization an individual manager must overcome in getting results. *Finally, the game goes by the tick of the clock.* Just as there are only so many minutes to play, there is only so much time for the organization to get results. This, truly, is the mark of the professional manager: not just getting results but getting results within the necessary time period. Consequently, the schedule is an important tool in the practice of managing by objectives. A schedule is a timetable, a list of details that must be accomplished to complete a large-scale mission. All the planned details are timed for start and finish in order to coordinate the interrelationship of these details with the clock and the calendar. Utilization of materials is signaled with the schedule. Production of units is started and stopped with the schedule. The flow of inventory to the warehouse and to distribution centers is guided by the schedule. The hiring and working of manpower is executed by the schedule.

The time baselines shown in Figure 1-1 represent the amount of scheduled time required to achieve each phase in the sequential phases of the M.B.O. process. A time baseline is a scheduled period of time in which planned work must be done. It signals all details that must be complete before passing into the next phase. It defines points of progressive development between interfaces of the phases. Time baselines can also provide an opportunity for managerial review of conflicts, over-laps, omissions, and difficulties before going any further with a project. For example, a practitioner who has just completed phase 3, validating the objective, discovers that a supplier cannot deliver material within a normal time because of a labor strike. The time baseline between phases 3 and 4 allows for a management review to reconsider the time expec-tancy of the commitment in question. This would mean either extending the time for completion, changing suppliers, or eliminating the commit-ment as stated. Time baselines within a schedule are used in the practice of managing by objectives for getting hundreds of details completed toward the ultimate objective. They provide plateaus for management review in the sequential phases of the process. Time baselines are indis-pensable in the practice of M.B.O.

What Makes M.B.O. Work?

Economic life without productive work directed toward some purpose is meaningless, dull, and sterile. It is within the nature of man to engage in purposeful activity. It provides him with satisfaction, especially when directed toward a common good. This common good may be manifested as perpetuation of the enterprise, customer satisfaction, or employee security. Purposeful activity that follows a course of action to some end is compatible with man's deep urge for growth, development, and life. This is motivational! Managing by objectives follows man's inherent pro-gressive principle of changing disorder to order, unfinished to finished, disorganization to organization. Man's purpose, in other words, finds expression in reaching and achieving higher levels of good. The work situation becomes an opportunity for him to exercise this process. What makes M.B.O. work is that it fills man's deep desire to accomplish; M.B.O. gives him the opportunity and the process to select what is to be accomplished, how it is to be accomplished, and when. Achievement for man in the work situation must not be a mere possibility but rather a certainty if economic life is to be meaningful, stimulating, and fulfilling.

Many organizations have understood this basic need of man and have set standards of accomplishment far beyond a realistic expectancy, be-lieving that the formidable challenge will spur people to work that much harder. More often than not, this plan does not work. If an individual works very hard, accomplishes a great deal, but never quite reaches the formidable goal, he takes the attitude, "What's the use?" The standard he can never hope to reach loses all meaning for him. Take the case of the general manager of a paper mill company who set a goal for his production manager of 15 percent cost reduction every year. Considering the cost of materials, supplies, labor, and overhead, this was an almost impossible task. In the first year, the production manager achieved about 10 percent reduction. Although actually a good job, apparently it did not meet the general manager's expectancy. The next year he was asked to continue his 15 percent cost reduction. By the middle of the year the impossibility of ever reaching the goal became apparent and discouragement set in. Three months later, the production manager quit and the general manager had to replace him with someone else. The general manager soon discovered that the replacement was not nearly as good as the man he had had before. In fact, the production manager who left turned out to be extremely effective and successful in another firm. It had been the general manager's notion that people would be spurred on by an extremely high goal, but he forgot that most of us need the satisfaction of achievement and an impossible goal makes it very difficult to experience this.

Managing by objectives requires of the work situation reasonable and attainable accomplishments. It forces planning at every level.

M.B.O. STRATEGY CREATES A MANAGEMENT SYSTEM

The five sequential phases described in the previous section provide a framework within which to think about and visualize the job of managing as an integrated whole. This framework helps to break some of the large job complexities down into simple and understandable segments, forming a foundation for management by system. The purpose of this section is to explain and illustrate how M.B.O. is a strategy that creates a management system within the organization. Three topics will be used for this explanation: (1) the concept of a management system; (2) the M.B.O. strategy as a management system; (3) feeder-objectives: elements of the M.B.O. strategy. The concept of feeder-objectives, which will be used in later chapters, is introduced, described, and illustrated in this section.

Concept of a Management System

The story is often told about a group of blind men who were assigned the task of describing an elephant. Because each blind man was feeling and analyzing a different part of the body, a heated argument developed among the men as to what an elephant is like. One had his hands on the tail and claimed the elephant was like a rope. Another had his hands on the body and argued that the animal was a large, soft, and flabby wall. The third had his hands on its leg, leading him to claim it was like the trunk of a tree. Each was sampling one aspect of the totality. Each failed to grasp the totality in spite of his correct description of his individual sample. What is fascinating about this tale is the role of the storyteller, who has the ability to see the whole elephant as well as the correct sampling of each blind man. He alone can see how ridiculous their separate inferences are concerning the totality.

The ability to see the whole, the parts, and their interrelationships is the art of conceptualizing a system. A system is defined[18] as an organized combination of things or parts forming a complex or unitary whole. The following are examples of systems:

1. *Solar system.* Sun, planets, earth, moon, and astroids orbiting in prescribed paths to give order, form, and conditions to sustain life as we know it.

2. *Circulatory system.* Heart, spleen, lungs, and capillaries connected with veins and arteries to allow blood to flow to carry on cellular processes.

3. *Restaurant system.* Chefs, cooks, busboys, cashiers, waitresses, and facilities organized to convert raw food to a finished product for customer consumption and satisfaction.

4. *Production system.* Machinists, toolmakers, operators, set-up men, maintenance men, janitors, machines, and facilities organized to process raw materials for finished products for inventory to be sold in markets.

Each system has a purpose, a composition, and a framework for fitting its parts together. In management systems, the manager designs and organizes all the elements so as to guide, integrate, and control all resources toward some objective. Managers take unrelated resources, disorganized facilities, and unused skills and build a framework for accomplishing a mission. The systems approach requires that he arrange unrelated and nondirective parts into a useful and meaningful set of steps to contribute to the enterprise as a whole. The manager's ability to grasp and relate individual parts to a totality gives him a conceptual overview for handling the complex parts of his job. To illustrate, imagine someone showing you, one at a time, the parts of a photograph taken of the elephant mentioned previously. Each of the parts, like a puzzle piece, is interesting in itself but you would like to see the whole photograph. If you are not given the parts so you can arrange them in their proper places, you must form an image in your mind of what the various parts would look like if put together. You must form a conceptual overview of the picture based on just one part. The restaurant manager must "see" the impact on customer satisfaction when raw food does not arrive on time, the union cook is going on strike, or the waitresses are becoming angry over lack of tips. The production manager must "see" the impact on inventories when machine downtime is excessive, material reject rate is high, or established schedules are not followed. How well a manager can form a conceptual overview of his many individual responsibilities determines to a great extent how well his contributions relate to the enterprise. How well all managers' contributions relate to the enterprise determines the extent to which a management system exists for accomplishing objectives.

Managing by objectives when practiced by an organization creates a structure that allows management a vantage point from which it can view the whole system while observing the contributions of each of its parts. The five sequential phases provide managers with links for relating the hundreds of individual contributions toward an overall large-scale accomplishment. Like the elephant storyteller, management sees the totality and correctness of each blind man's descriptions. However, unlike the elephant storyteller, management allows each blind man to know and understand the totality and how each description fits into the whole.

M.B.O. Strategy as a Management System

The terms "tactics" and "strategy" have often been used in management to describe maneuvers and approaches to solving problems. Strategies have been overall plans of higher management to achieve some objective, and tactics have been individual plans of lower management that contribute toward the objective. Strategy sets the long-range and broad plan, and associated tactics define the many short-range maneuvers required to implement the strategic plan. Tactical-strategic interrelations are the connections among the many short-range tactics necessary to implement a long-range and large-scale strategy. Tactical-strategic interrelations bridge individual plans to the overall larger plan. How well tactical-strategic interrelations are set up and operate determines to a large extent the development of a management system for focusing and reaching an objective. Riggs[19] considers these interrelations in terms of managerial efficiency. He defines this efficiency as the degree to which the relative value of tactical choices accomplishes the intended effort. To illustrate, the owner of a wholesale distribution center has decided that the purchase of more trucks will best satisfy his strategic objective for growth within the next five years. He wants his business to grow to a definite level within this period. He is willing to take the risk that new trucks will shorten delivery time and increase his market share. He expects the new trucks to reach new outlets and give him an attractive return on investment. His decision to buy trucks to reach a five-year growth objective, rather than to rent, lease, or subcontract them, has been a strategic one. Now he must make tactical choices to carry out his strategic decision. A few of the many tactical-strategic decisions he must make are the following: type and cost of trucks; routes of travel to potential customers; material-handling services and unloading procedures for the customer; frequency and schedule of deliveries; maintenance and insurance provisions; hiring and placement of drivers. How well the owner carries out these tactical choices will determine how closely he will meet his strategic objective. This is a measure of his managerial efficiency at systemizing the many individual tactical decisions toward his overall strategy of using new trucks for company growth.

The five cascade phases of managing by objectives illustrated in Figure 1-1 constitute a systems approach for integrating individual tactical planning and decision-making to an overall large-scale mission. The traditional system elements of totality, input, output, process, structure, and control are observed in this strategy.

1. *A totality.* A mission, aim, or function is conceptualized when an overall, long-range, promising objective is selected from among several alternate good ones.

2. *Input.* Individual resources are selected on a short- or long-range basis and related to an overall plan. These resources can be selected from within or without the enterprise.

3. *Output.* Results for which the strategy was organized. A set of conditions or services yielded from the processing of inputs.

4. *Process.* Transformation required to change inputs to outputs. These are the many activities that make possible the conversion of resources. They are the many tactical choices that are made to give direction to utilization of resources in the sequential process.

5. *Structure.* The connection of all system elements to perform the mission. Tactical-strategic interrelations are connected and blended together on a timetable to give an integrating structure to the strategy.

6. *Control.* Criterion or standard of measurement that compares intended output with actual output. Quantity and quality of results of the strategy are placed on a status-reporting basis. Progress is monitored and corrected when needed.

TABLE 1-1

Systems Overview Capabilities[20]	Strategic Value and Use for Management	Wholesale Distribution Center (Example)
1. Predictability	Foresees end from pre-scribed beginnings	Capital outlay now for 20 new trucks to improve sales 20 percent per year
2. Completeability	Foresees connective in-process steps to a conclusion	Annual 20-percent sales growth reaches 5-year sales volume plan
3. Reachability	Foresees results are attainable	20-percent annual growth from 10-percent expansion of old market and 10-percent penetration of new market
4. Visibility	Relates constituent parts into sequential whole	Decrease in delivery time by 4 hours will yield annual 20-percent growth in sales
5. Interfaceability	Conceptualize gaps between boundaries of in-process steps	Preventive truck maintenance program reduces breakdown and idle time 50 percent
6. Reliability	Identifies strengths and weaknesses	Best delivery time in market could be offset by union unrest
7. Supportability	Relates individual plans and tactical-strategic connectors toward overall accomplishment	Increase in delivery time results from good employees, preventive maintenance, loading and unloading procedures
8. Measureability	Grasps progress indicators and timetable	Monthly sales reports by truck by route
9. Controlability	Senses deviations within prescribed limits	Monthly sales reports acted upon by sales manager
10. Improvability	Foresees correction actions to stay on course	If share of market optimized, subcontract delivery system to other wholesalers with different product line

The process of managing by objectives facilitates a systems view of the organization as a whole (the strategy); the operations and performance of each department, section, and manager (the tactics); and the inter-related contributions among the departments, sections, and managers (tactical-strategic connectors). An organization that allows these processes to operate within the heart and core of managerial work soon discovers several emerging strategic overview capabilities. These capabilities provide a system overview of the strategy in operation. Table 1-1 summarizes these capabilities and their value and use for management.

Feeder-Objectives: Elements of the M.B.O. Strategy

This section will introduce the concept of feeder-objectives as examples of the tactical-strategic interrelations described in the previous section. Tactical-strategic interrelationships are the connectors among the various parts of a strategy that make it work. They are individualized but co-ordinated action plans of a section, department, or manager. These connectors are called *feeder-objectives* to convey the idea that completion of these individualized plans by a manager or department feeds into the overall organizational plan. Each feeder-objective acts as a source of supply to the entire strategy. The supply of individual contributions "flows" or "adds" to form a total contribution, in a manner similar to tributary streams that flow and add their contributions to lakes and oceans. Examples of feeder-objectives are seen in Figure 1-2. Cash flow is directed toward an ultimate objective of revenue or cash position in a wholesaler distribution center but requires the collective contributions of buyers, inventory controllers, and salesmen. Manpower flow is directed toward an ultimate objective of manpower manning level in a large corporation but requires the collective efforts of recruiters, interviewers, testers, trainers, and developers. Treatment of patients flow is directed toward an ultimate objective of patient care in a hospital but requires the collective contributions of doctors, pharmacists, nurses, and aides. One can readily see that feeder-objectives must be formulated in every area where performance and results directly affect an organization's ultimate objective. The feeder-objective concept provides many useful features in the systems approach.

1. It links individual managers to the enterprise.
2. It interlocks departmental contributions with managerial levels.
3. It provides individual participation for large-scale accomplishment.
4. It signals the start and stop of individual contributors in the flow process.
5. It blends performance outputs of several flow processes.

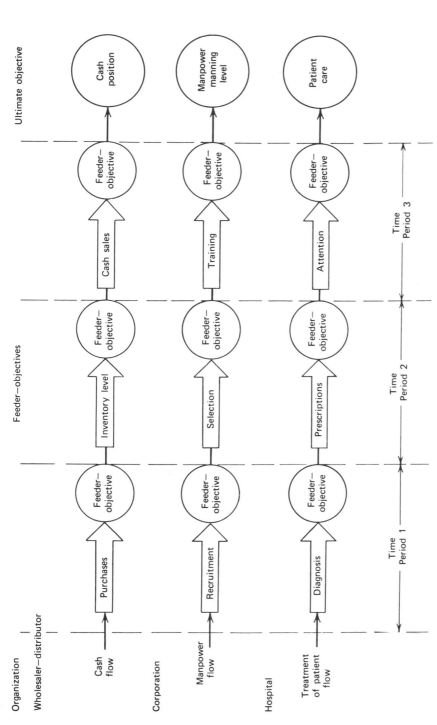

Figure 1-2. Feeder-objectives within a system's flow processes.

This concept and its useful features will be illustrated with another example: profit improvement. There are four ways[21] to achieve profit improvement: increase sales volume, increase price margin, reduce capital investments, or reduce costs. Determining the amount of profit and when it must be received within the company involves the objective-setting strategy for directing the organization's mission. Let us assume that the organization needs to make a profit through an 18 percent reduction in costs while holding volume, price, and capital outlay constant. See Figure 1-3. This 18 percent reduction is broken down into smaller percentages and assigned to three categories: travel expense, waste rejects, and material costs. Each of these categories represents a set of reduced cost results that must be met to achieve 18 percent reduction in costs. Each category is formally written and represents a feeder-objective to all departments. The means and methods of attaining these feeder-objectives are the action plans within the departments. Each action plan contains a series of activities under a schedule, which, when implemented, will achieve the results specified in the feeder-objectives. The category of waste rejects is formally stated as "reduce ½ percent per month waste rejects for the next 12 months for all production departments." The category of travel expense is formally stated as "reduce ½ percent per month travel expense for the next 12 months for all staff departments." The category of material costs is formally stated as "reduce ½ percent per month material costs for the next 12 months for all purchasing departments.

Once the feeder-objectives have been attained by individual managers and departments, the sum of all results should contribute to the overall organization's 18 percent cost reduction. Thus one can see that an individual production department that meets a feeder-objective of ½ percent per month is linked with the organization's 18 percent annual cost improvement. Since other individual departments or managers have the same cost commitment, they are said to be "interlocked" with each other in the same direction. The feeder-objective concept allows all departments to participate in a large-scale undertaking.

The feeder-objective concept is the basic unit of an objective network. A network is defined as a system of functionally connected segments and parts whose individual actions and interactions affect other segments, which, in turn, affect the system. Each separate segment is a link whose output is needed by other links in the system. The organization chart is a network form. It captures the total management structure, displays the levels of authority, and identifies positions of incumbents. A company that practices managing by objectives among all managerial levels can link each individual's feeder-objectives into a network of objectives. The

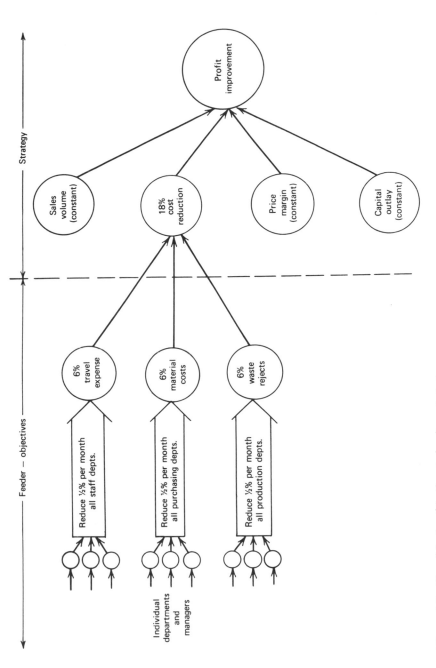

Figure 1-3. Use of feeder-objectives to implement strategy.

network shows the interrelationships of objectives, subobjectives, and feeder-objectives in the various levels of a traditional organization chart, as shown in Figure 1-4. As used in Figure 1-4, the objective network can support formal and rigid lines of authority by connecting individual work plans and their contributions in a total flow system. This tends to promote a sense of teamwork which clarifies the organizational structure.

The M.B.O. strategist does not ignore the chain-reactive effects of feeder-objectives in his strategy. He recognizes that as the performance of a feeder-objective increases, so should the performance of the entire flow process increase, assuming the feeder-objective is truly linked and interlocked with the expected output. If the contribution of the feeder-objective is not increased in quantity or time, it no longer feeds or contributes but is a constraint in the strategy. It will hold back and prevent the contributions of other feeder-objectives. For example, the production function must manufacture a product in term of its output per unit cost. If inventories are reduced or increased without a view toward meeting the entire system's objectives, such as marketing, then output per unit cost goes up or down independent of the system of which it is a part. The production function controls output per unit cost but is unrelated to marketing. The production function is a constraint on marketing. On the other hand, if the per-unit cost goes up or down as a part of an overall strategy of the system, the production and marketing functions are linked and both are resources for the system. The performance of the total system goes up as the performance of linked individual feeder-objectives goes up. Conversely, it will go down when the performance of the linked feeder-objectives goes down. The interactions among the feeder-objectives require phasing and juxtaposition to create a positive chain-reaction effect. Simply pushing the cost per unit down with lowered inventories may be wrong in terms of stockout frequency which disrupts and has a negative effect on the marketing function. The managing by objectives strategist develops his overall strategy as a "best fit" among the various parts that will make it work.

The systems management approach for managing by objectives requires feeder-objectives to be "tied" together toward the system's objectives. The feeder-objective concept is integrative; that is, it exists solely for the purpose of uniting with other feeder-objectives to form a "locked effort" toward an ultimate end. It is interdisciplinary because it cuts across established functional boundaries and routines. In addition, it provides a priority of control since the good of the system preempts the good of any one of the feeder-objectives. This discourages managers from trying to enhance their own personal performance at the expense of the overall system. Because the feeder-objective approach is concerned with

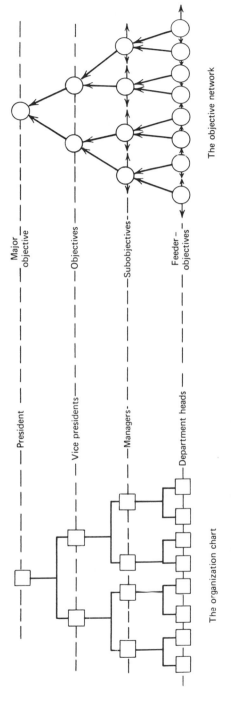

The organization chart

The objective network

Figure 1-4. The organization as an objective network.

President

Vice presidents

Managers

Department heads

Major objective

Objectives

Subobjectives

Feeder objectives

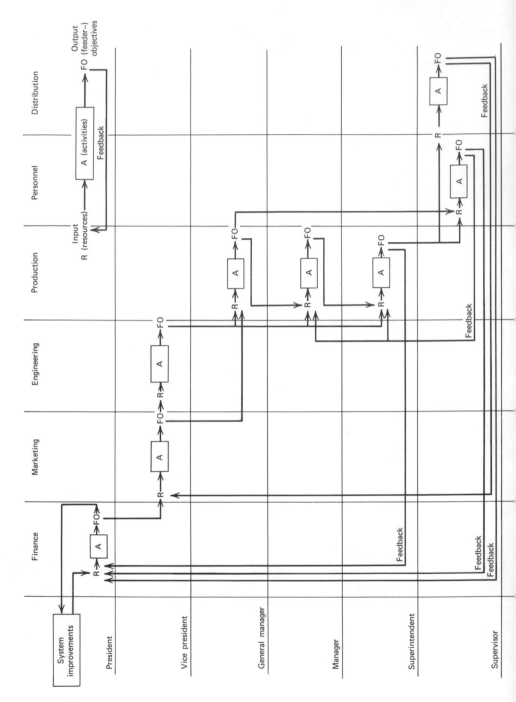

level interactions among managers, it thus provides a basis for building a framework. Several system elements are important in building this framework: the number of feeder-objectives in an organization; the size and scope of each feeder-objective; the critical nature of the feeder-objective; and the input-output relationships among management levels and functions. An increased number of management levels and functions within an organization will increase the complexity and variation among the feeder-objectives. This, in turn, creates a greater need for synthesis or connection among the many units. A company that truly practices managing by objectives as a total management effort will assure the connection and interlocking among its many feeder-objectives in various levels, as illustrated in Figure 1-5.

M.B.O. STRATEGY EVALUATES ORGANIZATION'S PERFORMANCE

The use of the strategy of managing by objectives is an effective means of evaluating a company's performance. Specific performance factors, such as revenues, operating income, net earnings, cost profiles, and return on investment, can be measured and precisely identified as to sources making contributions. Together these factors reflect the basic purpose of management's existence: to maximize profits and perpetuate the enterprise. This section will describe briefly how managing by objectives provides an easy means for measuring the performance of individual managers and how the total effect of all managers is a measure of the organization's performance.

M.B.O. Measures Performance of Individual Managers

A generalized evaluation is not enough for ascertaining how well a manager has performed. In spite of all the activities and efforts directed toward setting and using standards, we find that performance standards for managers are few indeed. Yet this is where standards are needed most. However, our ability to measure performance seems to decrease when we are faced with such intangibles as leadership, judgment, variety, creativity, initiative, and wisdom. How then can we go about measuring performance when the parameters are difficult and the conditions are continually changing? To compound the difficulty, managers have little incentive to improve their performance unless they know the specific areas in which they are falling behind. Unless there is some way in which a manager can see for himself how well he is doing, striving for improvement becomes a happenstance. Only when a manager can read his own indicators and identify deficiencies in work in progress can he catch his own errors and provide correction. The manager must maintain a constant check on work that is undertaken many levels below him and often thousands of miles distant; thus he must be able to check quality and quantity of performance without being on the spot himself. Management by distance is now a way of life. The central problem in measuring managerial performance is to have a reliable test of individual performance while operating in a system.

A basic principle in the practice of managing by objective is to assess progress in terms of what one is trying to make progress toward. This is the heart and core of a manager's work. Assessing and regulating work in progress and appraising results obtained is the very function of performance measurement and evaluation. To evaluate is to determine the outcome of performance. To manage by objectives is to establish a future set of results to be accomplished and to report work in progress toward its attainment. Variances over and under what was intended form a practical and reliable test for measuring performance. For example, phase 5 of the M.B.O. strategy provides feedback or status reporting that enables comparison of actual results with intended results within a time period that is corrective. That is, deficiencies or shortcomings are reported early enough for remedial action. The manager who has set for himself a $\frac{1}{2}$ percent per month reduction in operating cost at the end of a current year, as illustrated in the previous section, has specified a set of performance results to be accomplished. He proceeds toward achieving these results, getting monthly evaluations and reports of progress. Actual performance less than that expected within a period or actual performance equal to or greater than performance expected within a period is easily measured. Variances provide a basis for corrective action as the manager makes progress during the entire year. Several things are happening when these variances are reported and acted upon. For one, managers get a periodic check of their performance against a plan to which they are formally committed. For another, managers can sense quickly emerging conditions or changes that may fault their ultimate aims. When these occur, a manager may select alternatives. The manager who prescribed a $\frac{1}{2}$ percent per month reduction in cost may have expected to achieve this by holding his inventories down. If a new condition arises, such as a new marketing effort that increases customer orders, he may want to switch to waste reduction. This he does while still maintaining his monthly set of results.

M.B.O. Measures Total Effects of Individual Managers

The evaluation of an organization's performance is based on the effectiveness with which a firm employs its resources toward an established set of objectives. Because management is wholly responsible for the total operation of the firm and for the collective acquisition and employment of the firm's resources, it makes sense that overall company performance be measured and determined by the total effects of individual managers. The performance variances of individual managers, described in the previous section, provide a company with information at any given time on the flow of activities, the execution of plans, and the completion of feeder-objectives for the entire system. In effect, the measurement of variances in implementing feeder-objectives of all individual managers is a measurement of total management performance. This includes both the individual and interactive performances among managers. A shipping department that is not able to meet a delivery schedule, according to its feeder-objective commitment, will experience a performance variance. This will have an impact on several people: the production manager who is controlling inventory; the sales manager who made a commitment to a customer; and the transportation manager who was prepared to deploy his vehicles. The total performance variance of shipping, production, marketing, and transportation provides an evaluative status for each function as well as their interrelations. This is a measure of overall performance. Catching variances early is a primary responsibility of the manager in whose area they occur.

Managing by objectives as a system strategy allows variances in different areas to be spotted early and reported in order that corrective measures may be taken. The firm "sees" where it is going and its current rate of progress. Studies and analyses may be made if deficiencies, irregularities, bottlenecks, errors, failings, internal friction, or poor coordination are reasons for the variances. Overall evaluation of the organization based on individual variances is not only critical; it is the only evaluation that really counts.

Management measures the effectiveness of utilizing its resources in achieving objectives with this overall evaluation. The M.B.O. system's overview and the status of the interrelations of each functional part provide the means to measure accurately the total managerial performance of a complicated and dynamic enterprise. Weston[22] describes several tests that have been used to appraise this overall performance. They are summarized as follows:

1. *Profitability measures.* Return on investment, profit margin on sales, return on net worth and pre-tax profit.

2. *Operational measures.* Productivity, total costs, inventory turnover, cost reduction, and fixed-asset turnover.

3. *Marketing measures.* Gross sales, net earnings, cash-to-sales percent share of market, and sales per employee.

4. *Growth measures.* Competitive ratios, earnings per share, current ratios, and total debt to total assets.

These measures when taken alone can be misleading and unfair. For example, profits can and should be used in measuring total management performance, but consideration must be given to what is involved in producing profits, how the profits tie in with other company objectives, and in what way each manager contributes to making the profit. Many a glowing profit-and-loss statement on a short-range basis has hidden such management shortcomings as drop in company morale, trouble with suppliers, deterioration of equipment, and high turnover of experienced and skillful personnel. These ills have a long-range effect on the profitability gauge.

Commitment to profits must be weighed against the relative merits of short-term and long-term effects. It might be disastrous to concentrate on immediate results to the detriment of future needs. The ultimate requirements of the company must be flexible and broad enough for each individual to carve out some work plan that allows him to exercise his ideas, needs, and leadership abilities. The management by objectives strategy is geared fundamentally to reach and meet the company's long- and short-range programs; yet this strategy also requires individual commitment to a personal set of results that yields benefits to both the company and the individual employee. This contribution is documented and forms the basis for appraising both the company and the individual.

SUMMARY

This chapter has attempted to provide a perspective from which to view the material that follows. Thus it has been little more than an outlined presentation, establishing the conceptual framework of the methodology of managing by objectives for use in an organization. We defined managing by objectives and described four principles of operations. How companies have used the concept and the benefits they have received were discussed. How to manage by objectives is a systems approach to planning and procuring results for an organization. This chapter showed how a management system emerges whereby individual managers can link their individual plans to those of the firm. The concept of feeder-objectives was introduced and defined as the interrelations in a system that give it a structure for organizational clarity and meaning.

GUIDE QUESTIONS FOR THE PRACTITIONER

1. What are the four basic principles that form the foundation of the practice of managing by objectives?
2. What is meant by an objective? A feeder-objective?
3. What is your understanding of the strategy of managing by objectives?
4. Distinguish between individual performance objectives and company objectives.
5. Explain why managing by objectives is a conceptual strategy.
6. List the five fundamental phases of the M.B.O. strategy.
7. What insights are obtained for getting results from an overview of the M.B.O. strategy?
8. List the ways you think the technique can help you be a better manager.
9. In what way is a management system created within a company when M.B.O. is practiced? What are the specified outputs?
10. Contrast the number of results possible with different degrees of management participation.
11. What are the measures of managerial performance and how can managing by objectives reach them?
12. Explain the "pace" theme of the conceptual strategy of managing by objectives.
13. Discuss how feeder-objectives are links for motivation.
14. How can managing by objectives be used as a profit improvement program in your company?
15. List and explain six benefits possible with the correct application of the M.B.O. strategy in an organization.

REFERENCES AND NOTES

1. Alfred P. Sloan, Jr., *My Years with General Motors.* MacFadden-Bartell, New York, 1965, pp. 46–47; 53–55.

2. Peter F. Drucker, *The Practice of Management,* Harper and Brothers, New York, 1954, p. 121.

3. National Industrial Conference Board, *Managing by and with Objectives,* Research Study No. 212, 1968, pp. 21–26.

4. *Ibid.,* p. 57.

5. Dale D. McConkey, *How To Manage by Results,* American Management Association, New York, 1965, pp. 88–95.

6. LeRoy A. Peterson, "Establishing Objectives," in H. B. Maynard (ed.), *Top Management Handbook,* McGraw-Hill Book Company, New York, 1960, pp. 181–199.

7. Dale D. McConkey, *op. cit.,* pp. 84–87.

8. J. J. O'Hea, "Colt Heating & Ventilation Limited," in John W. Humble (ed.), *Management by Objectives in Action,* McGraw-Hill Book Company, New York, 1970, pp. 30–47.

9. Dale D. McConkey, *op. cit.,* pp. 96–100.

10. Lansing P. Shield, "Directing the Attainment of Objectives," in Maynard (ed.), *op. cit.,* pp. 302–316.

11. Herman W. Steinkraus, "Motivating," *ibid.,* pp. 351–371.

12. Harold F. Smiddy, "Deciding," in Maynard (ed.), *op. cit.,* pp. 267–297.

13. B. J. Pascoe, "Royal Naval Supply and Transport Service of the Ministry of Defense," in Humble (ed.), *op. cit.,* pp. 61–77.

14. National Industrial Conference Board, *op. cit.,* pp. 38–55.

15. *Ibid.,* pp. 27–37.

16. J. Russell Duncan, "Building and Retaining a Top Management Team," in Maynard (ed.), *op. cit.,* pp. 847–886.

17. C. Northcote Parkinson, *Parkinson's Law,* Houghton Mifflin, New York, 1967, pp. 2–8.

18. Dan Voich, Jr., and Daniel A. Wren, *Principles of Management-Resources and Systems,* Ronald Press, New York, 1968, pp. 21–29.

19. James L. Riggs, *Economic Decision Models,* McGraw-Hill Book Company, New York, 1968, pp. 7–13.

20. Practitioners in the managerial field will recognize the use of jargon to describe the systems capabilities. The use of jargon is kept to a minimum. Where used, jargon is defined and explained.

21. Phil Carroll, *Profit Control,* McGraw-Hill Book Company, New York, 1962, pp. 10–16.

22. J. Fred Weston, "Evaluating Company Performance," in H. B. Maynard (ed.), *Handbook of Business Administration,* McGraw-Hill Book Company, New York, 1967, pp. 3-72–3-79.

2. Trends Affecting Direction and Methods of Managing

Growing Dilution of Effort. Neglecting Opportunities as a Result of Crisis Management. Uncoordinated Planning within Managerial Levels. Constant Increase of Costs. Tendency To Tolerate Mediocrity. Growing Disparity Between Employer and Employee Goals. Imbalanced Organizations. Summary. Guide Questions for the Practitioner. References and Notes.

The period that man has now entered has been called the age of cyberculture, the postindustrial age, and the age of automation. It is a time of unprecedented change that will bring a jolting shock to methods and techniques of managing. It underscores the necessity for a company to organize and operate as if it existed within a "temporary society," as described by Bennis.[1] According to Bennis, we are in a period of cultural transition in which management must be flexible enough to move in and out of the economy as if the economy were temporary. The changing nature of technology, human needs, and social interactions generates strong trends in the business environment that affect an organization's strategy for completing plans. Consequently, an organization must address itself to these strong trends in order to grasp the conditions that may prevail during the period for which objectives are to be set and to establish appropriate methods for reaching them. Unfortunately, many organizations overlook or give little emphasis to this important requirement. The organization gets so involved in day-to-day operations that there is a tendency to forget undercurrents that cause drifts in undesirable or unknown directions. These undercurrents, at first, consist of trends in the consumer market, technological innovations, social redirections, and changing competitive profiles. Later, they emerge in the organization to produce critical management problems such as scarcity of competent managers, low employee morale, and obsolete or unnecessary products or services. Trends can affect the kinds of problems, opportunities, and expectancies involved in practicing successfully any method of managing. They can have a disruptive effect on both direction and operations of a company.

This chapter identifies seven trends in the business environment that affect methods of management. They are (1) growing dilution of effort; (2) neglecting opportunities as a result of crisis management; (3) uncoordinated planning within managerial levels; (4) constant climbing costs; (5) a tendency to tolerate mediocrity; (6) growing disparity between employer and employee goals; and (7) imbalance of organizations. Here we examine what these trends are, discuss the impact they have on an organization, and show how a conceptual understanding of the strategy of managing by objectives provides insight for handling these trends. Several practical methods also will be included to provide an M.B.O. approach for reversing these trends. For each trend, the methods are the following: (1) M.B.O. Rule for Focus, (2) M.B.O. Rule for Future Action, (3) M.B.O. Rule for Interlocking Functions, (4) M.B.O. Rule for Progressive Cost Improvement, (5) M.B.O. Rule for Stretching Performance, (6) M.B.O. Rule for Aligning Divergent Objectives, and (7) M.B.O. Rule for Balancing Organizations.

GROWING DILUTION OF EFFORT

Changes in business are uncertain, hence unpredictable. Products, services, and methods often become obsolete before they reach the final stage of planning. Innovations force a faster pace in business growth, resulting in greater complexities, cross purposes, multiplicity of goals, and a variety of possible directions. Van Horn[2] calls it a catatonic state of affairs because of changing business coherence. We now have hundreds of thousands of people devoting their full time to making obsolete our present products, services, and methods of doing business. They are reaching out for new products and services. Not only are more new ideas generated each year, but they are also applied sooner. "Future shock" is the term used by Alvin Toffler[3] to describe the emerging super-industrial world, the rise of new businesses, subcultures, life-styles, human relationships—all of them temporary. Future shock is the dizzying disorientation brought on by the premature arrival of the future. It is a time phenomenon in which innovations and change occur in the society with such rapidity that society does not have time to complete its orientation and adjustment to the innovations and changes immediately preceding. A single change triggers several changes, forming a chain reaction. As aircraft get bigger and faster, the logistic support facility problem compounds at a faster rate. Management attempts to keep pace with this tempo and complexity by stretching wider and wider its scope of activities. Managers compress within hours or days the work that formerly took weeks or months. A manager must give time and attention to many more items over a wider spectrum of activities. He literally "spreads himself thin" over many responsibilities. *He ends up by doing many things and doing none of them well.*

Business, generally, is evolving and developing into patterns new and different from those of the past. The "temporary societies" are influenced to a large extent by these evolving patterns. In turn, this influences and molds the type and quality of management needed. The current technical and social revolutions have made the manager's job formidable. He finds himself faced with many variables that he must sort and act upon. These variables are found in job content, human relationships and effort, the company and its relationship with stockholders, labor relations, and government with its controls and the requirements of the business community. Such variables have complicated the task of the manager. He expends prodigious amounts of energy, time, and money to operate legally and competently as these variables make demands on him. Historically most, if not all, of these variables are active and demanding. In an attempt to avoid running afoul and to bring order and progress to these intricate and interweaving demands, the manager spreads his time and energy across the entire spectrum. As a result, dilution of effort occurs and the trend for more dilution appears to be the prospect for the future.

The practice of managing by objectives forces a manager to face this spectrum of demands and to proceed to sort, select, and concentrate on the critical few. It forces a manager to deploy his limited resources where they count most. It also forces him to focus upon those variables that the enterprise needs for survival and growth. The practice identifies and separates the many trivial and insignificant variables. This separation is called the *Pareto effect,*[4] named after the Italian economist Vilfredo Pareto. The Pareto concept says that it is uneconomical to devote the same amount of time and attention to the inconsequential that one devotes to the critical. The Pareto principle translated to management funtions directs concentration to the few critical tasks which should receive the most skillful treatment because such functions produce the most good to the organization. Managing by objectives requires in its practice the assignment of priorities and weights to those objectives most important to the organization. From a list of a manager's potential accomplishments, the critical few are separated from the trivial many, as illustrated in Figure 2-1.

The manager recognizes that out of the total spectrum of objectives possible, he must commit himself to the critical few that most benefit the organization. These few are not always obvious but are often found to involve a key customer, a star salesman, the production foreman, receiving and maintaining good services, meeting schedules, and keeping

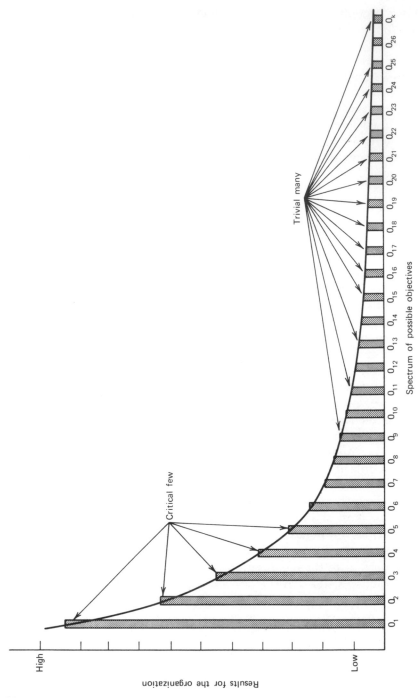

Figure 2-1. Concentrating effort for greatest results.

costs at rock bottom. The trivia are not always obvious, either, but they frequently appear in such areas as small customer orders, community involvement, career development, drop-in visitors, lengthy telephone calls, and the nuts and bolts of inventory. One method for sorting these two categories, based on the Pareto principle, is called the *M.B.O. Rule for Foucs*. This rule is described as follows:

M.B.O. RULE FOR FOCUS

1. List all the demands that face a manager.
2. Arrange the list in order of importance.
3. Select the top 20 percent as the critical few.
4. Identify the remaining 80 percent as the trivial many.
5. Spend most of your effort on the critical few.

The 20/80 percent M.B.O. Rule for Focus has shown, on the average, that 80 percent of the results in a situation can be attributed to 20 percent of the possible causes. The 20/80 percent breakdown has been derived and popularized by H. Ford Dickie of the General Electric Company[5] and designated as ABC analysis. Dickie used this analysis to divide inventory into classes according to dollar usage. The A class, upon which attention is concentrated, includes high value items whose dollar volume typically accounts for 75 to 80 percent of the material expenditures although representing only 15 to 20 percent of the quantity volume. The proportions are reversed in passing from the A class to other, less important, classes. In a later chapter, the Situation Action Model will provide an addition method for separating classses in order of importance.

Thus objectives can be set giving top priority to vital considerations, leaving matters of lesser importance to be dealt with later. The M.B.O. Rule for Focus helps reverse the trend toward dilution of effort and satisfies completely one of the basic principles of managing by objectives: *The greater the focus and concentration on the results one wants to achieve on a time scale, the greater the likelihood of achieving them.*

NEGLECTING OPPORTUNITIES AS A RESULT OF CRISIS MANAGEMENT

Operating a business is tough. Making key decisions is enormously difficult. Risks enter in as an essential part of planning and getting the work out. Every company seems to run into a certain number of troubles and complications that might be interpreted as crises. The terms "crisis," however, suggests major difficulties of the kind, for instance, that could lead to bankruptcy or organizational failure. As Sibson of the Sibson Company[6] has said, "Most businesses have one problem in common—they have too many problems to handle." In order to solve these problems, management must expend energy, ingenuity, and time. Most managers consider any sudden difficulty a crisis. It is not. The problem a manager faces at any one time is merely a materialization of symptoms. The crisis itself has been long in the making, usually the result of months or years of delay in facing up to solving problems once and for all. Many managers put off problem solving for one of two reasons: Either the cure is painfully slow, or the manager lacks the courage to do what has to be done. It is the nature of crisis that it seldom arises from a single cause but comes about from a variety of causes, one central and the others contributory. One may be financial and the others nonfinancial. Lippett and Schmidt[7] describe in considerable detail how nonfinancial factors contribute to crisis growth.

The crisis can be regarded as a problem situation. If a crisis has been long in the making, it follows that problems have long been standing without solution. The following principle underscores the growth of a crisis:

A crisis is in the making when the rate of problem generation is equal to or greater than the rate of problem solution.

The trend toward generating more problems than a company is able to solve sets in motion the crisis situation that moves the enterprise toward liquidation and bankruptcy. This trend toward problem generation saps and drains the energy and time of managers. It involves the manager so fully that he has little time to consider alternatives or opportunities. Crisis management may even be defined as total involvement in problems of the past, leaving little or no time to look into the bright opportunities offered by the future. Pursuing a reasonable number of opportunities is almost by definition the entrepreneurial task. What then is the reason for most companies' failure to pursue a reasonable number of these opportunities? The answers are many and varied; among them are unwillingness to take risks, insufficient personnel, and lack of competence. Probably the major reason, however, is preoccupation with recurring problems—preoccupation, that is, with a crisis situation where the rate of problem generation exceeds the rate of problem solution and the company never catches up.

In order for a manager to manage, he must solve problems. An examination of so-called permanency of problem solutions reveals that problems reappear even though they seem to have been solved many times before. A manager begins to feel that he is not getting anywhere, that he is caught in a "rat race" where he must make too many decisions too rapidly. Consequently, problems are solved partially, incompletely, or temporarily, only to have the original problems reappear later. When a manager devotes most or all of his time to these problems, he is, in effect, caught in the circuit of the past and ignores and neglects the opportunities of the future. Since problem solving is resolving a conflict or overcoming a barrier in the past, the manager who devotes most or all of his time to these problems has become a "historian."

A crisis is complex because problems are complex. Probably people who come up with easy answers cause more problems than they solve. Many problems are not merely complex but are in reality complexes, that is, groups of problems referred to under one general name for the sake of convenience. A large problem is often settled by solving the smaller ones of which it is composed. For instance, an acute problem of high operating costs can be solved only by controlling the small, myriad strains on the budget of the entire operation. Recognition of problems is not always easy because it is part of the situation which generated it.

The practice of managing by objectives requires a manager, through the objective-setting process, to solve problems in a system of expectations. It changes the manager's orientation so that he looks toward the future instead of toward the past. Instead of devoting full time to solving crisis types of problems, the manager searches and identifies opportunities that will lead the company in new directions. He must still solve problems but he solves them with a view to shaping the future. Problem solving that shapes the future requires that new opportunities be an essential ingredient in the objective-setting process. Objectives that are not opportunistic are objectives that maintain the status quo and perpetuate the existing structure. Time and energy should not be wasted in solving problems for which there are no solutions or that are trivial to the needs of the enterprise. The indictment of the busy manager who does not experience results is not for lack of effort and time. It is because he devotes his time and energies to problems which are oriented in the past and have little relevance to current or future expectations.

One method for assisting an organization or a manager to keep future oriented is to follow the *M.B.O. Rule for Future Action*. This rule is described as follows:

M.B.O. RULE FOR FUTURE ACTION

1. List all the responsibilities required of a manager (job description).
2. Arrange the list into two categories:
   (a) Responsibilities requiring job review time for past performance

    (b) Responsibilities requiring action on current or future results
3. (a) For higher management, reduce time spent for category 2(a), not to exceed 20 percent of available time. Allow time for category 2(b) to reach 80 percent of available time.
    (b) For middle management, reduce time spent for category 2(a), not to exceed 50 percent of available time. Allow time for category 2(b) to reach 50 percent of available time.
    (c) For lower management, reduce time spent for category 2(a), not to exceed 80 percent of available time. Allow time for category 2(b) to reach 20 percent of available time.
4. For higher, middle, and lower management, delegate excesses in category 2(a) to subordinates.

The percentage breakdown of the M.B.O. Rule for Future Action has been derived from studies made by Ralph E. Lewis[8] on the percentage of time spent on future planning at the various echelons of a company. The M.B.O. Rule for Focus also supports this method. One of the long-range objectives of Colt Heating and Ventilation Limited[9] was for its executives to devote no more than 25 percent of their time to job review and 75 percent to looking forward. This meant simplifying job descriptions, identifying key performance areas, reducing the number of standards, and keeping performance appraisals brief. By reducing the amount of time spent in reviewing past performance and filling out forms, more time is left for dealing constructively with planning future improvements in the job.

To summarize, the current trend in management is to neglect opportunities to move the enterprise in new directions. The practice of crisis management prevents this opportunistic approach since the solving of problems is oriented toward "unmaking" the past. Managing by objectives guided by the M.B.O. Rule for Future Action is a practice that forces a manager to be oriented toward the future. When setting an objective, the manager is looking ahead. As he does, he takes advantage of new opportunities to meet the needs of the enterprise. He proceeds to recognize his problems and develops plans to solve them. The implementation of these plans blazes a trail for making the future what the manager wants it to be rather than perpetuating a past that shouldn't be. He places himself in the problem-solving circuit of the future, as illustrated in Figure 2-2.

UNCOORDINATED PLANNING WITHIN MANAGERIAL LEVELS

The purpose of all organizations is to unify effort, that is, to coordinate. The employment of more than one person toward a given end involves

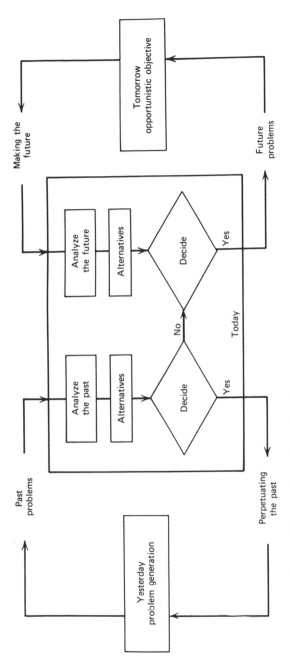

Figure 2-2. Problem solving circuits of the past and future.

specialization and division of labor. The purpose of organization is to integrate, that is, to assure that these specialties and divisions work smoothly, that there is unity of effort. Unity of effort means acting together in unison. For example, if two workers have been asked to lift and move some heavy objects, and if at first one lifts while the other moves, then they are not organized. When both lift and move together there is unity of effort, or coordination. Coordination, therefore, is the orderly arrangement of human effort toward unity of action in the pursuit of a common objective. In spite of its advantages, the division of labor, both horizontal and vertical, has some basic limitations. What this division does is to specify the activities that must be performed and who will perform them. At first glance, this might seem easy enough. For example, take four men rowing across a lake. Labor is divided so that John will steer, Harry will bail out the boat, Tony will pull on the right oar, and Jim will pull on the left oar. At first glance, this may seem to be all there is to it. But even this simplest boating experience will emphasize the fact that there is more to rowing across the lake than bailing, steering, and rowing. First, Toward what point on the lake are they heading? Second, How long should it take? Third, Are they performing all their activities in unison? Are the rowers pulling and the steerer steering in unison? Additionally, each may have quite different personal reasons for wanting to cross: Tony to see his girlfriend, Jim to pay a bill, John to visit a friend, and Harry to arrange for a service. Their decision to join forces and go together was a decision to form an organization. The organizational objective is to get the boat across the bay even though each private goal is different. What makes any organization work is that individual actions contribute to an overall accomplishment even though each person has his individual goal. The more difficult it is for functional members to perceive this relationship, the more difficult coordination becomes. As in the boating example, it might seem easy to determine the division of labor in a firm. The marketing manager sells to customers, the production manager produces the product, and the quality control manager assures quality. But is it so easy? Are these individuals working in unison? Do they have the same direction, the same objectives, and the same time pace?

Historically, the functional organization has been the formal structure that has broken the division of labor into different departments and subdepartments. Highly specialized activities of both individuals and groups have been assembled into functions, each function depending on the others and all operating only in closest coordination. Thus we have the engineering function, the research function, the marketing function, the purchasing function, the production control function, and other similar groupings. Carlisle[10] reports the obsolescent nature of functional organizations. The experiences of many companies are yielding evidence that functional formation, which has dominated industrial corporations for some time, has lost its value and is outmoded. The common occupational background of employees does provide an effective bond that encourages coordination and cooperation within the function but there is serious question as to whether any such bond exists between and among the functions. It is a natural tendency for functional organizations to emphasize their separate functional elements at the expense of the whole organization. Frequently, functional units treat their objectives and pursuits as primary, considering secondary the goals and objectives of the enterprise as a whole. The engineer makes a decision to complete a design. This decision affects production in terms of difficulty and cost, which, in turn, affects the salesmen, who must find customers to buy the product. The specialist, more often than not, is not part of a team. His record shows experience in which he has always set his own goals, planned his own work, and fixed his own schedule. For him to accept objectives that management selects and to meet someone else's time schedule is difficult. It often starts an inner rebellion that will either cause him to resign or to align his efforts in a nonconflicting direction. Assimilation of the specialist into the organization is frequently difficult and a common sense of purpose is not easily arrived at. The unilateral decisions of a functional organization tend to emphasize the functional objectives of the specialist without regard to their effects on the organization as a whole. Under functional organization, efforts to integrate across the functions to meet organizational needs are not always made. Theoretically, this task is the general manager's responsibility. However, the capability and skill necessary for coordinating not just effort but effort in unison toward objectives is not readily found in these managers. To add to the difficulty, organizations of the functional type do not as a rule develop competent general managers since each manager develops through his specific functional specialization.

These growing concerns raise some important questions about the usefulness of the functional form of organization. How many companies are truly unified in effort and well coordinated in desired directions? Is Parkinson's law of work elasticity[11] operating within managerial levels without the company's knowledge? Does each manager accomplish work to meet his personal goals at the expense of the company's objectives? Do companies allow their managers to wheel and deal with relative abandon, ranging so far afield from one another that there is little conflict?

The Olin Mathieson Company yields an example of a crisis of coordination. Its fifty-odd plants and enterprises were never effectively coordinated, and the power of the corporation was somewhat less than the sum of its parts. The incoherent enterprise is described by Richard Smith[12] as follows:

The company (Olin Mathieson) degenerated into a loose confederation of tribal chieftains. Executive vice-presidents proliferated. Division chiefs assumed the power and perquisites of corporation presidents. Product lines grew more exotic as one hand toyed with the atom, the other grubbed in the fertilizer business.

When there is no conflict, there is no coordination. How much waste is there in company time, energy, and money when the direction, scope, and contribution of individual managers from top to bottom are not coordinated? It is tragic to see how the untiring efforts of many competent managers and vice-presidents are diffused in different directions. It is equally tragic to note the result of their combined efforts for the enterprise. Managers are like vectors[13] with objectives (*O*) and drives (*D*). The vector resolution of several managers can produce a result for the enterprise smaller than any individual manager's contribution, as illustrated in Figure 2-3.

More often than not, the result of a scattered-force system is less than any individual result of a manager. Since work and activities are elastic (according to Parkinson), each manager will pace himself not only to meet his own time requirements but to give a "fit" necessary to satisfy his own personal commitments and needs. The "empire builders" will take directions most opportunistic for themselves rather than for the enterprise! How to bring about coordination among the functions and between the hierarchy levels is probably the most important single issue

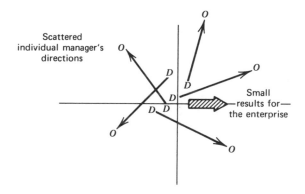

Figure 2-3.   Scattered managerial efforts yield small results for enterprise.

in organizational efficiency. The current trend is for organizations to experience more scattering, more disarrangement, and more fragmentation. The impetus toward complexity in products and polarization of personal goals is encouraging this trend.

The practice of managing by objectives requires interlocking action between people and departments. This is to combine functions into bundles to allow the combined activities to flow in a prescribed direction. The very nature of the interlock will make it seem that functions are being duplicated, but they are not. They are joined together with feeder-objectives to yield unison of action. One method of bringing about this unifying structure is to make use of "joint feeder-objectives." This technique is explained with the *M.B.O. Rule for Interlocking Functions*.

M.B.O. RULE FOR INTERLOCKING FUNCTIONS

1. List all the feeder-objectives desired by a functional manager.
2. Separate from the list those that can be completed only as joint efforts with other functions or departments. These are called joint feeder-objectives.
3. Negotiate and gain agreement to combine resources and effort toward achieving these joint feeder-objectives.
4. Assure that all managers on different levels of the hierarchy have a reasonable number of two- or three-way joint commitments.

Two-way feeder-objectives combine the efforts of two departments or managers toward a single commitment, whereas three-way feeder-objectives combine the efforts of three departments or managers. Some examples of two-way feeder-objectives are to reduce machine downtime 50 percent by machine shop and maintenance department; to reduce average handling time of customer statements 10 percent by billing department and mail room; to increase merchandise turnover in store from four to six within the current fiscal year by sales and inventory control. Some examples of three-way feeder-objectives are to achieve a product line mix in which 80 percent of sales is made by no more than 20 percent of R & D customers by marketing, engineering, and finance; to reduce frequency of lost time injuries from 21 to six per million manhours within six months of instituting a new safety program by production, maintenance, and safety.

Managing by objectives encourages extrafunctional understanding. The M.B.O. Rule for Interlocking Functions provides a method whereby managers can combine their efforts in a single direction. This encourages coordination and interlocking among the diverse functions and levels. The feeder-objective concept takes private and personal needs of the

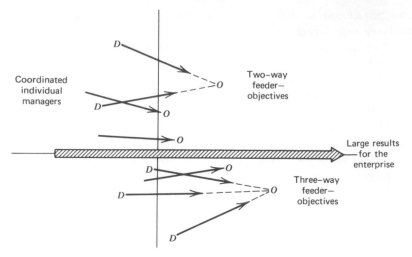

Figure 2-4.   Joint feeder-objectives coordinate planning within managerial levels.

manager into consideration but in a context of a management system. The concept of joint feeder-objectives results in a greater alignment among the various managers, yielding more efficient results for the enterprise, as shown in Figure 2-4. It fosters the attitude that all members of a company are mutually dependent, that no one individual can go charging out to wherever his "empire building" impulses lead him.

CONSTANT INCREASE OF COSTS

Today increase of costs is the rule rather than the exception. There is not a country in the world in which increase of costs has not been experienced. When revenues remain steady or decline while costs escalate, profits are diminished. Overcompetition or even wasteful competition has created tight markets in which price margins are very narrow. It is not unusual for companies to become desperate to salvage what they can for a respectable profit year. These companies have not paid close attention to keeping operating costs at rock-bottom levels and thus find themselves on the brink of disaster. News of cost cutting may indicate several conditions: the failure of a good many long-range plans, the existence of both profitable and unprofitable departments within the same company, the lack of a consistent cost-control program throughout the company, or simply cost mismanagement. The inescapable fact is that cost control is not a matter of choice for any company. It is part of the profit performance expected from managers. It is one of the ingredients for a company's continuing existence. The degree of profit making is, in the short or long run, directly dependent upon the extent to which a firm has developed a cost-managed system. Profits are the ultimate gauge for business survival and growth.

Cost control is a significant function of management. Ill-considered cost cutting and last ditch slashing are moves by panicked management. This panic may take the form of setting up a special and centralized group whose only existence is to conduct cost-reduction programs. As cost cutters, they are given license to proceed to prune where necessary. Usually they take drastic one-shot measures such as laying off workers, reducing overhead, consolidating operations, reducing wastes, eliminating advertising, cutting out training and development, reducing inventory, and curtailing public relations. These sudden one-shot cost-cutting moves may cause irreparable damage to company systems, functions, customers, personnel, and morale. For example, the insistence on substituting cheaper materials for more expensive ones may lose valuable longtime customers, which reduces sales volume but leaves the cost margin still high. The elimination of advertising and promotional programs may damage beyond repair the sales potential for short- and long-range needs. Hasty layoffs of staff personnel may mean that heavier demands in time and effort are made on line personnel, resulting in a slow-up or drop in productivity. When cost-cutting action is sudden and not well thought out, it may actually generate more costs and result in long-term damage to customers, employees, and the company itself. The usefulness of such "overnight" cost roundups is more doubtful than certain. They may aggravate present problems or even produce new ones. The crash approach to making spectacular cost cuts in one area can raise the costs in another area, at least in the short run.

Cost control must be considered as a way of life. It is not something a special group sets out to accomplish quite apart from in-plant activities. It is the heart and core of managing and, therefore, cannot be separated from managing. Cost control must be carefully established, thoughtfully applied, and continuously followed up as part of the on-going, day-to-day work of each employee. Nor is it a program to be carried out by a special group. Although it may be regarded as a program, it involves all groups, both management and employees. Costs are usually thought of in terms of facts, figures, and accountants, but primarily they are a matter of people working and performing efficiently. Every move an employee makes has an effect, no matter how indirect, on cost performance in his group or department. No supervisor can afford to overlook his greatest prospect for performing efficiently and keeping costs down, which lies in the way he reaches for results and how these results affect people directly. In this respect, the supervisor is in the ideal spot to keep costs under control. Under the stress of getting out the work, a supervisor often finds it difficult to plan and emphasize how costs will be the basis of his efficiency, but it must be part and parcel of his job along with his technical and functional responsibilities.

Cost control begins with the recognition of the need for cost control. It is not enough simply to tell people they must reduce costs. They must understand and accept for themselves why and how costs fit into the overall picture as well as into their individual jobs. Job security, job benefits, and job satisfaction must relate to costs and demonstrate a clear connection between causes and effects. Employees must believe in and understand this connection. This recognition of the need factor clearly may be the biggest stumbling block to making cost control a way of economic life.

Cost control requires the active participation of every employee in the enterprise. If costs are to be attacked at all, they must be attacked on all fronts by all personnel. The total cost picture is what counts. Many cost control programs have failed because only a certain percentage of the organization was involved. A prevalent attitude of department heads is, "I'm already down to the bone; it's the other department that needs to cut."

The practice of managing by objectives is an approach that not only plans a work accomplishment at the end of a period of time, but also builds into it the constraints and the limitations necessary to achieve this goal. Cost control is natural in managing by objectives since it provides a vehicle in which the need for cost improvement is identified. Additionally, participation, implementation, and control are phased and interlocked among personnel throughout the management system The focus capability of managing by objectives suggested by the M.B.O. Rule for Focus can give the cost improvement effort a precision and direction not normally found with other managerial strategies. In addition, cost targets should be formalized and coordinated in progressive steps: avoidance, reduction, and control. Cost avoidance is the elimination of a cost item anticipated and budgeted but not expended. Cost-control standards are guidelines set up according to average or best costs incurred in the past. They form the basis on which actual costs may be compared. Cost reduction is the deliberate attempt to work below the cost levels expected and allowed by the standards.

One method for giving the cost improvement effort successive stages of effectiveness is to follow the *M.B.O. Rule for Progressive Cost Improvement.*

M.B.O. RULE FOR PROGRESSIVE COST IMPROVEMENT

1. List cost improvement possibilities desired by a manager.
2. Separate from the list those that have high cost requirements.

3. Apply the three-step progressive rule to each cost item:
   (a) *Avoid* the costs where possible.
   (b) *Reduce* the costs from standards where and when possible.
   (c) *Control* the costs to standards where avoidance and reduction are not possible.
4. Write cost improvement requirements into a formalized statement of a feeder-objective.

For example, it is not "cut costs 10 percent next year with machine shop operations." Rather, it is "turn out 20,000 units of ×36 with no greater than 5 percent rejects while dropping unit costs from $2.50 to $2.25." The cost cutting pattern is built into the work plan itself. The manager controls and reduces costs as he carries out the technical and functional responsibilities of his job. The M.B.O. Rule for Progressive Cost Improvement provides an organized method to cope systematically with steadily rising levels of costs.

TENDENCY TO TOLERATE MEDIOCRITY

Peter Drucker[14] describes the danger of safe mediocrity as follows: "Few things damn a company and its spirit as thoroughly as to have its managers say: 'You can't get rich here but you won't get fired.' "

The first requirement of a good manager is the high value he places on performance, especially his own. The manager who sets his goals low or who tolerates indifferent performance in others is one who practices mediocrity. The manager who does not face up to his responsibility to exact from his employees their best performance and to get rid of people who cannot meet his standards faces this serious condition of mediocrity. Mediocrity is like a disease. It contaminates and spreads. To tolerate it in one subordinate will eventually infect all subordinates in the group. The mediocre employee is not one who does unacceptable work, nor is he regarded as deadwood or dischargeable; he is the employee who does barely acceptable work—enough to justify his employment but not enough for him to be called highly productive. He has an extra 20 to 30 percent productive performance he could deliver if he were motivated. The most tragic aspect of mediocrity is its contaminating effect on the supervisor himself. He who tolerates mediocrity in subordinates develops an equal tendency to tolerate it in himself. When the supervisor does not urge the subordinate to reach for higher levels of performance, it insidiously influences him not to stretch for higher levels of performance either.

All companies tolerate mediocrity. It is a question of how much and where—a tragic condition that can infect an entire management group, resulting in a general decline in performance of the whole enterprise. The precious competitive edge that all companies search out and hold on to has often been regarded in terms of site, facilities, services, and market position. These may be part of it, but competitive edge is not a static phenomena. It is continually changing. It is the "stretch" in performance that the enterprise makes continually. With the stretch, improved services, better timing, and unique marketing position result. It is the stretch in the performance of the entire enterprise that is, fundamentally, the competitive edge all companies seek and need. Additionally, this total stretch is the summation of the individual stretches of the employees of the company. If employees are not actively pursuing a continual stretch in performance, it is not likely the total stretch will exist.

Why have American business and industry fallen into this practice of tolerating mediocrity? Why is the trend toward mediocrity taking a greater toll among the ranks? Does planning and getting stretches in performance break the mediocrity trend? Three reasons are suggested for the practice of tolerating mediocrity: (1) shortage of qualified personnel, (2) practice of seniority within union ranks, and (3) difficulty of evaluating employee performance.

1. *Shortage of qualified personnel.* Probably the greatest reason for tolerating mediocrity is the shortage of qualified personnel within the ranks. There are many employees who need to be upgraded, updated, and developed. Time and money are not available for this effort. They are accepted on the job because the labor market may not offer anyone more qualified. Sometimes a manager is stuck with a mediocre subordinate in his ranks because potential employees from the labor market are below mediocre. Naturally he prefers the mediocre employee to the alternative.

2. *Practice of seniority within union ranks.* Seniority confers on its possessor a relative claim to available work or other benefits flowing from the enterprise. The collective bargaining agreement is a balancing mechanism among the interests of various groups of workers. Seniority grants preferential treatment to long-service employees almost at the expense of short-service employees. In times of business distress or organizational changes, the seniority rights of long-service employees provide protection against the company's attempt to weed out those causing the problems. As long as an employee with seniority does barely acceptable work, he is protected from the weeding out process.

3. *Evaluating employee performance.* Traditionally, performance appraisals center on the descriptor approach. A listing of descriptors such

as quantity of work, quality of work, ability to cooperate are itemized on one side of the appraisal. On the other side is a scale for measuring the degree of performance in each of these areas. The emphasis in this approach is on measuring effort and activities rather than results delivered. Supervisors are reluctant to participate in these types of appraisals. Most supervisors hate these procedures since they are forced to defend themselves in a confrontation with the employee appraised. Their defense is weak and often embarrassing since they have used subjective impressions as the basis of the evaluation. These subjective factors are difficult to define, let alone measure and prove. Supervisors prefer to avoid this type of confrontation. They tend to give acceptable or even high ratings even when they know the employee has serious deficiencies. In other words, they practice mediocrity. Add to this difficulty the tendency of supervisors to mix and confuse potential performance with actual performance. The temptation for supervisors is to give high ratings for actual performance when they really are looking at potential performance. They say, "I know he hasn't done the job quite as well as it must be done, but I know he can do it." Potential performance should not be confused with actual performance. The former is capacity and ability to do work, the latter is actual measurable work completion on the job. The former is a prediction and projection of likelihood, the latter is a matter of fact, truth, and history.

A prime requirement of managing by objectives is identifying in advance the results to be accomplished on the job. These results must be clearly defined as attainable yet also provide a challenge. They must constitute the stretch in performance required of all individuals. In the objective-setting process, there is a meeting of the minds between a supervisor and his subordinates on what this stretch entails and how to go about accomplishing it. The subordinate knows what is expected of him. He has agreed to work to attain this end. Through this process of planning and achieving stretches in performance, the mediocrity trend is reversed. That is, striving toward higher achievements pulls the subordinate away from the complacent mediocre level that was allowed and tolerated in the work environment. A period is assigned for measurement of these stretches to see how well employees are doing. Failure to reach expected goals reflects on the individual, the supervisor, or both. It is the results that evaluate the individual. The supervisor is no longer in the embarrassing position of having to undertake a confrontation on highly subjective factors. Mediocre performance can be readily identified and corrective action taken.

Many of today's leading behavioral scientists believe that the average normal individual is functioning at not more than 10 to 20 percent[15] of his potential; 80 to 90 percent of his capabilities, talents, inherent resources, and abilities have been rarely used, if ever. The average person has 80 to 90 percent prodigious reserves that he can call on at need. Often many of us are shocked to discover the tremendous energy, enthusiasm, and capacity to function that are released when we are vitally interested in a project we want to accomplish. This inherent 80 to 90 percent potential is the total sum of energies, qualities, and abilities that, when released, can give individuals tremendous performance on the job. Management, should, therefore, actively seek ways and means to release this potential stored within human beings. It is a false notion that if one works at maximum potential, he will be prevented from going further. As one works to his maximum potential, that potential increases steadily. The old adage is true: Give the busy man the job to do and he gets it done. Why? The more he does, the more he is capable of doing, and the more he is capable of doing, the more he does. One begets the other. Conversely, the less he does, the less he is capable of doing, and the less he is capable of doing, the less he does. Performance and potential are interrelated and inseparable. Each is a determinant of the other. When performance is increased, potential is unfolded. When performance is decreased, potential is stored. This inherent potential in people holds tremendous promise for creative productivity, satisfying relationships with people, and reversing the trend toward mediocrity. We have yet to understand *fully* how to release this stored potential.

One method to use in releasing this potential and breaking the trend toward mediocrity is the *M.B.O. Rule for Stretching Performance.* This rule utilizes three major steps to release potential for higher levels of performance: (1) identify inherent potential, (2) unfold and develop the potential, and (3) utilize the developed potential.

M.B.O. RULE FOR STRETCHING PERFORMANCE

1. *Identify employee potential.*
   (a) Make a list of performance responsibilities required of an employee.
   (b) Allow employee to select those of *great interest* to him.
   (c) Allow employee to add responsibilities he wants and needs.
   (d) Consolidate list and organize as feeder-objectives according to priority of interest. Keep the list short.
2. *Unfold employee potential.*
   (a) Build a 5 to 15 percent performance stretch within each feeder-objective that is of *high interest to the employee.*
   (b) Make each performance stretch realistic, letting there be a high probability of success.

(c) Select objectives for employees that are new (opportunistic) and traditional (problem solving).
3. *Utilize employee potential.*
   (a) After a successful initial 5 to 15 percent reach, a series of 5 to 15 percent stretches should follow in the same performance area.
   (b) Allow individual to reach highest job growth possible.
   (c) Plan a series of performance stretches in allied areas.

The practitioner of managing by objectives has four basic elements he can use to set his 5 to 15 percent performance stretch. These elements, illustrated below, are the following: (1) Decrease time to complete a job; (2) decrease resources needed; (3) increase quality of the performance; and (4) increase quantity or output.

1. *Decrease time*
   Research Engineer
   Contribute feasible marketing ideas at the rate of one per quarter.

   Stretch Performance to:
   Contribute feasible marketing ideas at the rate of one per month.

2. *Decrease resources*
   Salesman
   Follow up on new inquiries while holding sales expense to 5 percent of total sales.

   Stretch Performance to:
   Follow up on new inquiries while reducing sales expense to 3 percent of total sales.

3. *Increase quality*
   Welder
   Perform welding operations using acetylene equipment on 1½-inch flat steels with 7 percent weld rejects.

   Stretch Performance to:
   Perform welding operations using acetylene equipment on 1½-inch flat steels with 5 percent weld rejects.

4. *Increase quantity*
   Truck Driver
   Operate three motor trucks: 1½-ton cargo, 5-ton dump, tractor trailer.

   Stretch Performance to:
   Operate five motor trucks: 1½-ton cargo, 5-ton dump, tractor trailer, ¾-ton utility, 10-ton cargo.

Growing Disparity between Employer and Employee Goals

Most of the techniques of motivating workers have been dominated by what is loosely called the "human relations movement." This movement searches for the reasons workers behave as they do and postulates how management should treat them to get greater productivity. It recognizes the plain truth that, for most people, work is no fun at all. The emphasis in this movement is on the individual, and jobs are designed to meet his needs. This approach has certainly given us greater insight into motivating workers, showing us how to get an employee more excited about his work and indicating the factors that influence job satisfaction and morale.

But a problem remains even after motivation has been instilled. How is motivation to be sustained and raised to higher levels? How can one recharge, replenish, and regenerate the drive once the highly satisfying original work has been completed? How does one keep the motivation from fizzling out? Does a manager re-evaluate changing needs of workers and reorganize to meet these needs? What about the thousands of work assignments that cannot yield employee satisfaction yet must be done? As automation and mechanization of work procedures continues, the number of jobs that are dull and unsatisfying, yet necessary, is increasing. Sustaining motivation is the major problem in motivating workers toward higher achievement. The trend toward automation carries with it a trend toward monotony, routine, repetition, continuous, uninterrupted work, and low level of skill requirements. As these factors continue to grow, the job of instilling and sustaining motivation becomes even more crucial and difficult. Management is taking a hard look at traditional job designs and methods improvement in order to consider job content and automation in the light of human needs. The components of motivation, such as pride in work, job meaningfulness, identification with the product and the company, are given careful attention. The "sense of achievement" component is not a criterion for job design and reorganization in the work setting.

The strategy of managing by objectives, when properly used, recognizes that "sense of achievement" must be planned into the work and projected on a time scale.[16] Jobs, both satisfying and dissatisfying, can be laid out in such a natural way that plateaus or time periods exist to relieve the sense of dissatisfaction. These plateaus can be planned with a view toward replenishing and recharging a declining motivation. They allow an individual to see and to experience the set of results he has achieved, thus reinforcing his motivation for achieving the next set of results. Also, these plateaus can be used for appraisal periods, informal discussions of work completion, time-off periods, or natural leveling points in the work progression itself. However, in order for the sense of achievement component to have an effect, the work must be challenging or interesting. Simplification of jobs practically eliminates any interest and challenge. The sense of achievement component of motivation will work only when there is a combination: challenging work and a plateau from which the employee can see how he is progressing. In addition, the employee must somehow be made to feel that personal needs are taken care of. This is based on a simple truth, as described by Myers:[17]

Ideally every employee should be able to think of himself as an entrepreneur, not working for a company, but working for himself within a company.

Employees work primarily for themselves and only secondarily for their employer. Their wages, desires, and personal needs do not usually fall within the framework of company needs. An employee goes to work for a company with a set of expectancies that may or may not coincide with the set of expectancies the company has for this employee. A disparity exists between these two expectancies. The wider the disparity, the more difficult the motivation. Since it is natural for employees to want variety, novelty, and change, we can expect this disparity not only to exist but to fluctuate within both wide and narrow limits, as shown in Figure 2-5. As between two vectors[18] that represent directions and expectancies of the employee and the employer, an angle of disparity (d) or difference exists.

The actual result for the company is the resultant of the two forces: employee drives toward their goals and employer drives toward their objectives. Motivational intensity increases when the angle of disparity between these two forces becomes small.

The question is not whether a goal disparity exists between employee and employer, but rather how wide, how varied, and how amenable to change this disparity is. The goals of employees are continuously changing as a result of influences outside the enterprise. Take, for example, education. Surveys have consistently shown that the more education a worker acquires, the less satisfied he is with factory work and the less satisfied he is with work that was previously satisfying to him. As a result, he readjusts his expectancies, which, in turn, increases the angle of

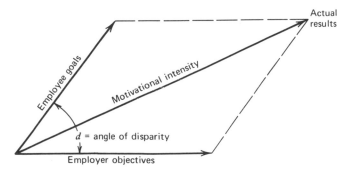

Figure 2-5. Motivational intensity changes with disparity.

disparity. Similarly, the employer is continuously reassessing and re-evaluating his own expectancies. Surveys have shown that the disparity angle shown in Figure 2-5 becomes wider and motivational intensity becomes weaker when employee expectancies are disregarded and employer objectives are ignored.

Managing by objectives recognizes that perfect alignment between company expectancies and employee expectancies is virtually unattainable. If it should be attained at any point, it will last only briefly. The changing nature of both parties' needs makes coincidence of the vectors a highly improbable event. The objective setting process, however, attempts to explore and assess the breadth of the differences. The supervisor tries to measure this difference when he sits down with his subordinate and asks: "What are your personal goals?" "What do you expect from your job?" "Why did you come to work for this company?" Answers to these questions give the supervisor an idea of the breadth of the disparity and what must be done to bring about a closer alignment. The supervisor must realize that the disparity can change and take several positions, as illustrated in Figure 2-6. Each position of the vectors will yield a different motivational intensity toward actual results. Those employers are most unfortunate who hire employees whose goals can never be met within the confines of the enterprise. This type of employee has the most difficult motivational problems to solve. It would be better to leave these employees at the door—on the outside. The supervisor should strive to move both vectors or states of expectancies to a closer alignment, as indicated in case I. Motivational intensity becomes stronger as disparity becames smaller. The employee is accomplishing his own personal goals while at the same time meeting the employer's objectives. Conversely, motivational intensity becomes weaker as disparity increases, as indicated in case III. The employee is attempting to meet his own expectancies but is in disalignment with his employer. It is when objectives of both employer and employees are brought into alignment in content and time phase that greater contributions are made to the enterprise. Motivational intensity is high when both the employee and the employer win. The objective setting process of the practice of managing by objectives measures this angle of disparity and attempts to bring about an alignment.

One method for aligning employee and employer interests is called the *M.B.O. Rule for Aligning Divergent Objectives.* It is based on the third principle of managing by objectives cited in Chapter 1. This principle is the following: *The greater the participation in setting meaningful work with an accountability for a result, the greater the motivation for completing it.*

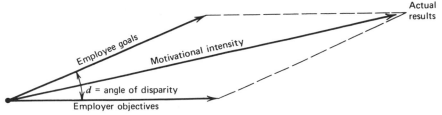

Case I: close alignment; high results; strong motivation

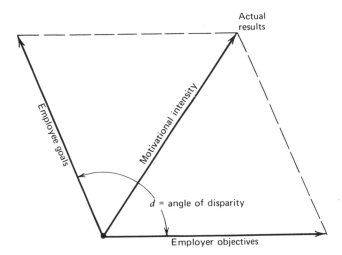

Case II: wide alignment; moderate results; moderate motivation

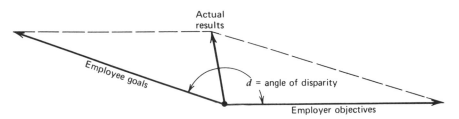

Case III: very wide alignment; poor results; weak motivation

Figure 2-6. Motivational intensity caused by employer and employee disparity.

M.B.O. RULE FOR ALIGNING DIVERGENT OBJECTIVES

1. Supervisor makes a list of requirements needed by the organization.
2. Employee makes a list of personal goals and job interests.
3. Supervisor and employee together select items from both lists that require similar actions and parallel activities to achieve.
4. A feeder-objective is established by both supervisor and employee based on matched items.
5. Unmatched items are dealt with by the supervisor as unilateral requirements of the organization.

If supervisor and employee are not able to match any items on their lists, there is serious doubt whether the employee is properly placed. This indicates that the employee's motivation will be a continuing problem. The M.B.O. Rule for Aligning Divergent Objectives is a form of participative management. It allows members of a group to take an active part in influencing and contributing to decisions. Organizations in the past, because of their formal structure, tended to be autocratic in nature. Those in authority complied with the rigid requirements of the structure, thus discouraging employees from contributing toward decisions that might affect them. The practice of participative management recognizes the following truth: *Employees find great satisfaction and need fulfillment when they actively participate in plans and activities that effect them.* The extent to which widespread participation should be allowed in a company depends on the definition of the situation and the styles existing in management. Organizations operating under union constraints may find it difficult to put this principle into practice to its full philosophical extent, although the collective bargaining contract can be regarded as "legalized participative management." Many factors or prior commitments may exist which may not allow this participation. Nonetheless, whether or not employees can participate, the involvement and participation of total management is an absolute "must" in the practice of managing by objectives. If a management system is to be created within a company in which each member of management makes a contribution, then each member of management must be involved.

Participation and involvement by individual members of the management staff does not mean separate decisions on what to do, however. It means that *management members share the opportunity to make a decision that affects all of them.* An agreement will tend to narrow any disparity among management personnel. This narrowed disparity creates a greater alignment within the hierarchy for organizational teamwork and coordination. The M.B.O. Rules for Aligning Divergent Objectives and for Interlocking Functions provide practical approaches for achieving this teamwork and coordination. Involvement and participation by total management form a vital part of the objective-setting procedure.

IMBALANCED ORGANIZATIONS

An organization is a structure of resource utilization established to meet the system's objectives. Ideally, organizing should begin as soon as objectives are set and a logical framework for assembling and grouping resources is established. The purpose of establishing an organization is to enable the resources to work more effectively as units. Unity of command is based on the idea that no one can do an effective job if he is subject to conflicting directives. Hence the organization structure defines reporting relationships, duties, and authority. A system of authority emerges, giving some idea of the decision-makers acting in the enterprise. The organization chart becomes a representation of the organization, indicating how the work is broken down into various functions and products; showing how people in the company are to work together; identifying job positions and names of individuals assigned to execute the duties of each position; and showing relationships among levels of authority and channels of communications flow. The concept of division of labor is exploited since an operation can be made more efficient by dividing the work. Functions and specialists are assigned in such a way that proficiencies and efficiencies are maximized in the course of time. The organization chart also shows how the work is delegated and controlled through people. Assignment of work, granting of authority, obligation to perform, location of decision-makers—all are formalized in the organization chart. The vertical and horizontal channels of the chart are considered formal since they are legitimate ways through which directives and reports flow. This formality provides links by which connection and coordination are effected. The organization chart becomes an important tool for management of the enterprise.

In viewing the organization, there is a tendency to consider it as a static and quiescent structure, rather like a photograph in which people, objects, and the environment are captured and frozen. This is a misleading conception; the organization is more like a motion picture—dynamic and changing. People vary in their roles; objects and equipment change; and the environment is continually altered. The organization chart is an inadequate representation of the organization that actually exists. Its principal deficiency is its inability to show the dynamic nature of work completion by individuals who vary in their drives, pressures, and activities. As mentioned earlier, the organization chart is a picture

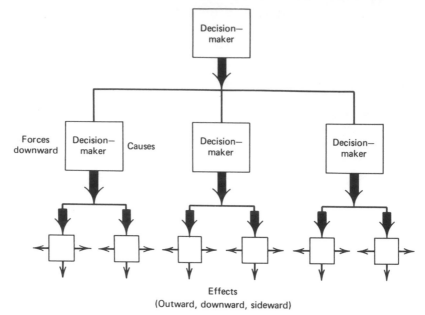

Figure 2-7. Decision-makers are stress forces in the organization.

of the system of authority. If one views it as a dynamic system, each decision-making manager acts as a force applied downward into the organization. This is illustrated in Figure 2-7. The collective forces of the decision-makers tend to stress the organization at the point of application, causing fluctuations, imbalances, and disunities. The strength of the force or decision varies from manager to manager and results in horizontal as well as vertical stresses in the entire organization. It is this dynamic nature of the organization that makes unity of action in a focused direction difficult. To integrate organization effort by coordinating the efforts of all parts of the system is easier said than done. How to get individuals to perform the right action at the right time is the key to the "quantum jump" in results for the enterprise. Over a period of time the stresses exerted by the stronger decision-makers lead to acquisition of many functions and responsibilities, resulting in an imbalanced organization, as shown by manager C in Figure 2-8.

Traditionally, unity of action has been attained by either the directed method or the voluntary method. In the directive coordination approach, the individual is told what to do and when to do it. Litterer[19] calls it "hierarchal coordination" since activities are linked by organizing them under a central source. A master plan is evolved by a central authority and tasks are linked to this authority on a time-phased basis. Formal

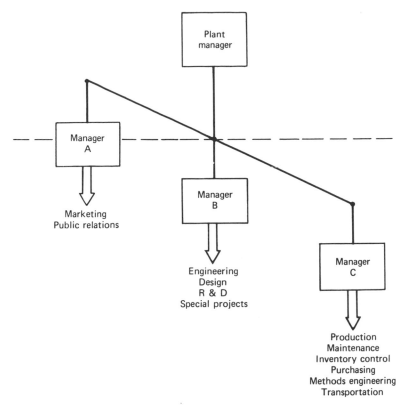

Figure 2-8.   Imbalanced responsibilities result in imbalanced organization.

procedures and policies are written up and coordinated work is attained through these procedures. The individual finds himself responding to numerous unrelated one-man acts of control. Paper-shuffling and evasions of decision-making rapidly spread. Individuals become cogs in a vast organizational structure.

In contrast to directive coordination, in which the individual is told what to do, is voluntary coordination. Here the individual is allowed to see the need to coordinate and waits until he can take the action to effect it. This approach sets the stage for the exercise of authority and power. It becomes a power base for those who will grab it. It is no wonder that in those companies that practice this approach highly motivated individuals use their newly acquired power base to impose their personal needs and wishes on the state of corporate life. Competition for power is characteristic of the organization man in voluntary, permissive organizations. Under these conditions, the organization tends to cluster around the power usurper. This results in fragmenting the managerial functions and processes, such as planning and control, which are normally structured in the functional forms of organization. Although this approach may appear useful for finding the leaders of the organization, it poses many problems. First, the decision-maker is not aware of all the factors outside his domain that might affect his particular situation. Besides, he has a relatively great need for independence. This individual will act independently and will tend to ignore outside factors unless he needs them to attain his ends. Second, coordination becomes a happenstance. That is, voluntary coordination, interlocking, and dovetailing occur infrequently. The extra effort, thinking, and time necessary to effect coordination usually are not expended. Finally, a sense of timing is lost. A manager may plan and drive in a very desirable direction, pulling and pushing his group with him, but he is lost in his own personal schedule, ignoring how his efforts affect other groups. His timetable is precisely identified but out of phase with other timetables. A manager must stand at a point in time looking forward to the objectives he wishes to achieve. He must also relate his own time point to those of other managers by looking sideward and backward to gain a sense of phasing, cycling, and moving as part of an entity. The inability to coordinate with other managers on a timetable basis leads to disruptions. It results in greater power-playing among the structural units so that the organization becomes hopelessly imbalanced, as illustrated in Figure 2-9. If work gets done in this organization, it is usually accomplished by dominant personalities, with others forced into the role of "sacrificial lambs." Instead of a dynamically changing, well-balanced structure that allows all managers to influence the organization, a static, imbalanced organization is created.

Managing by objectives, in practice, is a combination of the voluntary and directive approaches to organizational coordination. (1) It is voluntary, in that managers are expected to initiate and reach out for developing opportunities. (2) It is directive, in that managers once committed to a pursuit must interlock and dovetail in a timetable with other managers. (3) It is voluntary, in that managers are allowed to vent their personal drives and needs in goals and day-to-day work. (4) It is directive, in that managers obey the reality principle. They strive within the overall system's boundaries they themselves helped formulate. (5) It is voluntary, in that managers can exercise power and authority through a set of expected results. (6) It is directive, in that the power exercised is not the result of individual impulses but part of a system of activities designed to reach a set of objectives. Power is generated or attenuated on the basis of the type and significance of the results rather than on the dominating nature of the manager's personality.

A method of eliminating the tendency toward imbalance within an

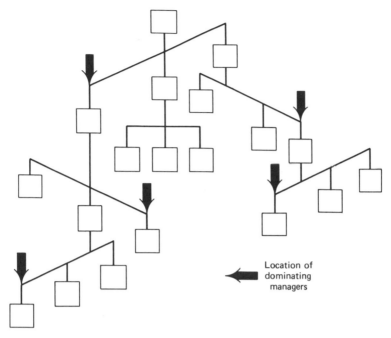

Figure 2-9. Imbalanced organization results from uncoordinated managerial dominance.

organization is to follow the *M.B.O. Rule for Balancing Organizations*. This rule is described as follows:

M.B.O. RULE FOR BALANCING ORGANIZATIONS

1. Each manager makes a list of major functional responsibilities of his position and of the subordinates reporting to him. He identifies them by brief titles and makes a list of minor responsibilities.

2. Manager rewrites each major responsibility as a feeder-objective, being guided by the M.B.O. Rules for Focus, Future Action and Aligning Divergent Objectives. All minor responsibilities should be combined under one low-priority feeder-objective.

3. Manager uses the organization chart to get a good balance or spread as follows:

   (a) Keeps the number of feeder-objectives for all managers about equal.

   (b) Includes at least three joint feeder-objectives for each managerial position.

   (c) Keeps number of subordinates reporting to each manager approximately equal.

(d) Holds the number of organizational levels under each managerial position about equal.

Managers with more responsibilities than they can handle tend to be overwhelmed for lack of time. With lack of time, coordination and interlocking become a happenstance not likely to occur. The managing by objectives practitioner acquires a systems style of defining a set of expectancies for the future but gets together with other managers to build an overall system for the company, using their personal commitments as building blocks. He may also take the approach of deciding (with other managers) what the overall system's requirements may be and proceeding to find the building blocks necessary to get there. The managing by objectives practitioner will not be swayed by pressures to "zag" when he knows and chooses to "zig." He will not be rebuked for taking control and dominating in pursuit of an objective since the organization expects this because of prior involvement, agreement, and commitment. Rules, regulations, and restraints on behavior are bound up in the commitments made through the objective-setting processes. The M.B.O. Rule for Balancing Organizations serves as a vertical and lateral integrator among the various groups. The feeder-objective is the vehicle for each manager to relate and connect to the overall system. The feeder-objective concept allows the manager to select his opportunities and directions. It also aligns these directions and feeds the results into an overall contribution.

SUMMARY

Strong currents and trends are pressures that move the enterprise in directions not often known beforehand or desired. These trends create conflicts and disruptions that are disconcerting to the manager. This chapter has identified seven trends in the business environment that are affecting current methods of managing. The practice of managing by objectives provides a useful basis for dealing with these trends. Several rules emerge in the practice that help the manager to reverse the trends and provide a capability vital to the success of the organization.

GUIDE QUESTIONS FOR THE PRACTITIONER

1. Are there any disruptive trends operating internally or externally in your company? If so, list them in the order of their seriousness, together with developing problems.

2. How certain are you that these trends are operating against your organization? What is the evidence, or the indicators?

3. Do you see any effort being made in your company to handle these disruptive trends?

4. What improvements or benefits would you expect if something were done to reverse these trends?

5. List the benefits that your section, department, or company could reap if problems resulting from these trends were solved.

6. List the improvements that you have identified as being possible within your company.

7. Using the M.B.O. rules described in this chapter, assess the impact of and the actions you need to take in dealing with the following trends:
   (a) Growing dilution of effort.
   (b) Neglecting opportunities as a result of crisis management.
   (c) Uncoordinated planning within managerial levels.
   (d) Constant upward climb of costs.
   (e) Tendency to tolerate mediocrity.
   (f) Growing disparity between employer and employee goals.
   (g) Imbalanced organizations.

REFERENCES AND NOTES

1. Warren Bennis, "Organizational Change Operating in the Temporary Society," *Innovation*, No. 1, May 1969, p. 8.

2. "How's Business? Latest Nationwide Survey," *U. S. News and World Report*, December 14, 1970, pp. 20–21.

3. Alvin Toffler, *Future Shock*, Bantam Book Co., New York, 1970, pp. 9–12.

4. J. M. Juran, "Universals in Management Planning and Controlling," *The Management Review*, November 1954.

5. H. Ford Dickie, "Hard-Nosed Inventory Management," in Donald G. Hall (ed.), *The Manufacturing Man and His Job*, American Management Association, New York, 1966, pp. 238–254.

6. Robert E. Sibson, "The Problems You Shouldn't Solve," *Management Review*, February 1969, pp. 29–31.

7. Gordon Lippitt and Warren H. Schmidt, "Crises in a Developing Organization," *Harvard Business Review*, November–December 1967, pp. 102–112.

8. Ralph E. Lewis, *Planning and Control for Profit*, Harper and Row Publishers, New York 1970, pp. 3–8.

9. J. J. O'Hea, "Colt Heating and Ventilating Limited," in Humble (ed.), *op. cit.*, pp. 41–44.

10. Howard M. Carlisle, "Are Functional Organizations Becoming Obsolete?" *Management Review,* January 1969, pp. 2–9.

11. C. Northcote Parkinson, *op. cit.,* pp. 2–8.

12. Richard A. Smith, *Corporations in Crisis,* Doubleday and Company, Inc., New York, 1963, p. 21.

13. The illustration of vectors with sense, direction, and magnitude has been adapted from a well-known principle of physics and was previously used by Weber and Karnes as effective leadership, a resolution between Service and Profit, *Industrial Leadership,* Chilton Co., New York, 1959, pp. 10–19.

14. Peter F. Drucker, *Managing for Results,* Harper and Row Publishers, 1964, pp. 145–147.

15. The measure of human potential is difficult. The following two books support the theory that potential utilization is between 10 and 20 percent:
    Herbert A. Otto, *Guide to Developing Your Potential,* Scribner and Sons, New York, 1967, p. 11.
    J. D. Batten, *Beyond Management by Objectives,* American Management Association, New York, 1965, p. 14.

16. David C. McClelland, *The Achieving Society,* Nostrand Co., Inc., New York, 1961, pp. 20–24.

17. M. Scott Myers, *Every Employee a Manager,* McGraw-Hill Book Company, New York, 1970, p. 46.

18. See note 13 on the use of vectors.

19. Joseph A. Litterer, *The Analysis of Organizations,* John Wiley and Sons, Inc., 1965, pp. 218–220.

3. Finding Objectives

Looking Ahead For Improvements. Techniques for Making Improvement Forecasts. Situation Action Model. Summary. Guide Questions for the Practitioner. References and Notes.

Managing by objectives is concerned basically with the future. The past is beyond control. The strategy starts from the point at which a company finds itself and prepares for the future. The conceptual strategy allows managers to look ahead, to search out, plan, and expect a certain set of results. To set objectives is to make a future commitment for the enterprise. This commitment includes people, money, facilities, time, and resources. Naturally, the value of this commitment is high because the stakes are high! Finding an objective cannot be left to caprice. A knowledge of the past and the present is desirable since it provides a perspective for judgments and projections. Present-day decisions should be sequential decisions. These are a series of related steps or problem-solving adjustments to bring a department or company from achievements today toward an anticipated set of achievements tomorrow. Problem solving is correcting and adjusting performance. Each adjustment is a change. A series of changes is a movement. A movement is a direction. The manager either makes this process deliberate and purposeful or suffers the consequences of finding himself where he never dreamed possible or desirable.

The concept of formulating objectives is inherent in any decision-making context. As O'Dell[1] put it, "Every business decision is a prediction. The executive looks for a set of results based on the conditions he arranges." The objective sought in a decision is implied rather than explicitly stated or formalized. Some form of end result is a necessary part of the decision-making process. A series of these implied decisions, in addition to solving their immediate concerns, can and does provide explicit impact on the entire operation. This is, however, without forethought or planning. *The failure of managerial decision-making to set formally and deliberately explicit objectives represents a great deficiency in the art of managing.*

The purpose of this chapter is to introduce a methodology for finding objectives for an enterprise through the concept of improvements. Finding objectives was identified as step 1 in the conceptual methodology of managing by objectives described in Chapter 1 and illustrated in Figure 1. In this chapter, four sections consider finding objectives: (1) "Looking Ahead for Improvements," which includes long-range, short-range, and immediate improvement forecasts; (2) "Five Useful Techniques for Making Improvement Forecasts"; (3) "Management Models for Improvement Forecasting"; (4) "The Situation Action Model," an integrated management approach for the identification of a potential list of attractive objectives. Several M.B.O. rules and guidelines are included in each area to give the reader a fundamental understanding of this first step in the practice of managing by objectives.

LOOKING AHEAD FOR IMPROVEMENTS

Organizations are likely to get so involved and preoccupied with the present and past that their directions are ill defined. The first implication for any organization in looking for directions lies in the mission of improvement—improvement from the standpoint of the interest and needs of the enterprise. Improvement connotes the idea of excellence, and the idea of excellence has not only been encouraged by John Gardner[2] but urged as a constructive action. He says the following:

> Excellence implies more than competence. It implies a striving for the highest standards in every phase of life. We need individual excellence in all its forms— in every kind of creative endeavor, in political life, in education, in industry— in short, universally.

The mission of improvement must be the very foundation for any planning effort. It is the foundation for the practice of managing by objectives. It recognizes the following simple truth:

Even though the future of an organization is uncertain, the organization must act and react to make it better than it has been in the past.

Looking into the future is an attempt to visualize changes that, once adopted, will improve the existing situation. In the context of this mission of improvement the search for opportunities and alternatives is part of the manager's job. The manager seeks improvement in the following traditional categories:

1. To increase share of opportunities available.
2. To develop new products and services.
3. To lead other organizations in the technology or professions.
4. To reach a needed level of operational services.
5. To increase volume of sales, customers, clients, or prospects.

6. To provide a needed return on investment.
7. To reduce waste and costs.
8. To improve the quality of products or services.
9. To strengthen the organizational image.
10. To improve morale in the work force.

A decision to adopt a set of improvements formalized into objectives must be a result of analysis and evaluation based upon the enterprise's needs. It begins by forecasting and looking at what lies ahead and determining how a company can make use of this future situation.

The look ahead often involves a capacity decision. To adopt a set of improvements is to relate end results to the resources and capabilities of the firm. It is also to improve existing capacity. A capacity definition may be one or several of the following:

Technological Capacity. Technological skills and know-how for the conception, design, production, and use of products and services.

Production Capacity. Facilities and equipment types and layout for flexible manufacturing designed for changing markets.

Manpower Capacity. Type and availability of employee skills and degree of employee willingness to work under a variety of conditions.

Capital Capacity. Cash position, budgets, assets, and ability to raise capital to support competitive projects engaged in by most companies.

Marketing Capacity. Creating and maintaining markets through promotion, service, and distribution.

Management Capacity. Effective in-house application of the managerial processes of planning, organizing, and controlling resources on all organizational levels of the enterprise.

Information-Processing Capacity. Data generation, storage, and retrieval within a timetable for effective communication and decision-making.

Reaching an objective is determined or restricted by how well existing capacity is translated into results. A company must appraise and define "what it is" as it addresses itself to "what it can be." Objectives set and reached can be viewed as successive units of capacity added as "chunks" to the organization. Conversely, objectives set and reached can be viewed as new units of capacity that does little, if anything, for the existing business. In some cases, this capacity may even subtract or dilute an existing capability. The future direction of a company or department may be thought of as the future direction of existing capacity. Initially, airlines defined their business as the "airline industry." Later in their development, they considered themselves to be in the transportation business. Today, many airlines are redefining their operations as the recreational business, since new capacity chunks such as hotels, car rentals, and resorts have been added to their initial capability. The practitioner of managing by objectives should outline, describe, interpret, and set forth the capacities that exist within an organization as he proceeds formally to find new objectives or to add new capacities.

Improvement forecasts are the vital element in planning and establishing objectives for the firm. The strategy of managing by objectives uses these forecasts as a basis from which to collect alternatives for creating a management system. Creativity, intuition, and rationality form the basis for making these forecasts. As one faces the future, one faces complexity, obscurity, and confusion. In spite of this, an objective must be found and a commitment must be made; improvement forecasts provide the method. These can be classified in many ways. One classification is by time period, that is, (1) long range, (2) short range, and (3) immediate. These categories are interrelated. Collecting alternatives from each of these categories to form the basis for setting objectives requires a systems view from future segments of time, as illustrated in Figure 3-1. This section will examine in detail what these three categories are and how they can be used in developing a potential list of objectives for an organization.

1. Long-range Improvement Forecasts

The long-term view of improvements is usually concerned with the fundamental issue of any company anywhere—self-preservation. In what state should the company be preserved? What changes from its present state are necessary? Looking ahead—3 years, 5 years, 10 years, 15 years—what ought to be the entity of the business? Economic, social, and political trends and indicators must be considered and interpreted since the long view must take into account technological changes, competitive position, new product developments, capital expansion, and new equipment acquisitions. The long-term plan with regard to a department, section, or function should deal with its long-range preservation. The head of a department—engineering or quality control, for example—must bear in mind the state of the art of his function, the direction it is taking, new skills that are emerging, and the effects of obsolescence. He must look for changes that will improve his effectiveness in the total system. Long-term improvement decisions are usually trade-offs over immediate and short-range gains. The manager must weigh carefully the acquisition of value on the short-range basis versus value over the long-term period. For example, reducing inventory by cutting down production may reduce

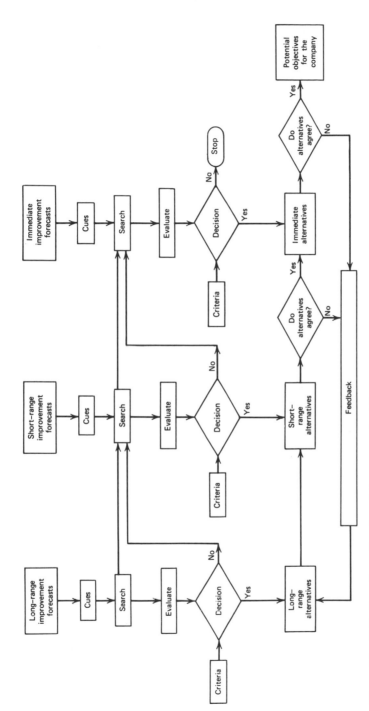

Figure 3-1. Collecting alternatives from future segments of time.

73

costs in the short run if full production capacity is not a factor. Reduced inventories, however, reduce the advantage for ready shipments and quick services to customers over the long term.

Curtiss-Wright[3] followed the practice of seeking short-range profits while ignoring and refusing to spend money on long-range development and changes required in the aerospace industry. Ex-President Hurley insisted that if Curtiss-Wright could not break even on a project in 2 or 3 years, it was not worth doing. A creeping paralysis developed within the company because it refused to look at the long-range picture. At first, the company dropped out of airframe production. Later, it stopped aircraft-engine production entirely, and finally, it ended up as a spare-parts business. One might well ask how long the company can survive until it comes to a sputtering end.

Long-term improvements must be capable of measurement in terms of the consequences to the enterprise as a whole. In order for a long-term improvement to be adopted, its anticipated effects on the organization must be clearly recognized and understood. Long-term improvement forecasts provide guidelines by which management can evaluate its own performance. These forecasts force management to think about present-day problem solving in the context of long-range survivability. The chronological scope of a forecast should be governed by the objectives sought. The 5-year forecast has traditionally been a useful rule.[4] On the other hand, the 5-year forecast may be too long or too short for the purpose intended and the information available for this period. A useful way to determine the length of the forecast is to follow the *M.B.O. Guideline for Long-range Forecasting:*

M.B.O. GUIDELINE FOR LONG-RANGE FORECASTING

Select and decide on long-term improvements within the time period that valid and useful information is available.

A company that embarks on a 5-year plan when information is available for only a 3-year forecast is pursuing a course based on guesswork, conjecture, and hope. To fit the time period to the information available is to provide management with confidence in regard to its long-range course of action.

2. Short-range Improvement Forecasts

Long-range improvement forecasts largely deal with the organization as a whole for a future period of time. Questions must be raised concerning the consequences of these long-range forecasts in the short run and for the individual departments and functions of the enterprise. Short-range improvement forecasts deal with smaller changes, shorter time periods, and consistent delivery of results. A long-term improvement may be to increase the share of the market from 23 to 30 percent. A short-term improvement may be to prevent profit fluctuations from dipping below 12 percent after taxes. Or a long-term improvement may be to make a technological breakthrough in metallurgical conductivity. A short-term improvement may be to maintain a consistent sales volume of pre-packaged electrical conductors with the same customers. Uncertainty, risks, and unknowns for the short range are not so great as for the long range. Therefore, critical changes needed in the organization should be considered short-range rather than long-range goals. The chronological scope of short-range forecasts should be governed by two considerations: the availability of useful and valid information, and the importance of achieving an improvement within a desired period of time.

Montgomery Ward's[5] postwar needs for growth and improvement within segments of time were not coupled with useful and valid information. Sewell Avery, chairman of the board, expected a financial crash as devastating as in 1929. His faulty information caused him to hoard cash year after year for a collapse that was never to come. As a result, Montgomery Ward opened no new stores, sales remained at the same level, and its arch competitor, Sears, Roebuck, moved into the market and built new stores on prime sites. In 1946, both chains had sales around the billion-dollar level, and in 1961 Ward's sales remained frozen at that level while Sears' rose to $4.3 billion. Both companies needed to grow in the postwar period, but they based their methods of accomplishing this on two different types of forecasted information.

The 1- to 2-year period for short-range forecasts traditionally has been a useful rule.[6] On the other hand, this may be either too long or too short for short-term needs. A useful way to determine the length of the forecast is to follow the *M.B.O. Guideline for Short-range Forecasting:*

M.B.O. GUIDELINE FOR SHORT-RANGE FORECASTING

Select and decide on short-term improvements within the time period in which consistent and critical results must be achieved by the company and in which valid information is available.

A company that embarks on a 2-year cost-improvement program based on 2-year breakeven cost data of newly installed capital equipment is pursuing a course of action within a time interval and based on valid information.

3. Immediate Improvement Forecasts

The immediate forecast deals with urgent problems covering periods of 3 months, 6 months, 9 months, or 12 months. It involves looking ahead and setting up performance standards that can guide a manager, department, or company to a specific improvement within a very short period of time. For example, in financial budgeting, forecasts set up standards by which management can judge its own performance independent of factors not under its control. Immediate improvement forecasts can range from accepting a production run to quoting price on a single order, or from submitting acceptable contract proposals to reducing weld rejects in a welding shop. Immediate improvement forecasts are achievements expected to be accomplished within a relatively short period of time. To be sure, immediate improvements have short- to long-range implications. Lower price quotations in contract proposals may be an immediate objective. The consequences of the contract award can be far-reaching, however. The reduction of weld rejects may have an immediate effect on the quality acceptance of a product by a customer. The long-range effect may be to change the company's percentage of the market. Improvements, whether long range, short range, or immediate, interact with each other in their effects. Yet value accrued within the specified time period must remain the major criterion for adopting an improvement measure. A useful way to determine the length of the period for an immediate forecast is to follow the *M.B.O. Guideline for Immediate-range Forecasting:*

M.B.O. GUIDELINE FOR IMMEDIATE-RANGE FORECASTING

Select and decide on immediate-range improvements within the time period in which realistic performance standards can be set up for solving critical organizational problems.

Commitments on either a long-term, a short-term, or an immediate basis have effects on balance, speed and progress in certain directions. Conflicts among the alternatives offered by the three time spans will always emerge. The manager must resolve these conflicts on the basis of company need. The decision to adopt a future set of improvements always leaves some regret or uncertainty as to whether the conflict resolution is optimal. The decision to pursue an objective does not stop the search for additional improvements. In many ways, this is a concept of "progressive looking ahead." The adoption of an objective to be accomplished in any one period is a best selection for value from many alternatives offered by the three time spans. Balance of value is defined as greatest return for effort from actions taken during a current year consistent with a company's long-term interest. No action should be taken to divert an expected gain from a future year to a smaller gain for the current year. Similarly, no action should be taken to divert an immediate gain for the current year to a smaller gain from a future year. This rule for balance of values requires a progressive view toward making commitments. Some corporations get into difficulties not from inherent flaws in the practices of decentralization, centralization, or diversification, but rather from the inability to find the balance of value among these three concepts. Corporations go to extremes in these practices and lose the balance of value. As time goes on, reassessment of the value expected from the three segments of time must continue, as illustrated in Figure 3-2.

The quality of an objective is very much influenced by the changes and needs brought about by time. A manager assesses the impact these changes and needs will have on his objective program with progressive evaluation after each period. His continued improvement forecast gives him an inventory of alternatives from which he can make progressive changes.

TECHNIQUES FOR MAKING IMPROVEMENT FORECASTS[7]

The principal aim of improvement forecasts is to provide a reliable estimate of future conditions on the basis of which objectives may be set. A good forecast is a set of realistic expectations. These expectations are essential to the practice of managing by objectives. Obviously, the methods to be used to determine these expectations are influenced by several factors: the number and type of assumptions to be made; knowledge of, background in, and understanding of the field and the industry; amount and validity of information available; time and facilities available to the forecaster; ability to sense the factors and forces controlling demand in the market; and skill in interpreting qualitative and quantitative trends and movements that cross, run parallel, or diverge from each other. Improvement forecasts are never precise! At best, they provide a structure of expectations without much detail. The skillful forecaster always forecasts the market before attempting to forecast his own company's role in the market. The progressive forecasting concept, discussed earlier, provides a way of both validating the expected structure of the market and providing pertinent details for a manager's own company. The M.B.O. practitioner will use as many aids as possible to help him

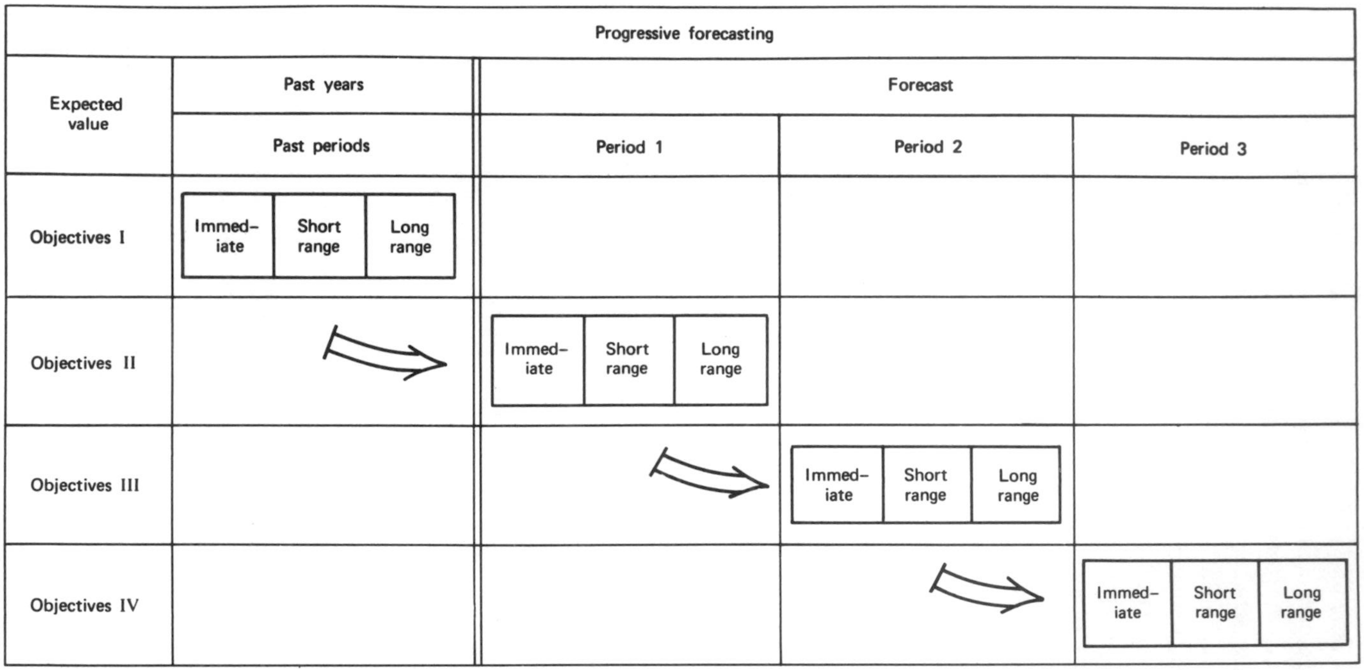

Figure 3-2. Improvement forecasts must be progressively balanced for value.

determine future structure. These several aids can be cross-checked with results. The more intimately acquainted the practitioner becomes with the field to be forecasted, the more valuable his forecast will be.

Several methods[8] are available to the forecaster to help him look ahead for improvements that may serve as a basis for objective setting. They are (1) the consensus method, (2) the problem-areas approach, (3) the maximize opportunity method, (4) numerical methods, and (5) management models. We do not intend to go into these techniques in detail. Here we present only an outline, but in the references we suggest several books that deal with these techniques in greater depth.

1. The Consensus Method

This approach relies on opinions held by a group, committee, or conference concerning the future. It is a highly subjective approach and relies on both the experience and the intuition of the participants. Each individual contributes his opinion as to the improvements he deems necessary during some future time. He makes this contribution on the basis of problem trends he has observed or experienced. His intuitive judgments are integrated reactions made up of experience, know-how, and reflection. Data used by the individual are biased and individualistic. When several such individuals are brought together, the consensus approach combines and averages the contributions of each participant. Each contribution is a single estimate. The estimates are compared to find those that have high consensus. The coordination of the various estimates can help in deciding whether a single direction can be agreed to by the participants. For a number of years, The Lockheed Aircraft Corporation,[9] a manufacturer of airframes and missiles, has used a forecasting technique called "prudent manager forecasting" as part of its long-range forecasting procedure. This involves a small group of seasoned specialists from within the company representing such functions as administration, engineering, marketing, and finance. These specialists hold conferences during which they attempt to anticipate and estimate the purchasing decisions that will be made by potential customers. This is a form of the consensus method. Obviously, the participants in the consensus method must be carefully selected for this activity since each represents a resource for the improvement forecast. Participants may be assembled as homogeneous or heterogeneous groups. Homogeneous groups might consist entirely of executives, engineers, salesmen, foremen, or planners. Heterogeneous groups might consist of members from each of the homogeneous groups within a firm or outside the firm. The selection and assignment of individuals to groups for consensus improvement forecasting will be governed by the nature of the forecast and the areas of improvement deemed critical. The pooling of experience and judgment, the ease and simplicity of the contribution, and the involvement and participation of individuals who may ultimately set the objectives help to provide a motivational climate in which objectives can be most easily reached. The disadvantages of the approach—reliance on opinions, lack of objective data, and non-numeric averaging—must be weighed against these valuable advantages.

2. The Problem-Areas Approach

In this approach, the process starts with the identification and collection of areas that have high problem-generation rates, that is, areas in which problems recur and are difficult to solve. This approach is critically needed in companies practicing crisis management. A crisis was defined earlier as the situation that exists when the rate of problem generation exceeds the rate of problem solution. Improvement forecasting using the problem-areas approach involves an analysis of the types of problems, histories of these problems, problem trends, and probabilistic occurrences. Future solutions are searched for in order to eliminate these problem trends once and for all. This approach is also a grass-roots approach, since it involves examining the opinions, data, reactions, and reports in the areas where problems are generated. Probable improvements and future solutions are solicited from those who are part of the problems as well as from those who merely relate to the problem. The Otis Elevator Company[10] for many years has made use of field information as a forecasting tool; the company has had considerable success in the areas of new elevator equipment and control over inventories. The company relies on information supplied by field personnel within various districts making up ten zones. This information is collected, checked, and consolidated at the home office to arrive at company totals.

The use of outside consultants can also be most useful in terms of assessing the nature of grass-roots problems and suggesting viable directions and problem solutions. Problem definition is important before the search for improvements can begin. A manager from an unrelated section may prove useful in providing an objective view of effects of related groups as well as in formulating the problem. This approach involves a historical analysis of the problem to see what the record has been in the past. Variables and constraints in terms of personnel, methods, equipment, facilities, and resources are identified for cause-effect relationships. The identification of causes of problems represents a significant step toward an improvement forecast since the elimination of problem causes are potential solutions. Enlisting the aid of people close to problem-generation sources as well as outside people stimulates the motivation toward improvement since getting rid of the problem might make life easier for all concerned. It does not make sense for any objective-setting program to plan future improvements without addressing itself to current problem confrontations and conflicts.

3. The Maximize Opportunity Method

A careful study of existing and potential customers for information on expected consumption, purchases, and needs is another useful method for making improvement forecasts. User-expectation surveys provide data and profiles from which opportunities for developing new products, new services, and other improvements can be identified. The National Lead Company[11] goes directly to the consumer in forecasting the market for new and undeveloped products. The firm interviews executives from a sample of companies to collect favorable or unfavorable responses on purchases of potential products. It also conducts mail surveys, using a larger number of samples, to get a response from interested customers. In each case, the greatest opportunity for a new product is carefully determined as a basis for forecasting.

The maximize opportunity approach focuses upon opportunities that are innovative for the enterprise. It searches outside the company for improvements that would make the best use of internal resources. The improvement forecast is, in effect, an attempt to maximize resources by scanning possible applications outside the company. In this respect, markets are not necessarily existing and ready to be exploited. Often, markets are created by merger, one company devoting its underutilized resources to the unexpected applications for consumer use offered by the other company. This is one reason that companies pursue programs of acquisitions and mergers. True, it is often to supplement internal growth and complement existing activities, but in many cases it is a substitute for internal growth. Acquisitions are seen as quick means of spreading existing overhead, buying skillful management and technical know-how, and expanding through acquiring capital equipment and facilities. A special study[12] conducted by the National Industrial Conference Board reported the following cases: A chemical manufacturer that had a policy of buying smaller companies because of its relatively limited product line; a food company that merged because its overhead could support additional new products; and a beverage firm that acquired two companies because its franchise base limited the area it could serve.

Improvement opportunities can be identified by any member of the enterprise's management. A deliberate program for collecting opportunities is basic to the objective-setting process of managing by objectives. Making the future happen requires ideas—improvement ideas. The maximize opportunity method is a deliberate effort to organize brainstorming for innovative ideas. This is not to suggest that the managing by objectives practitioner need be a creative genius like Edison, Sloan, or DuPont. Improvement ideas can range from breakthroughs that cause the company to progress by leaps, to minor innovations that advance the company by increments. Improvement forecasts, using the maximize opportunity approach, are made according to the following steps:

1. *Identify the totality of customer needs in a market.* This is accomplished through user-surveys, mail questionnaires, interviews, and telephone checks.

2. *Find customer needs that company can serve.* This is accomplished by removing from the totality of customer needs the needs that cannot be served.

3. *Link capabilities of company to needs that can be served.* Resources of the firm are identified and matched to needs that can be served. This matching takes into consideration the magnitude and timing of both customer needs and company resources.

4. *List constraints and limitations on matched needs.* This step involves identifying competitors, governmental constraints, community demands, and political influences.

5. *Arrange according to maximum opportunity the list of matched capabilities and customer needs.* Several criteria are used to find maximum opportunity. These are profits, return on investment, utilization of capacity, market penetration, company image, and product leverage.

6. *Formulate maximum opportunities as company objectives.* This is accomplished through the formal process of setting objectives according to the steps outlined in Chapter 1.

4. Numerical Methods[13]

The use of numerical forecasting methods employing ratios, statistics, and mathematics has become popular among many companies. Movements within a company or in the economy can be measured and projected with a reasonable degree of accuracy. The projections can identify what variables will exist, the magnitude of the variables, and deviations from known directions. This can be most helpful for improvement forecasts since new directions and deviations from present conditions will suggest new approaches and improvements a company can adopt. These methods attempt to establish a numerical series, a formula or mathematical equation that connects the pattern of variables in an economic movement with the company's role and interest. Numerical methods tend to be more objective than non-numerical ones, and when properly used are reliable and useful for estimating trends and growth. The quantification of the factors and the relationships has a tendency to give clarity and precision to the forecast. For example, with methods previously discussed, assumptions are verbalized. With numerical methods, assumptions are quantified as either constraints or limitations in the series or equation. Numerical methods generally demand the skills of a specialist since statistics, mathematics, and computers are the tools necessary for their use. Salesmen, production men, executives, and administrators may not possess these skills. Numerical methods can be used as a basis for comparing improvement forecasts of one period with those of another period. The objectivity offered by this approach permits verification by other forecasters, which tends to build validity of the forecast. The relationships within a company that are critical to the needs of the enterprise are not left to questionable intuitive judgment. The numeric description of these relationships makes it easier for management to check results. Of course, there are also many dangers in using numerical methods. Numbers tend to oversimplify and at best should be regarded as indicators. The numerical methods, in themselves, are based on assumptions that could fault the entire forecast in spite of its precision. We give only a partial description of numerical methods for improvement forecasting here. A more rigorous and detailed treatment of these methods can be found in the references. The methods that we describe briefly are the following: (1) graphical extrapolation, (2) semiaverage method, (3) method of moving-averages, (4) trend method of least squares, and (5) method of exponential smoothing.

1. *Graphical extrapolation.* Graphical extrapolation is extending into future time the average line found by plotting past data patterns. The graphical scatter chart resulting from this plot shows both the individuality of each point and the general trend of all points, making it extremely useful in making improvement forecast decisions. This is illustrated in Figure 3-3.

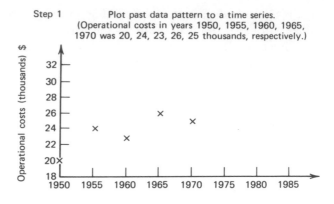

Step 1   Plot past data pattern to a time series.
(Operational costs in years 1950, 1955, 1960, 1965, 1970 was 20, 24, 23, 26, 25 thousands, respectively.)

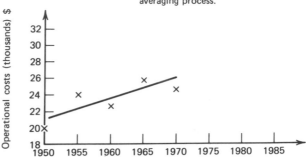

Step 2   Draw a line through the data that represent a visual averaging process.

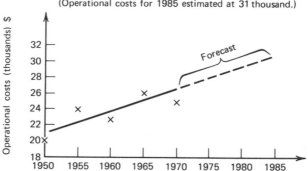

Step 3   Extend the drawn line to the period to be forecasted. (Operational costs for 1985 estimated at 31 thousand.)

Figure 3-3.   Forecasting with graphical extrapolation.

   2. *Semiaverage method.* Another simple numerical method that is not dependent upon an individual estimate is the semiaverage method. This makes use of the arithmetic mean $(\bar{x})$ for extending into future time a past data pattern. This is illustrated in Figure 3-4.

Split past data pattern of a time series into two equal parts. Compute totals (Σx) for each half. Divide totals by number of years in each semiperiod (N).

Year	Sales Volume (Millions $)	Semitotals	Semiaverage $\left(\bar{x} = \dfrac{\Sigma x}{N}\right)$
1953	10.0		
1954	10.5		
1955	11.2		
1956	12.0		
1957	13.4	$\longrightarrow$ 110.6	$\dfrac{110.6}{9} = 12.3$
1958	13.5		
1959	12.5		
1960	13.3		
1961	14.2		
1962	14.5		
1963	14.8		
1964	15.1		
1965	14.8		
1966	14.8	$\longrightarrow$ 137.9	$\dfrac{137.9}{9} = 15.3$
1967	15.2		
1968	16.0		
1969	16.1		
1970	16.6		

Step 2   Plot semiaverages and connect with line.

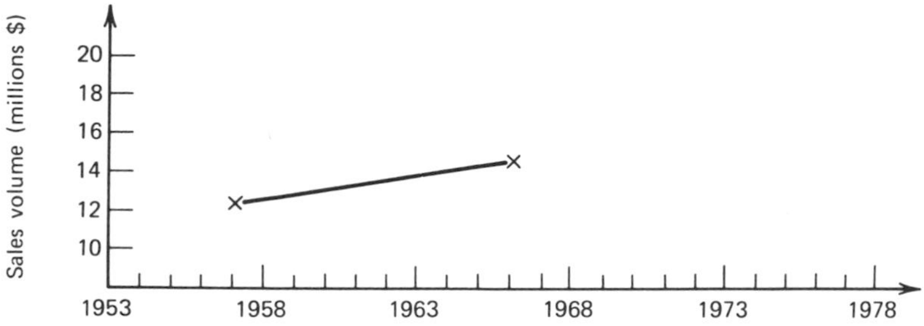

Step 3   Extend the drawn line to the period to be forecasted. (Sales volume for 1978 estimated at 18 million.)

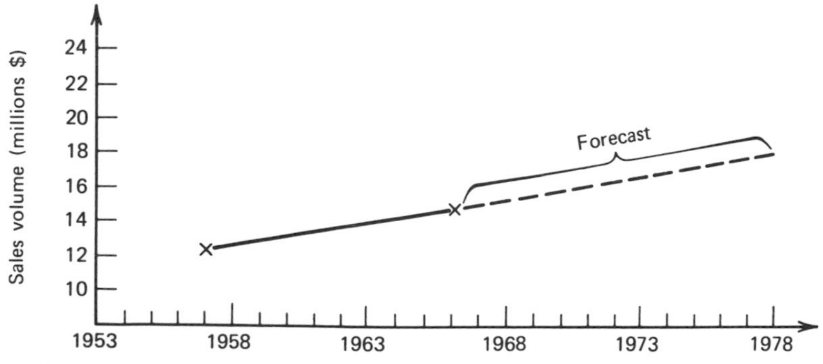

Figure 3-4. Forecasting with the semiaverage method.

3. *Method of moving-averages.* In the moving-average method, the trend is obtained by smoothing out the fluctuations of the pasta data pattern by means of a moving-average. To obtain a 5-year moving-average, in Figure 3-5, the first 5 years are added. Each succeeding total is moved by omitting the first year of the preceding period and including the year that follows the last year of the preceding period. The moving-average is computed by dividing the 5-year moving total by 5.

STEP 1.   Compute a series of moving totals by adding 5-year spans progressively (column 3).

STEP 2.   Compute an average for each total by dividing by 5 (column 4).

(1) Year	(2) Boxes Shipped (Number)	(3) 5-Year Moving Total	(4) 5-Year Moving- Average
1950	34	—	—
1951	62	—	—
1952	41	197	35.4
1953	22	207	41.4
1954	38	203	40.6
1955	44	207	41.4
1956	58	220	44.0
1957	45	252	50.4
1958	35	249	49.8
1959	70	276	53.2
1960	41	247	49.4
1961	55	274	54.8
1962	46	279	55.8
1963	62	306	61.2
1964	75	319	63.8
1965	68	331	66.2
1966	68	342	68.4
1967	58	343	68.6
1968	73	353	70.6
1969	76	—	—
1970	78	—	—

STEP 3.   Plot the actual data and the 5-year moving-average (trend).

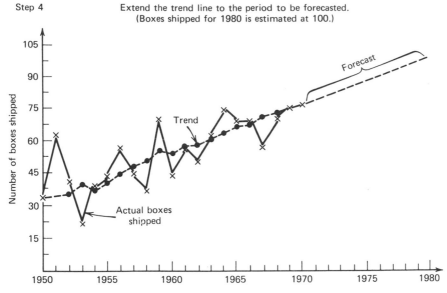

Figure 3-5. Forecasting the method of moving-averages.

4. *Trend method of least squares.* This method may be used to compute straight trend lines. Estimates of trend are calculated in such a manner that the sum of squared deviations from actual data is at a minimum; hence the term least squares. It is based on the formula for a straight-line equation:

$$Y = a + bX$$

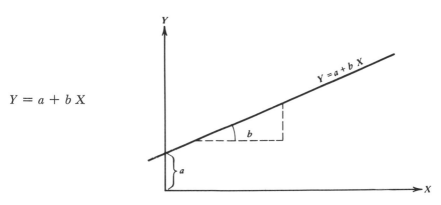

where

Y = the variable undergoing a trend
X = the variable causing the trend

a = the value of Y when X is zero; height of the straight line above the horizontal axis.

$$a = \frac{\Sigma X^2 \, \Sigma Y - \Sigma X \, \Sigma XY}{N \Sigma X^2 - (\Sigma X)^2}$$

b = the amount of change in Y that occurs with each change in X; the slope of the line.

$$b = \frac{N \Sigma XY - \Sigma X \, \Sigma Y}{N \Sigma X^2 - (\Sigma X)^2}$$

N = total number of variables

STEP 1. Calculate values of X^2, XY, Y^2 (columns 3, 4, 5).

(1) Field Districts Reporting (X)	(2) No. of Equipment Failures (Y)	(3) X^2	(4) XY	(5) Y^2	(6) Failure Trend
1	1	1	1	1	1.19
3	2	9	6	4	2.47
4	4	16	16	16	3.11
6	4	36	24	16	4.39
8	5	64	40	25	5.67
9	7	81	63	49	6.31
11	8	121	88	64	7.59
14	9	196	126	81	9.51
$\Sigma X = 56$	$\Sigma Y = 40$	$\Sigma X^2 = 524$	$\Sigma XY = 364$	$\Sigma Y^2 = 256$	

STEP 2. Calculate values for a and b; failures = $a + b$ (districts).

$$a = \frac{(524)(40) - (56)(364)}{(8)(524) - (56)^2} = .55$$

$$b = \frac{(8)(364) - (56)\,40}{(8)(524) - (56)^2} = .64$$

STEP 3. Set up trend equation and calculate values for failure trend (column 6).

$$\text{Failures} = .55 + .64 \text{ (districts)}$$

STEP 4. Forecast using failure trend equation when 20 districts report.

$$\text{Failures} = .55 + .64\,(20) = 13$$

Figure 3-6. Forecasting with trend method of least squares.

Since X is the independent variable, estimates of long-time trend may be calculated as soon as the values of a and b have been determined. This is illustrated in Figure 3-6 and with the following example: The number of field districts that report equipment failures follows a data series (columns 1 and 2). It is required to estimate the number of failures when 20 districts are reporting.

5. *Method of exponential smoothing.* Any forecasting method attempts to smooth out fluctuations in a past data pattern. In exponential smoothing, the constant alpha (α) smooths the fluctuations by giving weight to the time period that appears significant. This method is based on the following exponential-smoothing forecast equation:

$$F_n = F_{n-1} + \alpha (Y_{n-1} - F_{n-1})$$

where

$\quad F_n =$ forecast for next period

$F_{n-1} =$ forecast for previous period; can be calculated by a simple average of the most recent N observations. The moving-average can also be used.

$Y_{n-1} =$ actual value for latest period before forecast

$\quad \alpha =$ smoothing constant $(0 \leqslant \alpha \leqslant 1)$

$\qquad \alpha = 0.8$ when more weight given to recent values
$\qquad \alpha = 0.2$ when more weight given to past values

STEP 1.   Determine forecast for previous period F_{n-1} by calculating a simple average between 1962 and 1968.

$$F_{1962-68} = \frac{\Sigma X}{N} = \frac{44 + 48 + 56 + 62}{4} = 52.5$$

STEP 2.   Establish actual value for latest period before forecast (Y_{n-1}).

$$Y_{1970} = 66$$

STEP 3.   Decide on value for smoothing constant (α).

$$\alpha = 0.8 \text{ (heavy weight given to recent values)}$$

STEP 4.   Estimate the number of boxes to be shipped for 1972 with the exponential-smoothing forecast equation.

$$F_{1972} = F_{1962-68} + .8 (Y_{1970} - F_{1962-68})$$
$$F_{1972} = 52.5 + .8 (66 - 52.5)$$
$$F_{1972} = 63 \text{ boxes}$$

Figure 3-7.   Forecasting with method of exponential smoothing.

Exponential smoothing is a weighted-average method for allowing the forecaster to assign greater or lesser importance to an old forecast relative to current values. An example of this method is given in Figure 3-7 with the following: The number of boxes shipped for the periods 1962, 1964, 1966, 1968, and 1970 are 44, 48, 56, 62, and 66, respectively. Estimate the number of boxes to be shipped in 1972.

In summarizing the discussion of techniques for making improvement forecasts, it should be clearly noted that companies do not rely exclusively on any one approach to the exclusion of others. Although the preceding descriptions have been devoted to single methods, most company applications require more than one method. That is, most firms take a multiple-method approach, adopting those techniques most useful for making the type of improvement desired. This multiple-method approach appears rational since forecasting tends to pyramid from the specific locus of a department to a broad range of future concerns, as suggested in the following forecast ranges:

Extensively broad.   Economic, political, and social indicators
Very broad.   General business conditions
Broad.   Specific industry movements
Narrow.   Products, services, and consumer needs
Very narrow.   Individual company directions
Specifically narrow.   Needed specific future improvements

Those companies that elect to rely on a single method to find their improvements usually experience consistent results. This is often, however, an oversimplification. The multiple-method approach offers a more realistic and reassuring series of checks and balances.

5.   Management Models for Improvement Forecasting

Management models are structural representations of variables in the real world of work in a form that displays and makes ready a given set of conditions for decision-making. The representation is intended for analysis, study, measurement, and manipulation in order to determine the best course of action from many possible courses of action. A model is a valid representation if it includes as much information as necessary for a particular purpose. It becomes an aid to seeing certain features of a system and to seeing the effects of the system when variables are forces of change. Models provide feedback to improve decisions, reduce uncertainty, identify conflicts, build confidence, and make predictions. It is this last prediction function that is useful in improvement forecasting. The model is a picture of the situation that the manager manages. To be sure, it is not a very good picture since it is oversimplified. The model has but few dimensions, whereas the managerial situation is multi-dimensional. The model has clearly defined boundaries, whereas the managerial situation is not so clearly separated from its environment. The model contains only a few variables and a few facts, whereas the managerial situation is a complex system of men, materials, money, machinery, and methods. The model, at best, is an attempted simulation of a situation. Through it, the manager wishes to test a decision or to see a certain cause-effect process.

Several types of models have been developed.[14] Each represents a structure that is intended to aid managers to grasp a situation in its entirety, to change some of its conditions, to control processes and operations designed for achieving objectives, and to test decisions. A brief discussion of five types of management models follows.

1. *Iconic or physical models.* These are models that contain a physical representation of a real situation. The representation looks like the real thing in miniature and gives a visual picture of relationships in three dimensions. Physical models may be life-size, smaller, or larger. A scaled-model car is a miniature representation of a real car. When several of these model cars are set on a street intersection designed to scale and are made to collide, a management model has been set up on the basis of which forecasts can be made as to possibilities for improving street design, setting up new traffic patterns, or both. A three-dimensional, scaled-down replica of a production system in which work flows as a result of equipment, people, machines, methods, and processes is a model of managerial situation from which to judge the effects of changes in schedule, equipment locations, or work flow. A proposed layout is tested for improvements in the management model before making the real changes. Each part is constructed as a template and moved as a variable for distance, time, output, frequency, cost, and working conditions.

2. *Graphic models.* Graphic models are two-dimensional graphic representations of a real situation. Usually they depict one aspect of the situation for demonstration or manipulation. Replacement-planning organization charts are graphic models. The divisions and the positions of the chart provide a structure for the managerial situation. Transfers, promotions, retirements, and replacements by incumbents are the manipulations of the variables within the managerial situation in order to find the best arrangement. In-flow process operations charts for production planning provide examples demonstrating a situation needing change. The elements of operations, delays, storage, transportation, and inspec-

tion are manipulated to determine the effects of rearranging work to gain efficiency and increase motivation. Moving these variables provides insights into possible improvements over an existing situation. The breakeven chart is a graphic model. Fixed costs, variable costs, and total revenues are variables that can be moved in the chart in order to see how the breakeven point moves and what its effects on profits and losses are.

3. *Network or schematic models.* Network models deemphasize the importance of physical or visual relationships and stress connective input/output flow relationships. A network model provides an overview, showing the parts and the interactions among the parts. A systems flow results with network models. A computer program flow chart depicts the configuration that is necessary for data to flow and arrive at a set of computed results. A PERT network diagram is a panorama of the events and activities necessary to complete a project. A method to change these events and activities is to manipulate time by either extending or contracting it.

4. *Mathematical models.* Mathematical models deemphasize the importance of visual and flow situational descriptions and stress manipulative value of quantitative factors. Relationships, limits, and constraints are set up in the form of equations or symbols to improve the accuracy and quantification of results. In decision-making situations, mathematical models predict outcomes resulting from changes in existing operations. Breakeven mathematical equations are an example of quantifying profit as a relationship between sales and cost. The effects of a decision to change one or the other can be observed and studied. Linear programming equations structure the allocation of resources and the effects when these allocations are changed. Decisions are made in linear programming to determine optional use of resources.

5. *Probability verbal models.* Probability verbal models deemphasize the importance of visual, flow, and quantification relationships and stress cause-effect relationships. These models are structured in essay form, using words to capture causes and effects, and they apply a logic to thinking and analysis. Variables are assigned a probability or rank order in order to analyze changes and effects. More will be said later about this model because it will form the basis of an illustration of the objective-setting processes.

Management models are purposeful activities for structuring situations in such a way that problems are obvious, opportunities emerge, and choices to reach out and select alternatives are made available. The real

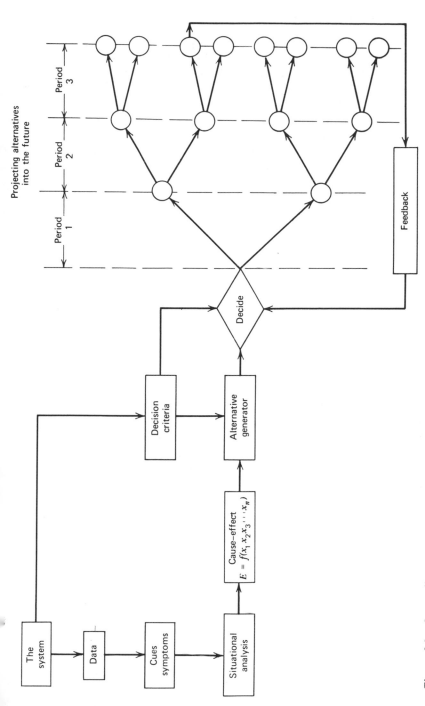

Figure 3-8. Cause-effect processes as source of alternatives.

value of a management model is that it produces a set of alternatives from which objectives may be selected. Improvement forecasts are alternatives projected into the future with future conditions kept in view. A model that yields few alternatives limits the quality of decision-making. On the other hand, a model that yields many alternatives can help bring about high-quality decision-making through optimization. The search for and evaluation of all possible courses of action have been traditionally carried out through the effective methods of brainstorming and idea accumulation. An additional method is the cause-effect approach, which is basic to the structure of a probability-verbal model. Alternatives are generated from an extensive analysis of the cause-effect relationship in a situation, as illustrated in Figure 3-8.

THE SITUATION ACTION MODEL

The situation action model offers another way of finding objectives. This model, a form of the probability verbal model described in the preceding section, is a structure that contains several related steps: (1) collecting effects from a situation analysis; (2) determining causes of situational effects; (3) finding eliminators of (alternatives to) causes in the situation; and (4) choosing the best eliminator (alternative). These steps are illustrated in Figure 3-9. The logic behind this sequence of actions is clear. One cannot select a course of action or an objective until he has examined the situation he is in. Specifically, he cannot set a course to follow unless he knows where he is. As in navigation, plotting a course requires locating two positions—where one is and where one is heading. It seems more useful to start where one is since resources, existing commitment, and current capabilities must be considered in any future context. From this known point, an objective is set and a course of action is plotted. By following in sequence the enumerated steps of the situation action model, the practitioner of managing by objectives has a useful and practical tool for finding objectives for his organization.

1. Collecting Effects from a Situational Analysis

A situational analysis is a deliberate method of raising questions and collecting data about the company's immediate situation and how it arrived there. It is an analysis of significant trends and changes occurring within the organization and a forecast of where the company is heading as a result of these conditions. The purpose of the situational analysis in

Situation Action Model (with case example)

Situational Problem: *Production department unable to meet production quota*

Decision Matrix

Effects (Symptoms)	Causes (Conditional Forces)	Eliminators (Improvement Alternatives)	Standards To Decide*				Total Rank Across	Best Alternative (Objectives To Be Completed)
			Customer Effects	Sales Volume	Union Unrest	Feasibility		
1. Backlog excessive	1. Machine idleness and downtime high	1. Use preventive maintenance program	3	2	2	3	10	*Second objective:* set up preventive maintenance program
2. Schedule slippage	2. Unsequenced ordering of parts	2. PERT ordering of parts from vendors	2	1	5	1	9	*First objective:* PERT ordering of parts from vendors
3. High overhead	3. Excessive travel expense	3. Set up travel expense control	6	7	6	6	25	
4. Turnover excessive	4. Low motivation	4. Design jobs for job enrichment	5	5	4	5	19	
5. High grievance rate	5. Contract violations by supervision	5. Train supervisors in labor contract	7	6	1	4	18	
6. Loss of key customers	6. Product breakdown disrupts customers' operations	6. Improve design reliability	1	3	7	7	18	
7. Reject rates high	7. Careless errors among employees	7. Motivate and train employees	4	4	3	2	13	

* Rank order; probabilities; or percentages can be used for assessing alternatives against the decision standard within the column. Here the rank-order method is used.

Figure 3-9. Situation action model for finding objectives.

collecting and analyzing information and trends is to identify and inter- pret both the directions in which the company is drifting without choice and the directions the company can take if an organized and deliberate plan can be adopted. This approach discourages picking objectives out of thin air and relates objective setting to the needs of the enterprise. The analysis will disclose a series of facts, both strengths and weaknesses, relating to services and product requirements. It will also provide in- formation as to the company's resources and capability of delivering these services and products. The manager raises many questions in order to collect a variety of viewpoints about the situation; from these opinions he identifies the needs and deficiencies of the enterprise. These needs and deficiencies, if left unattended, can cause the firm either to drift in some un- wanted direction or actually to change in some undesirable way. Several methods can be useful in uncovering symptoms of problems in a situ- ation—for example, conducting audits, collecting statistical data, hold- ing conferences, making purposeful observations, analyzing reports, and interviewing individuals. However, asking questions is the heart and core of diagnosis. Hodnet[15] once remarked, "To know what to ask is already to know half." Asking questions is like sharpening a knife. Each apt question helps sharpen the blade to cut the problem precisely. There is no easy system for formulating questions. Questions follow a pattern of thinking and analyzing. The seven basic guidelines have always been useful: Who? When? Where? Which? What? How? and Why? These questions do not plumb the depths for specifics needed to understand the situation, but they can give the questioner a good grip on situational effects. The skillful manager will find it easy to consider a situation as a whole, to raise the appropriate question, and to visualize possible improvement. Organized questions are valuable as a starting point since they can penetrate the problem and provide information that enables the questioner to examine different facets of the problem. To stimulate thinking and to help a manager get a good grip on situational effects, the following questions can be posed:

A. Problem analysis
1. What is the potential product obsolescence and length of product life?
2. What directives, policies, positions, and organizational conditions are impeding growth and performance improvement?
3. What problems can be expected within 3 months? 6 months? 12 months?
4. What changes can be made in job requirements to enlarge re- sponsibilities and currency?

5. What are the barriers that have prevented the company from reducing cost and being more efficient?

B. Opportunity analysis
   1. Where is the highest probable rate of growth for each product or service?
   2. Where are the possible technological breakthroughs and what are the effects on present facilities and equipment?
   3. Where is the greatest number of potential customers for volume sales with emerging new technologies?
   4. Where have product or service values closely aligned with customer needs?
   5. Where are the unique advantages over competitors' products that could be expanded?

C. Personnel analysis
   1. Who are the marginal or submarginal personnel who are draining the resources of the firm?
   2. Who are those impeding improvement and what can be done to help them better their performance?
   3. Who are the individuals who have ideas but have not been able to implement them?
   4. Who are the individuals who would double their performance if they were shifted to a new set of challenges?
   5. Who are the individuals who are too big for their small jobs or too small for their big jobs?

D. Schedule analysis
   1. When can existing commitments be moved up for completion?
   2. When can a new schedule be adopted for implementing a new idea?
   3. When can additional manpower be added to complete commitments earlier?
   4. When can cost targets be given to personnel to meet commitments?
   5. When can changes be included to reduce rejects and defects?

E. Methods analysis
   1. How can we regroup or alter the sequence of work assignments to reduce costs and improve schedule?
   2. How can we revise our layout for improved coordination and shortening distances?
   3. How can a rearrangement improve morale, satisfaction, and results?

4. How can a suboperation be modified, changed, or redesigned to incorporate the functions of other suboperations?
5. How can a major operation be improved by elimination of or modifying a suboperation?

These questions as well as additional ones can help the manager to identify the needs and deficiencies of the enterprise. They are particularly useful in discovering effects or symptoms of a situational problem. The following is a partial list of these effects:

Excessive backlog
Schedule slippage
Excessive pollution
Loss of key customers
High accident rates
High waste and spoilage
Excessive repairs
Interdepartmental disputes
Rivalries
Individual resistance
Low sales growth
High corrective work
Low inventory
High overhead
Excessive turnover
Loose quality control
High costs
High machine downtime
High material-handling costs
Production delays
High absenteeism
Insufficient dividends
High pilferage
High rejected rates
Low profits
High grievance rate
Sales volume off
Low morale
Continuous errors
Rumors
Poor public image
Overtime deterioration
Imbalanced organization

High rates of shipping returns
Ineffective advertising

2. Determining Causes of Situational Effects

Once an examination has been made of effects, symptoms, indicators, and other data pertinent to pinpointing the company's immediate situation, a search can be made for causes. Cause-effect relationships are identified within the situation. A cause is a conditional force acting on or dominating a situation. Obviously, there are desirable as well as undesirable cause-effect relationships. Those causes producing undesirable effects represent areas in which improvements can be proposed for reduction or elimination. Those causes producing desirable effects represent areas in which improvements can be proposed for continued growth. A greater understanding of cause-effect relationships can provide additional insight into the situational analysis. The following are some principles designed to provide a better understanding of these relationships.

The enormous importance of cause-effect relationships in objective-setting processes and to the ultimate commitments of the enterprise makes their analysis worthwhile. As Hodnet[16] describes it, "Solving problems by working from cause to effect is always working into the future." Causes are the producers of effects. Regarded in this light, they can be improvement forecasts. Every time a person says, "What would happen if we tried . . . ?" he is thinking and forecasting from cause to effect. Conversely, working from effect to cause is working backward in time. Every time the question, "Why did this happen?" is asked, a person is thinking and

Principle I. A single cause can generate an ever-widening chain of primary effects. These primary effects become causes of secondary effects.

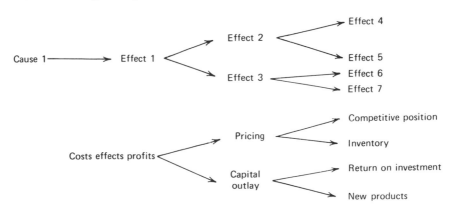

Principle II. A cause-effect relationship can be interchanged when directed toward a new objective or new situation.

Cause ⟶ ⟵ Effect

Sales — costs = profits
Sales — profits = costs

Principle III. When there are several optional causes producing variable effects, cause-effect relationships can be selected and directed toward an objective.

Cause 1 — Effect 1
Cause 2 — Effect 2
Cause 3 — Effect 3
Cause 4 — Effect 4

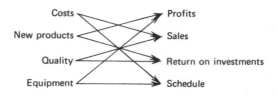

Costs — Profits
New products — Sales
Quality — Return on investments
Equipment — Schedule

Principle IV. A cause constraint occurs when causes hold back the completion of a desired effect.

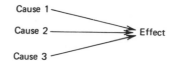

Cause 1
Cause 2 — Effect
Cause 3

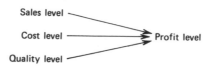

Sales level
Cost level — Profit level
Quality level

Principle V. An effect constraint occurs when causes hold back the completion of a desired cause.

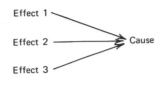

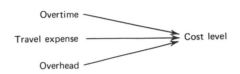

analyzing from effect to cause. Managerial analysis and problem solving follow this logical procedure. It is unfortunate that most managerial time is devoted to the past—that is, to analyzing from effect to cause—and thereby results only in unmaking the past. This was discussed earlier in the section on crisis management. It should be clear to the reader that a 180-degree shift in orientation will offer the opportunity to devote cause-effect analysis to improvement forecasts for a future period. The principles described earlier allow us to take this perspective. A desirable effect in the past can be targeted for the future by finding the cause and redirecting it. An undesirable effect in the past can be avoided in the future by finding the cause and eliminating it. Tracing cause-effect reasoning in the present situation provides a good basis for selecting objectives for the future. The following is a partial list of situational causes. According to principle II, they can also be effects in a different situation:

Shrinking economy
Negative attitudes
Strikes
Insufficient space
Poor timing
Poor methods and procedures
Mismatched job and employee
Unacceptable products
Too much quality
Insufficient lead time
High wage rates
Seasonal influences

Wrong materials
Lack of job skills
Not enough controls
Insufficient records
Low motivation
No preventive planning
Inadequate safety practices
Poor organization
Inadequate standards
Dominant personalities
Weather conditions
Old or faulty equipment
Lack of needed information
Bad layout
Insufficient inspection
Lack of coordination
No shipping schedules
Insufficient communications

3. Finding Eliminators of (Alternatives to) Situational Causes

Finding eliminators or alternatives should not be a hit-or-miss affair but a careful search for the specific action that will eliminate the undesirable cause or strengthen the desirable one. The search for causal variables and their effects provides a methodology for discovering alternatives for future improvements. An understanding of cause-effect relationships according to the principles described above can give insights into identifying eliminators of causes. Problem eliminators are possible improvements. Possible improvements are alternatives. Suggestions for eliminating or reducing a cause in a given situation emerge as alternatives for improving the situation. For every cause, there is a suggested alternative to oppose, eliminate, or strengthen the existing cause. A multiplicity of causes implies a multiplicity of eliminators and, in turn, a multiplicity of alternatives. Thus an "alternative generator" can be developed by identification and analysis of causal variables. The more causes a manager can identify, the more alternatives he can make available. The more alternatives a manager has, the better the quality of his decision for a future commitment is likely to be. A good decision-maker always asks, "How many more alternatives are there?" In this question lies the difference between a fair decision-maker and a first-rate one. The superior decision-maker does not accept three or four possible alternatives easily, even when they are good. Merely gathering a number of possible courses of action does not mean that the best course of action is among them. He not only searches for all the possible courses of action; he also develops a gradient among them to reveal those that are best. In addition, he recognizes that doing nothing is an alternative. He has a choice between maintaining the status quo or changing it. When the consequences of doing nothing appear better than those of doing something, then the good manager chooses to leave well enough alone. He is also the judge of when he has a sufficient number of alternatives to make a decision. He knows whether to stop at three, four, or ten alternatives, basing his judgment on the importance of time. Often the search for the "best" alternative can be a waste of effort as well as time. Often the "better" one will suffice. One can easily fall into the trap of continually putting off making a decision on the hope that the best alternative is just beyond the horizon. This delay can be disastrous! The amount of time available should be the guide to how many alternatives can be considered.

The superior decision-maker does not confine himself to extracting alternatives only from causal variables. He also uses traditional methods to bring about an interplay of aptitudes, resources, past experiences, and untried, novel ideas. If the principle holds true that the quality of decision is raised with an increase in the number of alternatives, then several methods and strategies for generating alternatives should be employed. These methods[17] are practical ways of finding eliminators (alternatives). Among them are the following: brainstorming, idea checklists, question checklists, and value analysis.

Brainstorming. Probably the most widely known and used technique among managers and companies, brainstorming is based on the principle that suspension of judgment allows the mind to free wheel. It is assumed that an individual can come up with more alternatives when he does not have to evaluate and weigh each alternative. The mind seems to pour out more ideas when this is the only function it is permitted to perform. There is a braking effect on ideas when more than one function is required of the mind. As with individuals, brainstorming within groups rules out criticism or evaluation for the same reason. The mutual stimulation felt by participants in a group can be very useful in accumulating alternatives. Whether brainstorming for alternatives is used on an individual basis or in a group, the technique is useful for accumulating ideas as potential alternatives for the objective-setting process.

Idea checklists. Another technique for accumulating alternatives involves idea checklists. This approach uses ideas as channels to establish new trains of thought. The lists of ideas serve to stimulate further ideas and lead to new directions. Idea checklists accumulate data from experience, prior solutions, strategies used with other products, memory, needs, sensitivities, and questions. The checklist must be developed for a particular function, department, or product. As one reads and reviews these lists with the particular problem in mind, the idea stimulates a chain of thinking which might result in an attractive alternative.

Question checklists. In a manner similar to idea checklists, question checklists provide another approach to thinking up alternatives. Instead of listing ideas to improve a particular function, department, or product, the company lists questions pertinent to a variety of categories and applications. These questions are intended to offer alternative points of view. The various answers to a question about a given function or problem may trigger a series of ideas useful in organizing a proposal for a course of action. Earlier, the questioning technique was suggested as a method of collecting symptoms or effects in a situation. Now it is seen as a valuable tool for generating fluidity and variability in thought processes. Both of these applications in the conceptual strategy of setting objectives confirm the value and indispensability of skill in questioning.

Value analysis.[18] Still another approach to the search for alternatives is value analysis. It is an organized approach to identifying the underlying function of a product, problem, or difficulty while considering the importance of cost and product quality. Secondary and tertiary functions are also identified. An evaluation is made of how well the function is accomplished. Ascertaining value applies to methods, parts, services, and procedures. That is, how does each part of the overall activity contribute to the basic function? Herein lies the value of generating alternatives, since any suggestions as to how to improve the function while maintaining cost and quality requirements also suggest other new ideas for consideration. A complicated situation may consist of several functions, each related to the others. The value analysis approach enables one to compare one function with another in terms of cost, quality, and time. This comparison results in a scale of value. Suggestions can be made on how to improve the value of these functions. Thus alternatives are generated within the function itself.

Deliberate creative techniques combined with information and good judgment can be used to generate alternatives for the objective decision process. Creative techniques are personal matters. One technique can work well for one person but not for another. The situation action model has a logical structure of effect, identification, cause determination, and alternative generation. But it offers flexibility within this structure for each individual to pursue a method useful and meaningful to him as he reaches and identifies his future objectives.

4. Choosing and Deciding on the Best Alternative

The final step in the process of finding the objective using the situation action model of Figure 3-9 is to select which alternative is best suited to the objective-setting procedures. Painstaking effort and analysis have gone into the process up to this point. The challenge now is to evaluate the alternatives to find the best few. This means a decision must be made to weigh the alternatives in terms of value, payoff, or utility—utility of a gamble, as Brincklose[19] puts it. One of the chief differences between an objective program that produces outstanding results and one that produces mediocre results lies in the utility or payoff weight that is assigned to the various alternatives. To determine which alternative has the greatest payoff, we need decision criteria or standards for action. These are measures for weighing utility. They are guidelines by which an alternative or eliminator is judged as to its value in and applicability to the situation. The weights that are assigned to each alternative on the basis of a standard for action are verniers or degrees of priority. A payoff matrix or decision-making matrix can be a useful way to represent how the weights will be allocated to each standard of action, as illustrated in the situation action model of Figure 3-9. This is a grid on which the alternatives are placed with the standards placed in an adjacent position. Finding the alternatives that best meet all necessary standards is the process of optimizing. A numerical ranking procedure, probability assignments, or percentages can be used as the vernier for assessing how well the alternative meets the standard for action. A ranking procedure was used in Figure 3-9, which thus illustrates a ranking matrix. Alternatives are assigned rank numbers on the basis of how well they meet utility and payoff standards. The step-by-step procedure for developing the best ranking from the decision matrix is as follows:

STEP 1. Select the standards for action that constitute greatest utility in the situation or problem at hand.

STEP 2. Using a numerical ranking sequence, weigh each alternative in order of utility for each columnar standard, 1 for greatest utility, 2 for next greatest, and so on.

STEP 3. Continue the process of ranking each of the alternatives by columns until all standards that have been selected are covered.

STEP 4. Add horizontally the cell values to arrive at the total score in the total score column.

STEP 5. Select the rank number in the total score column for the alternative that best meets all criteria.

STEP 6.   If standards are to be given differences in value, rank the standards across in order of importance and multiply the cell value by this weight. Repeat steps 4 and 5. If standards are regarded as equal in importance, then ignore this last step.

The optimizing process is enhanced when a meaningful selection of standards has been made in relation to the problem or the situation. The following is a checklist of standards for action that will help to determine the goals or objectives to be set.

   a.   *Return on investment (ROI).* Increasing the rate or percentage of profit or interest returned to the enterprises as a result of undertaking an investment or capital commitment at some early period of time.

   b.   *Sales volume.* Increasing the amount of disposed of or sold products, services, or merchandise in an existing or created market.

   c.   *Cost benefit.* Maintaining minimal expense in the selection and deployment of resources, equipment, materials, methods, and manpower.

   d.   *Schedule.* Meeting a predetermined time program that projects events, operations, arrivals, and departures. A sense of pace is structured and reached.

   e.   *Feasibility.* Capable of being done or effected in a practical way.

   f.   *Customer effects.* Avoiding situations that would retard patronage of an enterprise.

   g.   *Competitive advantage.* Avoiding acts that will favor a rival enterprise that is engaged in selling goods and services in the same market.

   h.   *Employee morale.* Creating a climate and mood conducive to willing and dependable performance.

   i.   *Union unrest.* Avoiding actions disruptive to collective bargaining efforts.

   j.   *Community image.* Avoiding acts which give the company an unpleasant appearance in the eyes of the community.

   k.   *Legislative actions.* Avoiding illegal practices that may provoke legal action to retard or stop competition and growth.

   l.   *Cash position.* Creating a favorable and necessary situation in which the turnover of capital follows a cycle from cash to assets to receivables and back to cash, in sufficient time for the enterprise's use.

m. *Opportunities for improvement.* Exploiting uniquely timed situations for market growth expansion and diversification.

n. *Quality requirements.* Avoiding acts aimed at reducing the ability of a product or service to satisfy its specified design.

o. *Safety needs.* Avoiding activities that are unsafe and areas where safety standards are minimal.

p. *Tax benefits.* Avoiding acts that exceed the statute of limitations and bring about tax increases.

The foregoing criteria form only a sample list for the manager who is screening his options in order to discover potential objective areas. Probably the most important criterion for all managers to follow is opportunities for improvement. Such opportunities are built into the selection of alternatives because these alternatives are standards for action. For example, an opportunity to move into a new area by adopting a new product is assigned a weight and included in the ranking matrix. In this manner, when one solves a problem to meet an organizational need one also takes advantage of new opportunities. Intrinsic to the practice of managing by objectives is the desire to "leap forward" or take a "quantum jump ahead" in improvements. Incremental progress does not justify the commitment of time, money, and resources that must be made to employ the technique. Either the progress must be significant or another approach is indicated. The criteria for meeting and exploiting opportunities should be heavily weighted in the matrix solution of the model.

The steps of finding and evaluating alternatives for objective-setting processes must be directed toward greatest payoff. To determine what course of action has the highest probability of success is a major decision of the organization and its managers. The quality of results achieved from pursuing a set of objectives depends largely on how well the objectives are set and in how decisive a manner they are carried out.

SUMMARY

Managing by objectives is managing with the accent on the future. It requires looking ahead to what must happen in the enterprise. This chapter described the first step, finding objectives, in the five-step sequence in the practice of managing by objectives. The concept of improvement forecasts was described as an estimate of areas in which a company may find attractive objectives to follow. Several techniques and guidelines have been introduced and explained for conducting forecasts within a firm.

GUIDE QUESTIONS FOR THE PRACTITIONER

1. What is your understanding of the reasons for using a systematic and deliberate approach for finding objectives?

2. Why are improvement forecasts necessary for the M.B.O. practitioner? What types of improvement forecasts does your company use to find objectives?

3. What type of improvement forecast do you see as most useful for your section or department?

4. Explain what management models are and how they fit into the decision-making process?

5. Select a problem trend area as suggested in Chapter 2 and apply the situation action model to find objectives to break the trend.

6. Using the situation action model for your department or company, make the following analysis:
   (a) Collect effects or symptoms of problems and descriptions.
   (b) Determine what the causes are.
   (c) Find eliminators and suggest alternatives.
   (d) Using the decision matrix, choose the best alternative.

7. List the ways in which you think the ability to find objectives rationally improves the skills of a manager.

REFERENCES AND NOTES

1. William F. O'Dell, *The Marketing Decision,* American Management Association, New York, 1968, p. 130.

2. John W. Gardner, *Excellence: Can We Be Equal and Excellent Too?* Harper and Row, New York, 1961, p. 160.

3. Richard A. Smith, *Corporations in Crisis,* Doubleday and Co., New York, 1963, p. 11.

4. To treat adequately long-range profit planning would require a book in itself. Dale P. McConkey gives a detailed insight into the 5-year profit in his book, *Planning Next Year's Profits,* American Management Association, New York, 1968, pp. 87–94.

5. Richard A. Smith, *op. cit.,* pp. 6–9.

6. Dale P. McConkey, *op. cit.,* pp. 106–114.

7. The literature on techniques for making forecasts is voluminous. The three following books will provide the reader with greater depth into the techniques: Myron S. Heidingsfield and Frank H. Eby, Jr., *Marketing and Business Research*, Holt, Rinehart and Winston, New York, 1963; Robert Ferber, *Market Research*, McGraw-Hill Book Co., New York, 1949; James L. Riggs, *Production Systems: Planning, Analysis and Control*, John Wiley and Sons, Inc., New York, 1970.

8. National Industrial Conference Board, *Forecasting Sales*, Studies in Business Policy No. 106, New York, 1964, pp. 12–62.

9. *Ibid.*, p. 16.

10. *Ibid.*, p. 27.

11. *Ibid.*, p. 31.

12. National Industrial Conference Board, *Merger Policy in the Smaller Firm*, Studies in Business No. 10, New York, 1969, p. 21.

13. Numerical methods for forecasting are presented in outline form. The reader is urged to consult with books suggested in reference 7 for a rigorous and detailed statistical treatment of these methods.

14. James Riggs, *Economic Decision Models*, McGraw-Hill Book Co., New York, 1968, pp. 16–20.

15. Edward Hodnet, *The Art of Problem Solving*, Harper and Row, New York, 1955, p. 33.

16. *Ibid.*, p. 130.

17. Alex F. Osborn, *Applied Imagination*, Scribner's and Sons, New York, 1953, pp. 227–243.

18. Lawrence D. Miles, *Techniques of Value Analysis and Engineering*, McGraw-Hill Book Co., New York, 1961, pp. 1–18.

19. William D. Brincklose, *Managerial Operations Research*, McGraw-Hill Book Co., New York, 1969, pp. 81–91.

4. Setting Objectives

Formulatiing Objectives. Quantifying Objectives. Number of Objectives. Sample Objectives. Selecting Objectives for Highest Payoff. Entry Methods for Interlocking Objectives. Feeder-Objectives Set for Performance Stretches. Summary. Guide Questions for the Practitioner. References and Notes.

Clearly, central to a management by objectives effort is the process of determining just what it is a company, an organization, or an individual should accomplish within a specified period of time. The assumption that every manager knows exactly what he is trying to achieve is often incorrect. The truth is rather that directions and pursuits tend to get lost in the shuffle and bustle of managerial activities. Managers need to keep goals clearly in mind as well as the steps necessary to achieve these goals.

There has been a tendency among managers to regard setting objectives as a relatively simple process; it is deceptively simple, however. The formalization of a statement of objectives requires precision of thinking and forecasting as well as making commitments involving others; most managers are not accustomed to viewing the process in this light. Directing many people in a unified effort to reach a desired end is far from simple.

The previous chapter dealt with the rationale of making a situational analysis, collecting data, and defining areas in which to find objectives. The situation was analyzed in terms of four questions: What are our problems? What are our opportunities? Where are we drifting? and Where should we be going? Forecasting techniques were described and a situation action model was utilized to structure thinking in a logical manner to find the best areas for setting goals. This is the first step in the practice of managing by objectives as outlined in Chapter 1.

The second step is the specific process of setting and formalizing statements of objectives. This chapter will provide a clear understanding of this second step. It discusses the following subjects: (1) formulating objectives, (2) quantifying objectives, (3) number of objectives, (4) sample objectives, (5) selecting objectives for highest payoff, (6) entry methods for interlocking objectives, and (7) feeder-objectives set for performance stretches.

FORMULATING OBJECTIVES

Formulating meaningful statements of objectives takes careful thought and analysis. The intention of the objective must be clear and its focus well understood. The formal statement should not only specify the action to be taken but also stimulate it. The following are guidelines to assure careful formulation of objectives:

1. Defined in terms of results or conditions to be achieved rather than in terms of activities to be performed.
2. Written so that they can be analyzed and reviewed from time to time.
3. Limited in time so as to provide milestones of achievement.
4. Written forcefully, starting out with such terms as *achieve, complete by,* and *replace,* which suggest results or performance stretches.
5. Completed with an accountability assignment to a member of management.
6. Formulated in the light of past experiences.
7. Stated in positive terms, that is, in terms of what is to be done rather than in terms of what is to be avoided.
8. Stated concisely and briefly without complex and elaborate descriptions.
9. Designed to cover a single end result and not a number of commitments.
10. Communicated to managers involved when changed or modified.
11. Designed to coincide work resources, facilities, and skills that are available.
12. Planned to find the best fit among individuals and situations in deploying resources.
13. Written to meet organizational improvement requirements such as profits, opportunities, development of personnel, attainment of schedules, technical competency, return on and investment.
14. Assigned a priority to foster a sense of importance and value in the company.
15. Documented to provide "performance experience" for future goal setting.
16. Assigned a risk factor to indicate the confidence level of completion.
17. Written so as to be at least significant and perhaps critical to the individual as he carries out the responsibilities of his job.

18. Written in quantifiable terms that are easily measurable and hence easily reportable.

19. Designed as a commitment between the employee and his supervisor.

20. Written to embody the basic ingredient opportunity, which makes possible a leap forward in performance and results for the individual and the company.

To write a meaningful statement of objectives appears simple. But evidence from many companies reveals the contrary. They report that statements are more often fuzzy collections of commitments that eventually result in misunderstandings and misinterpretations. George Odiorne[1] observes this difficulty among many companies. Foggy statements of objectives are not explicit about the results to be accomplished, nor do they suggest a guide to action. A personal inspection of many of these statements will reveal them to be ambiguous. Thus they embody a built-in comfort for those who wish to find a way to escape the commitment. A statement of objective should not be a one-way commitment but rather a circular, two-way, flowing interchange of intentions among the many people who are involved. The selection of words is critical since words—even commonplace words and phrases—carry different meanings for different people, depending on where or when they are used and who uses them. There are many language barriers in the management-business-technical world. Words such as "total systems," "input," "indicator," "promotion," "supervisor," and hundreds of others pose interpretive problems in meaning and usage. One person, on the basis of his experience and education, may use these terms to mean something quite different from what his listener, on the basis of his own background, understands. The structuring of a statement of objectives, since it is to be communicated to several people, should be aimed at these specific people. Formalizing the statement carries with it the implication that all who are involved agree to the essence of the objective and the content of the statement. It is impossible to obtain agreement if the words used are vague, ambiguous, or misleading. In actuality, the meanings of words overlap and carry emotional connotations; they may be provocative, biased, attitudinal, and complex. A statement of objectives cannot be structured and worded ignoring the fact that people of diverse backgrounds are involved. The statement must relate to those involved in terms of how they feel and what they think. To ignore this is to ignore the two-way communication that is necessary.

QUANTIFYING OBJECTIVES

Throughout the history of management, the area of objectives has been the most neglected area of managerial activities. Today, managers everywhere will quickly show their lists of formalized objectives for a future period. There is no scarcity of objectives among managers. A careful examination of these objectives, however, reveals a wide variety of deficiencies. Some consist of platitudes, such as "improve efficiency." Others cover an illusively broad range, such as "experience continuous business growth." Still others deal with such nebulous activities as "improve communications." Broad generalities have increasingly crept in, used in such a way that a variety of meanings are implied. Because of the language in which they are phrased, these generalities can be manipulated to mislead and misinform, to twist and distort their real and precise intent. Inherent in these generalities is a range of possibilities that no one can refute or reject, yet there is nothing in them to give specific direction. Such generalities, lacking in specificity but accepted by all, are called "motherhoods." Motherhoods have a tendency to creep into statements of objectives because they *sound good,* are *readily acceptable,* and offer a *comfortable distance and range.* Although motherhoods or generalities are an acceptable part of our day-to-day language in management, they should not be permitted in a statement of objectives. Some examples of motherhoods are the following:

Improve managerial effectiveness
Achieve greatest efficiency
Increase profits
Attain highest quality possible
Increase share of market
Continue existing management
Render better customer service
Improve delivery time
Improve economic conditions
Complete study of new program
Lower production costs
Steamline procedures
Achieve technological leadership
Complete planning for future requirements
Maintain good labor relations
Cooperate in maintaining equipment
Decrease delay time
Increase sales volume

Communicate with other departments
Provide more timely assistance
Develop cost awareness
Maintain morale and attitudes

The lack of specificity in a motherhood renders the statement of objectives unmeasurable. Further, any objective that does not have measurable points will be difficult to control and to achieve. Managers tend to use motherhoods either because they are uncertain about possible goals or because they lack the information necessary to pin down exactly what is required. The following guidelines may be useful in eliminating motherhoods in statements of objectives.

AVOID.   Oversimplifications; sensational terms; understated or overstated words; opinions subject to change; exaggerations; inexactness; idealistic terms; terms that can take a range of meanings.

USE.   Words that indicate how much; terms that can be proved or demonstrated; precise terms designating actions can be controlled and measured; terms that lend themselves to clarification by percentages, ratios, numbers, averages, index numbers, correlations, and standard deviations.

Objectives must be quantified! The more concrete the information a supervisor can build into his objective statement, the more likely it is that he will be able to achieve a real meeting of minds among those involved. To refer again to the football game cited in Chapter 1, there is no ambiguity as to where the goal posts are located and in what direction the teams should travel. The field is marked so that each player can tell whether he is moving toward his objective or away from it. This precision brings clarity and meaning to football play. When management personnel do not know specifically where they are heading and how good a job they are doing, their results become divergent and their work inefficient.

The quantity of results—"how much"—is just as important as the type or kind of results. Quantified objectives that have measurable points built into the written formal statement specify both the quantity of results expected and the period of time in which they are to be achieved. Quantification of motherhoods translates them to conditions that must exist when a job is well done. Therefore, to the greatest extent possible, objectives should be quantified. Following is a list of dimensions that can be used for quantification:

Volume amounts
Units of production

Time units
Frequency rates
Ratios
Index numbers
Percentages or proportions
Averages
Number aggregates
Degrees
Phases
Percentiles
Quartiles
Deciles
Mean deviations
Correlations

Including these dimensions within the objectives indicates precisely the number of results that must be obtained. Furthermore, these dimensions can be broken down into subdivisions and projected on a time scale, providing points at which the status and progress toward achievement of the objective can be noted. For example, a 20 percent cost reduction in office supplies within 4 months can be allocated at 5 percent per month, and a progress chart can be developed to show present status and progress toward reaching this schedule. Where it is not possible to quantify the objective, activity indices can and should be used to give confidence and high probability that desired results will be reached. These activity indices should be used with care, avoiding vague and irrelevant statements. A sample list of these activity indices is given in Chapter 7 under status control.

There are many advantages to quantifying objectives in the objective-setting process. It might be useful at this state to say a few words about these advantages. *First,* quantified objectives define and clarify the elements of expected results better than any verbal description can hope to. They provide a better configuration of what is expected. "To improve morale" is a motherhood and a verbalized expectancy, but "to improve morale by reducing monthly grievance rate from 10 to 5" is a quantified objective and a specific target. A *second* advantage of quantified objectives is their built-in measure of effectiveness. The process of measuring progress toward an end result is difficult, if not impossible, with qualitative statements. Using a measure to describe a future result also provides a way of measuring the current activities that will make it happen. Management can see the relationships among data, resources, and skills needed to deal with different situations. The reduction of the grievance rate from 10 to 5 to improve morale suggests the relationship of several skills and activities, such as handling people, knowing the labor contract, and being able to nip trouble in the bud. A *third* advantage of quantifying objectives is that they then can be enlarged or reduced for progressive performance stretches. This is hardly possible with verbal descriptions. To improve morale by reducing the grievance rate from 10 to 5 for the first year implies a second-year effort to reduce the rate from 5 to 3. Reducing costs 10 percent for the first year suggests a progressive reduction for subsequent years. Quantitative techniques give the statement an intrinsic manipulative value; that is, results can be manipulated as to both direction and the speed at which they are achieved. A *fourth* advantage of quantitative objectives is that they offer a means of keeping unknowns and uncertainties at a given level. The quantitative feature helps us see the effects the results will have on other areas. To reduce the grievance rate from 10 to 5 implies the need for a sharper and better level of supervision. If training is necessary, how much will it cost? When can it be conducted? What will the program consist of? Implications derived from quantitative statements tend to make unknowns more knowable.

There are also limitations and disadvantages to the quantification of objectives. Numbers are tricky. They may suggest a precision that does not exist, or they may oversimplify. Mathematics, statistics, and other quantifying techniques are not generally known by the average man. The liquidity ratio of current assets to current liabilities is an excellent quantified measure to use in an objective statement. It assumes, however, that everyone involved understands this measure, which often is not the case. Those who do not understand may regard the statement as impractical, or perhaps too theoretical. It may also be argued that quantification of human judgment is not possible. The mechanical procedure offered by numbers is no substitute for an intuitive, mature, and experiential decision. Mature decision-making should not be thrown out the window. Rather, it should be complemented by numerical methods. A final limitation is the impossibility of quantifying certain areas of behavior and leadership that are known to be critical. Such leadership qualities as sincerity, open-mindedness, character, impartiality, and tactfulness are known to be important agents in achieving results. It may be argued that behavioral and leadership skills are not results to be targeted but resources and activities necessary to reach results. However, it must be appreciated that many supervisors do target these qualities in their objective programs. In this case, they are at best feeder-objectives, and performance indicators of some type should be used to assess the acquisition of the quality. For example, training skill can be measured with before- and after-examination scores.

These limitations are significant but do not outweigh the advantages and benefits offered by quantification. Statements of objectives must be formulated carefully with built-in measures.

NUMBER OF OBJECTIVES

The number of objectives to pursue during a coming period varies from company to company. There are several reasons for this. First, the scope of each company's objectives varies. A chemical company may set objectives for its profit centers and major departments for 5 years; a restaurant chain may set the same kind of objectives but limit the time to 1 year. The time required to accomplish a given set of results will vary among companies because the importance of their execution varies. Second, the nature of the job varies from company to company. Different product lines, types of markets, available resources, and company size will cause corresponding differences in the number and type of responsibilities the chief executive, functional staff, managers, and supervisors must manage within their organizations. The president of a small business that employs 500 has a job somewhat different from his counterpart whose company employs 40,000. A company that deals in defense products has a different set of responsibilities from one that deals in nondefense products. Finally, the importance of achieving the objective will vary from company to company. Most companies will agree that there are seven key result areas in which objectives should be specified. These areas are the following:

1. Profitability and growth
2. Market position and penetration
3. Productivity
4. Product leadership
5. Employee morale, development, and attitudes
6. Physical and financial resources
7. Public responsibility

Few companies will agree on the importance attached to each of the key areas within a given period of time. A pharmaceutical firm that has polluted a river for the past 10 years and is now concerned with possible litigation from the government and the community will place a greater emphasis on public responsibility within the next few years. A trucking firm that experienced wildcat strikes and excessive labor grievances will give greater weight to improving employee attitudes, morale, and satisfaction. A small tool manufacturer that experienced a decline in defense contracts must give a great deal of attention to market position and product leadership. The number of objectives most suitable will be unique to each company because each business differs in the type and number of improvements that must be made within a period of time.

Some authorities[2] on management have suggested the following rules to determine a proper number of objectives: No position should have more than 2 to 5; 6 to 10 should do the job adequately; 8 objectives for each of 5 major functions are appropriate. Each authority has his own definite idea about the number of objectives to be selected. The beginning practitioner of managing by objectives will tend to adopt a great number of objectives, thus violating the M.B.O. Rule for Focus. He achieves only a dilution of effort by spreading himself too thin. The best approach to determining the number of objectives to adopt is to follow the M.B.O. Rule for Focus, described in Chapter 2. This rule limits the number of objectives to the nature of the job to be accomplished, the criticality of the achievement, and the management level at which objectives are to be set. The rule supports the theory that the number of objectives should be kept small but significant in terms of results for the enterprise and the individual.

SAMPLE OBJECTIVES

This section provides a sample list of objectives to cover an entire organization. These objectives can be regarded singly or as two-way or three-way joint feeder-objectives for interlocking and coordination. Samples of functional objectives are also provided. The functions are finance, marketing, research and engineering, production, and personnel.

1. *Overall organization*
   (a) Achieve a 15 percent return on investment within 4 operating quarters.
   (b) Reduce cost during the current operating year 24 percent of approved budgets prorated 6 percent per quarter.
   (c) Maintain current asset to current debt ratio not less than 3.0 for the next fiscal year.
   (d) Achieve a net profit average at least 7 percent of sales and 11 percent of net worth.
   (e) Increase market position for nondefense items from 15 percent to 30 percent; maintain market position for defense items at current levels.
   (f) Achieve a product line mix in which 80 percent of sales is made by no more than 20 percent of R & D customers.

(g) Complete management controls reporting system of all operating divisions by April 1.

(h) Complete an operating and financial strategy statement for reaching objectives within 2 months for presentation to the Board of Directors at the May meeting.

(i) Obtain from research efforts two accepted improvements per month for 10 consecutive months to raise sales of product K 15 percent.

(j) Reduce plant operating costs to $.54 per 100 units produced by January 1.

(k) Develop technological capability to introduce two new products in market sector BB at end of 3-year profit plan.

(l) Reduce capital expenditures, class B, from $350,000 to $150,000 during the coming biennial.

2. *Finance objectives*

(a) Reduce by 2 days the 6-day time lag in preparation of division cost reduction reports using an agreed upon follow-through system.

(b) Achieve an average age of accounts receivable not to exceed 25 days.

(c) Restrict bad debt losses to less than 3 percent of reporting non-defense sales.

(d) Improve margin by 15 percent with same revenues but reduced costs of 30 percent.

(e) Increase 15 percent the working cash required in each of three banks at the end of the year by holding inventory levels at 80 percent capacity.

(f) Complete training of three replacements for key positions in accounting section by next June.

(g) Complete study and construct index of expense trends for all departments for the past 5 years and project anticipated expense of future at annual intervals. Set 10 percent reduction targets from this projected expense trends.

(h) Collect ten suggested cost-reduction ideas per month from each of six operating managers.

(i) Complete write-up and acceptance of company cost-reduction manual and distribute to all members of management within 2 months.

(j) Install five suggestion boxes in five company locations to collect employee suggestions for cost reduction in their job procedures.

(k) Collect from six operating managers long distance telephone call analysis and recommendations for controls of number, type, and cost of calls.

(l) Reduce dollar value of cost of returned material credits from an average of $20,000 per month in the preceding year to $15,000 per month in the coming year.

(m) Reduce current debt to tangible net worth position to 35 percent for proposed creditor portfolio.

(n) Reduce fixed assets to a level not to exceed three-quarters of the tangible net worth in the next 2 years.

(o) Improve profits to payroll margin from 5 percent to 10 percent within the next four profit sharing quarters.

3. *Marketing objectives*

(a) Implement proposed system B for processing and expediting the filling of back orders at the rate of ten per month until 90 percent of back orders are filled. Reinstate system A when back-order level is reached.

(b) Increase sales revenues of a new product 15 percent within 12 months by concentrating existing expense levels of promotions in New England.

(c) Increase merchandise turnover in store from 4 to 6 within the current fiscal year.

(d) Hold sales expenses this coming year to 5 percent of total sales while increasing sales manpower 10 percent.

(e) Secure 100 percent distribution in markets D, E, and F of district 3.

(f) Convince three wholesalers to introduce new merchandising under a prearranged monthly schedule.

(g) Increase occupancy ratio in hotel rooms from a yearly mean of 65 to 85 percent while maintaining rate structure.

(h) Complete training program A for all district representatives to assure readiness for distributing product Y at the first of the year.

(i) Reduce average handling time of customer statements by 10 percent.

(j) Complete painting of ten trucks with new advertising campaign within 1 month.

(k) Complete 75 percent follow-up calls of new inquiries within 3 days of initial inquiry.

(l) Reduce number of customer complaints on commercial business from 22 percent to 10 percent of orders billed. Dollars of settlement should not exceed 5 percent of total commercial billing.

(m) Improve sales per employee to $25,000 during the next 5-year profit plan.

(n) Achieve percentages of sales to consumer, industry, and government from 20, 28, 52 to 30, 35, 35, respectively.

(o) Complete a strategy statement within 3 months for giving two new segments of the market brand X image to be introduced next season.

4. *Research and engineering objectives*

(a) Decrease research effort ratio of feasible marketing ideas to actual marketing products from 10 to 5 within the coming fiscal year.

(b) Complete design and development of new prototype in 14 months within cost of $140,000 without farm-out work to vendors.

(c) Complete product design specification for product M within budgetary period.

(d) Supply three new products to marketing within the coming fiscal year with forecasted sales not less than $1.5 million.

(e) Get approval from three departments of production, plans for customer, costs, and schedule within 3 months.

(f) Complete PERT layout for contract B within the prebudgetary planning schedule.

(g) Complete value analysis job plan for three engineering sections during operating quarter.

(h) Increase diversification program with development and introduction of five new products within the small product line.

(i) Complete literature and patent search by end of year for five patentable ideas useful in entering new markets K, L, and M.

(j) Reduce research investment pay-out time from 3 to 2 years.

(k) Improve research know-how in section B by increasing Ph.D. hires by 20 percent.

(l) Reduce the R & D budget as percent of net sales from 4.5 to 3.5 in the next 5-year profit plan while maintaining services and new product development.

(m) Maintain lead competitor's position in market with four new product introductions in the next 5-year profit plan.

5. *Production objectives*

(a) Reduce frequency of lost time injuries from 21 to 6 per million manhours within 6 months of installation of new safety awareness program.

(b) Maintain overtime hours at the level of 5 percent of scheduled hours while completing emergency work program A.

(c) Reduce cost of pump and engine repairs from $10,000 to $5,000 per year per mechanic.

(d) Maintain a once-a-day contact with all subordinates at their work stations and hold a once-a-month work appraisal meeting in office with all subordinates.

(e) Complete construction of 5,000 square feet, 2-story approved addition to existing plan within cost of $45,000 by spring of next year.

(f) Master ten techniques in work simplification as related to machine-shop operations through a 6-month-by-monthly cost-reduction meeting for machine-shop supervisors.

(g) Reduce clerical labor costs in three departments by $50,000 with the installation of a data-processing system whose leasing and operational costs are not to exceed 50 percent of the projected savings.

(h) Reduce weld rejects of Hy-80 steels from 6 percent to 3 percent of all plates in assembly S.

(i) Maintain total heat losses at 5 percent of total heat transferred when changing from system A to system B.

(j) Deliver 16 units per day for less than $45.00 unit cost to shipping point B.

(k) Reduce inventory lead time from 3 weeks to 2 weeks while maintaining customer services.

(l) Reduce obsolete items and all adjustments to inventory to 6 percent of commercial sales dollars.

(m) Complete master schedule of sales and inventories for fiscal year 19xx to reduce stock-out frequency rate to $2\frac{1}{2}$.

(n) Complete by next year a vendor rating system to maintain price, delivery, and reliability at or below an index established for the past 5-year record.

(o) Achieve for the machine shop a process layout by 19xx to reduce material-handling costs to 22 percent of manufactured costs.

6. *Personnel objectives*

(a) Select five candidates in the third quartile from 25 trainees successfully completing supervisory training. These candidates to be temporarily appointed for 6 months at the new division.

(b) Reduce cost of recruiting each engineer from $450 to $250 while meeting requisition totals and dates.

(c) Complete preparations for labor negotiations by apprising all management personnel of needed contract changes; hold bimonthly meetings for discussions and conduct two simulated labor bargaining sessions to gain insights on strategy.

(d) At a cost not to exceed $15,000, conduct a sampling survey of the company's hiring image in three adjacent labor markets.

(e) Complete for distribution at the end of month x a 20-page, 10-topic industrial-relations policy manual for newly hired employees.

(f) Decrease termination rate of clerical employees from 25 to 15 percent.

(g) Increase outside correspondence answered from 25 to 75 percent within 24 hours.

(h) Read 12 new books in management by the end of a year at the rate of 1 per month.

(i) Complete course in statistics within the next semester with a grade of B or better.

(j) Set up and validate 5 standards of qualifications for new hourly employees.

(k) Complete within 3 months an attitude survey of labor-management relations among all employees within cost of $1,800.

(l) Reduce frequency of grievances by the end of the year from an annual average of 35 to 20.

(m) Complete planning, organization, and installation of an employee suggestion system at the start of next year's cost-reduction program.

(n) Complete training by December 19xx of 600 supervisors in 2-day seminars on managing by objectives.

(o) Reduce absenteeism record for next year from 8 to 5 percent.

SELECTING OBJECTIVES FOR HIGHEST PAYOFF

In practice, the improvement forecasts described in Chapter 3 are bound to yield several potentially attractive objectives with equal or near equal appeal. The decision-maker is faced with a situation in which he must select the objective or objectives that will give him the greatest return on his investments of time, money, and resources. Additionally, there may be long-standing objectives that he wishes to retain. For example, he may wish to adopt improvement objectives such as decreasing production costs by certain amounts, rendering better customer service in terms of both quantity and speed, and increasing the company's share of the market by extending geographical boundaries. He may also wish to retain objectives pursued in the past, such as maintaining stable employment at a certain level, retaining product leadership with percentage of the market, and preserving good labor relations. The decision-maker is faced with a list of attractive goals from which he must select those that will maximize his gain. Because of this wide assortment of attractive and useful targets, some companies adopt them all, causing a dilution of effort. This was described in an earlier chapter as one of the current trends in business. One of the fundamental principles of managing by objectives is to concentrate on the vital few while ignoring the trivial many. The M.B.O. Rule for Focus provides guidelines for avoiding dilution of effort.

A useful guide for the practitioner who wishes to select those objectives that will yield the greatest gain from a wide assortment of possibilities is to assign relative values and weights to these objectives. Through this method, he can get an idea of the whole picture, the pattern formed by all the possibilities together. This usually requires arranging the assortment of objectives in an array and weighing them according to utility or payoff.[3] The payoff array is simply a list of objectives according to some expected value. The array distinguishes between those objectives that have the highest payoff and those that have the lowest. Of course, payoff is relative; the value of anything depends upon its utility to the person who has it or wants it. Money is not an entirely objective measure of value because the value of money will depend on its utility to the person who has it or wants it. We must admit, however, that the value of money is high in businesses and companies because money is one of the objects of economic organization. The value of money will decrease in proportion to the amount already possessed or increase in proportion to the amount needed. Payoff values or weights may be assigned according to one criterion or several criteria that give the greatest utility to the practitioner. The selection of "cost improvement" as a utility criterion is illustrated in Figure 4-1.

Assortment of Objectives	Cost Improvement (Dollars)	Probability of Occurrence (Percentage)	Expected Payoff (Dollars)
Objective 1	d_1	p_1	$d_1 p_1$
Objective 2	d_2	p_2	$d_2 p_2$
Objective 3	d_3	p_3	$d_3 p_3$
Objective 4	d_4	p_4	$d_4 p_4$
Objective 5	d_5	p_5	$d_5 p_5$
Objective k	d_k	p_k	$d_k p_k$

Figure 4-1. Weighting objectives in a payoff array.

To make a choice among various possibilities involves a variable, probability of occurrence. This is risk. Risk is always present when deciding on some future event or some expected value. The higher the risk of failure, the lower the expected value; conversely, the lower the risk of failure, the higher the expected value, assuming equal dollars among all objectives. In making a decision, each objective in the payoff array is multiplied by the probability of occurrence to obtain expected payoff. Objective 2, which contributes $20,000 in reduced costs with an 80 percent probability of occurrence, has an expected payoff of $16,000. Objective 3, which contributes $50,000 in reduced costs with a 20 percent probability of occurrence, has an expected payoff of $10,000. Thus each objective is quantified to our preference and utility of outcomes are measured. This procedure is continued until all of the objectives have an expected payoff. Those objectives with highest expected payoff will now emerge from the assortment of possibilities for the decision-maker. Probabilities of occurrences should be assigned on the basis of past experience and historical data. Subjective assignments can be made in the absence of objective data provided a validation procedure is followed. This may take the form of a test sample or group verification.

The above procedure for calculating a payoff array, when reorganized in descending and ascending order of payoff, yields a rank order of an assortment of objectives. Those with highest expected payoff are assigned the rank of 1 and those with lowest expected payoff are assigned the rank number of the total number of objectives. The use of a second criterion for the same assortment of objectives will yield a second list of expected payoff with a subsequent rank order of its assortment of objectives. For example, if "time of completion" is used as a criterion of utility, a second array of expected payoff can be calculated and arranged in rank-order ascending or descending payoff, similar to the array for expected payoff of cost improvement. Analysis of the same assortment of objectives using two separate criteria of utility can result in two separate arrays of expected payoff. Each array is given a rank-order form numbered from lowest to highest. The practitioner may wish to investigate whether a correlation exists between the ranks. If the correlation is high, it suggests that the high-ranking objectives on both arrays are strongly associated with both criteria. If the correlation is low, it suggests that the objectives have little or no association with both criteria. This aids the decision-makers in selecting the objectives that represent the vital few.

The rank-order correlation coefficient,[4] which is a measure of association between two utility criteria in a payoff array, is calculated as follows:

STEP 1. Rank the objectives. Ten objectives, whose expected payoff is calculated according to Figure 4-2, are ranked from 1 to 10 for each of two criteria: cost improvement and time necessary for completion. Those with highest payoff are assigned rank 1, and those with lowest payoff receive 10. This results in two separate ranks from 1 to 10.

STEP 2.   Calculate rank-order correlation. Using the rank-order correlation formula, calculate the rank-order correlation coefficient rho (ϱ),

$$\varrho = 1 - \frac{6 \Sigma d^2}{N(N^2 - 1)}$$

where N is the number of objectives that are ranked, d is the difference between the ranks, and Σ is the summing of the differences squared. This operation is illustrated in Figure 4-2.

| | Ranks | | | Difference |
Objectives	Cost Improvement	Time for Completion	d	d^2
O_1	1	6	-5	25
O_2	2	3	-1	1
O_3	3	7	-4	16
O_4	4	2	2	4
O_5	5	1	4	16
O_6	6	8	-2	4
O_7	7	4	3	9
O_8	8	9	-1	1
O_9	9	5	4	16
O_{10}	10	10	0	0
Total			O	$\Sigma d^2 = 92$

$$\varrho = 1 - \frac{6 \times 92}{10 \, (100 - 1)} = .442$$

Figure 4-2. Calculation of rank-order correlation coefficient.

STEP 3.   Assess the correlation coefficient. The size or magnitude of the coefficient of correlation can be interpreted as the strength of association of a set of objectives with two different sets of expected payoff. A positive perfect correlation, $\varrho = +1$, means perfect utility. A negative perfect correlation, $\varrho = -1$, means perfect inverse utility. A zero correlation, $\varrho = 0$, means no association between the ranks. Values between these limits may be interpreted as follows:

Size of ϱ		Utility
.00 to	.20	Little or no value
.20 to	.40	Slight association
.40 to	.60	Useful value
.60 to	.80	Substantially useful
.80 to	1.00	Very high & definite value

Thus the rank-order correlation procedure can be a useful guide for the practitioner to measure the value of two sets of expected payoff arrays. In the previous problem, the coefficient .442 suggests that a useful association exists between the objective and the two criteria of cost and time. This will aid the practitioner in determining the critically few objectives having the highest expected payoff. Often a variety of criteria can be employed to search for expected payoff in many areas. The rank-order correlation coefficient can be an aid to finding which criteria are closely associated with each other. If this procedure is followed, the reader can see that an optimization occurs among several selected criteria. A suggested list of criteria is given in Chapter 3 under "Standards for Action."

ENTRY METHODS FOR INTERLOCKING OBJECTIVES

To create a management system within a company, the practitioner needs to develop an objective network in which each feeder-objective is aligned and interlocked with every other. This alignment and interlocking must begin where the objective-setting process takes root. There appear to be a variety of entry points to the network process, and each organization must decide for itself which is the most feasible and practical. The following entry points are used by many companies: (1) profit plan, (2) top-down, bottom-up system, (3) budgeting approach, (4) common objective approach, (5) appraisal by results approach, and (6) job descriptions approach.

1. Profit Plan

A profit plan's basic objective is to target and reach a desirable return on investment. A management group must target a profit level and keep their operations pointed in that direction. This group never loses sight of their objective: to finish a period of time with a profit. In the past, profit plans were often nothing more than fiscal plans. Financial objectives were set, and operating plans were evolved by functional heads to describe how the financial objectives were to be reached. This traditional profit-planning approach has a basic flaw, however. It fails to provide a motivational vehicle through which all members of the staff can align and interlock with these objectives. It fails to develop a motivational approach to profits, which should be a responsibility of all members of management. A profit plan could be an excellent vehicle for relating, involving, and committing personnel. Financial objectives should be a major part of the plan, but other objectives and targets from the major functions should be included. Each functional manager, rather than evolving a "how to" operational plan, must develop a set of objectives that becomes a part of the company's profit plan. Specific objectives are set up, aligned, and interlocked by such functions as marketing, engineering, manufacturing, research, quality control, industrial relations, and purchasing. All functions are directed toward a profit plan, which provides the point of entry for alignment and coordination. More will be said about the profit plan in Chapter 9.

2. Top-down Bottom-up System

The president of any company occupies a unique and important position. From his vantage point, he can oversee the entire operation as well as the parts of which it is composed. He is like the storyteller of Chapter 1, who sees both the whole elephant and its different parts. The president or general manager must make each of his subordinates understand that, although the subordinate's individual part description is correct, he cannot describe the entire operation correctly on the basis of it. The president or general manager is the one who has the overall view of operations and can judge how well they are going. The top-down system of initiating the objective-setting process requires that the president not only recognize the overall view but specify his own objective at the start of the problem solution. His position as president is symbolic. He initiates improvement in a common problem area and directs each succeeding level to provide subobjectives designed to meet the requirements of the preceding level. This process is continued until all levels are involved. Once the objective-setting process reaches the first-line supervisors, their objectives are passed up the line for coordination and approval, as illustrated in Figure 4-3.

The process is described as follows:

1. A conducts a situation analysis with his B staff. This involvement eventually leads to long- and short-range objectives for the entire enterprise in the areas of profit, return on investment, cost reduction, sales volume, and new products.

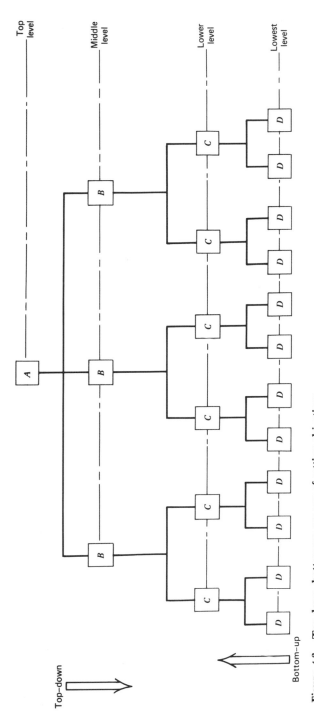

Figure 4-3. Top-down, bottom-up process of setting objectives.

2. B conducts a situation analysis with his C staff using A's objectives as major targets to support. This involvement with B's staff eventually leads to long- or short-range subobjectives for the lower to middle levels in the areas of forecasting, organizing resources, controlling, and operating.

3. C conducts a situation analysis with his D staff using B's objectives as major targets. This involvement eventually leads to feeder-objectives for the lower levels in such areas as costs, schedules, personnel, production methods, and motivation.

4. D, on the last level, begins the validation process by assuring his immediate superior C that the work implied by C's objectives can be accomplished. C assures his immediate superior B that the work implied by B's objectives can be accomplished. B assures his immediate superior A that the work implied by A's objectives can be accomplished.

5. The assurance process, which builds confidence and reduces the risk of failure, requires dialogues and conferences in which the participating managers enter into give and take discussions and make tradeoffs, concessions, and adjustments. This process cannot be exclusively top-down or bottom-up; rather, it is top-down, bottom-up, and sideward as well. Managers at all levels have an opportunity to review and influence the content of the objective before its adoption.

In practice, interlocking commitments to levels is far more difficult than implied here. The business of tradeoffs and concessions can become quite intense and disruptive. This is to be expected since coordinating and interlocking mean aligning individual drives and goals with overall company goals.

3. Budgetary Approach

Traditionally, the accounting department has been a key area in initiating the objective-setting process through budgets and financial commitments. The balance sheet or position statement of a company gives a financial picture of the firm at a specific moment of time. Assets and liabilities are listed in such a way that the financial health of the company can be seen quickly. Similarly, the income statement, which is a summary of income and expenses during a fiscal period, is prepared to show several important measures: revenues, expenses, expenses against revenues, and special nonrecurring items. Both the balance sheet and the income statements represent data from which budgetary planning is done. A budget is a future plan for allocating and controlling resources to meet an expected schedule. Good budgeting processes require participation and involvement by all groups responsible for the budget. Comprehensive budgeting[5] is profit planning via the budgetary approach. It is an annual profit plan documented by several accounting statements that indicate expected profit position. Comprehensive budgeting is also called drawing up a master budget. The sections or schedules included are the following: the budgeted income statement, which is a summary of income and expenses targeted within a coming period; the budgeted balance sheet, which is the anticipated financial position of the company on the closing date of the plan and in which assets, liabilities, and capital are projected for the period; and supplementary budgets, such as capital budgets, overhead budgets, cash budgets, sales budgets, operating budgets, and long-range budgets, which are included as expected positions of the company in a future period. Thus the accounting sections of a company, through budgeting performance analysis, can start the objective-setting process with appropriate schedules and participation.

4. Common Objective Approach

The common objective approach to entering the objective-setting process requires that all managers set their objectives simultaneously and independently. A directive is issued to all managers to get together with their subordinates by a predetermined date and agree on a set of objectives for a future period. It is requested that these objectives be submitted to an individual who is designated the *objective coordinator*. His responsibility is to collect and categorize objectives according to content, level, and functions. Common objectives as well as related objectives are identified, clarified, and accepted by the submitting managers. Those objectives that do not contain common or related elements are either discarded or negotiated. There are interface areas where commonalty is a must. For example, the selling of complex, technical products should not be split up between salesmen and engineers. It is a senseless battle to find out who is accountable for poor sales of the new product. This objective should not be split up since both engineers and salesmen are responsible for developing and marketing new products that give consumer satisfaction. The objective coordinator functions as a catalyst to assure that interfaces and common areas are brought together. Additionally, he sees that overlapping, redundant, and divergent objectives are brought into a single direction through negotiation and tradeoffs. Those objectives that cannot be brought into a common alignment are discarded from the objective program. The objective coordinator makes sure that progress and results are maintained during the implementation phase. He resolves disputes and helps individuals fulfill their commitments. Essentially, the common objective approach interlocks objectives through an objective coordinator whose existence in the organization is solely for this purpose. He is an individual of great importance in using this approach.

5. Appraisal by Results Approach

The appraisal by results approach has been widely adopted since it is very useful in reviewing performance in stimulating motivation. It is generally spearheaded by the personnel department. There are several variations on a common theme. The most prevalent variation is that in which the focus is on both the superior and the subordinate. The two begin the process by deciding jointly on ways performance can be improved. Jointly they develop short-term and long-term projects and ways in which performance can be measured. This approach is concerned with the results achieved by the subordinate rather than with any characteristics of his personality. Plans for implementation are evolved and approved. When the implementation period is completed, the subordinate evaluates what he has done and discusses it with his superior. The process is repeated for the next period with a set of new performance objectives for the individual. A comprehensive appraisal conference by superior and subordinate on results achieved forms the basis for setting new objectives for the next period. The process repeats itself through a cycle of performance review, objective setting, plan evolution, performance, performance appraisal, and setting of new objectives. Often the appraisal by results will be made in a context of group participation. The superior will discuss with his entire group ways and means whereby performance can be improved. With his group, the superior develops a network of performance targets, each individual setting his own goals to reach the targets. This variation of the appraisal by results approach emphasizes group processes to get people involved in the business of setting objectives. This group process descends through the hierarchy so that eventually the entire organization is setting objectives for a coming period. Thus the appraisal by results approach focuses on improvement of subordinates' performance. It provides a means through which an employee can understand what is expected of him and how he should go about achieving it. Interlocking occurs in the objective-setting process through superior-subordinate relationships, since in a management hierarchy everyone is superior to some but subordinate to others. A superior must set objectives jointly with his subordinates. He must, also, set objectives jointly with his boss. Thus interlocking occurs through people and throughout the levels of the organization. Similarly, interlocking is brought about in group processes through superior-group relationships, and this group interlocking permeates the entire management hierarchy.

6. Job Descriptions Approach

The problems of interlocking and alignment in an organization are problems of relating the organizational role each manager plays in the company. The organization chart shows basic divisions of work and who reports to whom. It does not give details as to what each individual is expected to do. The position description, which is a first derivative of the organization chart, details the duties and tasks to be performed by the individual. Position descriptions are concerned with defining an individual's tasks rather than with detailing how these tasks are carried out. Traditionally, the position description has failed to describe how the individual's responsibilities and tasks relate to and interact with other members of the group and the company. Traditionally, they have been written in such a way as to suggest complete independence from other positions. As a result, no common framework for relating and interlocking with other members of the group has been established.

Recently, however, position descriptions have come to be regarded as other than fixed statements of responsibilities. The new, dynamic view is that responsibilities change not only in terms of the requirements of the organization but also in terms of the relationships and roles of other individuals. The new approach to position descriptions enables personal and functional relationships among superiors, peers, and subordinates to be identified first through participation and group discussion. Positions, functions, and duties are related within a company framework. The objective-setting process begins with functional objectives at the higher levels of management. The process goes on through each subsequent level, defining and establishing relationships in position descriptions. The position descriptions are written flexibly to include objectives to be completed, performance standards necessary to reach objectives, and the duties required to meet both the standards and the objectives. Thus the new approach to position descriptions provides one method of interlocking and aligning various individuals in the organization.

Several entry points have been described for interlocking objectives. Company practice has centered on these six albeit with many variations. Often a company will use a combination of the approaches described above. The search for organizational coordination is an intense one. To get unity of action among management levels, functions, and personnel is a formidable challenge. The interlocking concept described here contributes significantly to this search.

FEEDER-OBJECTIVES SET FOR PERFORMANCE STRETCHES

The concept of the performance stretch built into each objective was described in Chapter 3. Its value is so great for the practice of managing by objectives that we describe it further in this section.

Attainable stretches are those attainable by each individual rather than by the majority or by the average employee. The stretch point must be designed to fit the latent potential within the individual rather than potential within a group. This is the feature that distinguishes setting standards of performance from setting objectives. The performance standard is designed to be attainable by the majority of persons working under the standard, but the performance stretch built into a feeder-objective must be attainable by each individual involved. Lethargy will develop when the level of attainability is so high that no one can reach it. Each individual finds a challenge at his own particular level, and all these levels must be made to relate to others in the same group. That is, the level of challenge for an individual must be set as high as he can reach but also must fall within an acceptable range of levels within a group. Group norms tend to give validity to the challenge level. An objective becomes formidable if it is related to objectives of others within the group. The leap-forward concept of setting objectives to stretch capability is aimed at discovering who can leap the greatest distance, or who can deliver the greatest contribution. This is a relative assessment. The performance stretch, however, is built into an objective set for the individual, using the group norm as a gauge. Although people differ widely in their ability to work and produce, an individual is always subject to the influences of the group in which he works. The group often strikes its own level of minimum or maximum acceptable performance. A manager must guard against undue influence on the individual, either in the level at which he sets his objectives or the manner in which he implements them. Supervisors who agree on a 5 percent reduction in costs will react when an overeager supervisor commits himself to a 10 percent cut in costs. Such a supervisor may be subjected to harassment and pressure from members of the group who want him to retreat to the level of the group. Group effects on setting performance stretches within objectives need not be deleterious, however, if it has been made clear that both performance stretch and attainability are expected by all members of management.

The normal curve has been a useful device for setting objectives in the challenge region and for relating this challenge to a group.[6] This bell-shaped curve offers a method of distributing a large number of people according to the laws of probability. A group average can be a useful guide to where the challenge range exists. This is illustrated in Figure 4-4. The curve suggests that 16 percent is the probability that members of any group will set and attain objectives in the challenge region as far as group norms are concerned. This does not preclude the challenge each individual has in his own objective. Within the whole group, 84 percent will achieve individual stretches but will relate to each other at distribution levels suggested by the normal curve.

Barnes and Anderson[7] give a ratio of best operator to poor operator as 2 to 1. The capacity of the best operator is roughly twice that of the poorest. Objectives set and accepted in the challenge range provide a measure for gauging low-level performance in relation to high-level performance. Effective utilization of personnel means developing the latent potential of subordinates in a planned progression. This is an orderly development and release of potential from lower levels of the

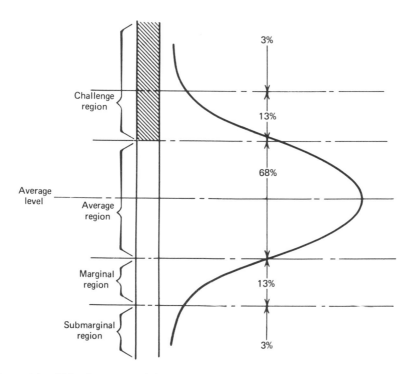

Figure 4-4. Objectives set to challenge personnel. Normal curve—Estimated percentage of personnel performing in various regions.

organization to upper levels. Performance stretches designed as a progressive ladder provide a natural vehicle for management development. The M.B.O. Rule for Stretching Performance described in Chapter 3 is a practical way to start and continue this progression for the individual. However, if the performance distribution of an entire group is known, the built-in performance stretch of each individual within the group can be more easily fit in. One way to find the performance distribution within a group is to follow the *M.B.O. Rule for Performance Distribution within a Group*.

M.B.O. RULE FOR PERFORMANCE DISTRIBUTION WITHIN A GROUP

1. Identify the best performer within a group. Validate this by comparing with other similar groups.
2. Identify the poorest performer within a group. Validate this by comparing with other similar groups.
3. Establish a midpoint performance level between the two.
4. Average performers of a group (68 percent) will be clustered around the midpoint.
5. High performers of the group (16 percent) will be above the midpoint.
6. Low performers of the group (16 percent) will be below the midpoint.

For example, a supervisor has fourteen electrical workers in his group. The best performer can wire 20 units per day. The poorest performer can wire 10 units per day. The supervisor can establish the performance distribution of his group as follows: ten workers will wire, on the average, 15 units per day; two workers will wire between 15 and 20 units; two workers will wire between 10 and 15 units. Thus the M.B.O. Rule for Performance Distribution within a Group provides a framework to assist in setting the challenge level of each individual as he relates to his group.

The process of stretching continuously for greater achievements has an effect on the lower levels of performance. The submarginal region, 3 percent of the group shown in Figure 4-4, represents "deadwood" which the company cannot justify keeping on the payroll. Deadwood employees are submarginal employees. They are unable or perhaps unwilling to make the progressive performance stretch required by the company. The process of stretching for improvement as a full-time job—month to month, year to year—will always uncover 3 percent deadwood. This is because the performance of the entire organization is continuously shifting upward. When the entire organization embarks on a progressive performance stretch of between 5 and 15 percent, as suggested by the M.B.O. Rule for Stretching Performance, a small group will not be able

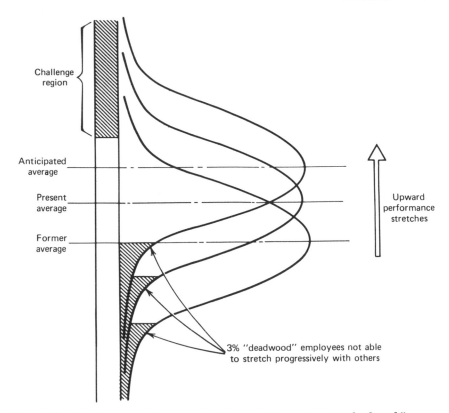

Figure 4-5.   Continuous performance stretches result in continuous "deadwood."

to keep the pace. This small, submarginal group is part of the marginal 13 percent. The stretch upward continually raises norms or averages, and by the same token it continually leaves behind a 3 percent deadwood category. This is illustrated in Figure 4-5 where the normal curve shifts upward.

SUMMARY

Objective setting is a process, not an event. Formalizing a statement of objectives must be meaningful to those committed to its implementation. This chapter described the second step in the five-step process of managing by objectives. It provided guidelines for selecting, writing, quantifying, and interlocking objectives for the organization.

GUIDE QUESTIONS FOR THE PRACTITIONER

1. What method do you use now to get management personnel involved in reaching for results? How do you assess the results?
2. Which method is the most feasible entry point to the objective-setting process with your management staff? Write a brief description of the procedure by which you will implement the following:
   (a) Profit plan
   (b) Top-down, bottom-up system
   (c) Budgetary approach
   (d) Common objective approach
   (e) Appraisal by results approach
   (f) Job descriptions approach
3. List three significant objectives that you and your subordinates wish to pursue for both short- and long-range results.
4. Write formal statements of these objectives, building in quantifiable terms in the challenge region.
5. Discuss with others how your objectives will meet organizational needs and provide opportunities for both short- and long-range projection.
6. List motherhoods used by your company in a statement of objectives and write an improved statement.
7. Set up a progressive 5-year plan in which annual performance stretches lead individuals or a section to a high level of achievement.
8. Appraise each individual in your section as to performance and potential performance and list experiences that might be useful in releasing this potential.
9. Develop an expected payoff table with your three objectives and identify a payoff array.
10. Using the rank-order correlation procedure and selected criteria, determine a measure of association among the decision-making criteria.

REFERENCES AND NOTES

1. George S. Odiorne, *Management by Objectives,* Pitman Publishing Co., New York, 1965, pp. 122–126.
2. Ernest C. Miller, *Objectives and Standards,* American Management Association, New York, 1966, pp. 43–45.

3. William Emory and Niland Powell, *Making Management Decisions,* Houghton Mifflin Co., 1968, pp. 109–113.

4. George A. Ferguson, *Statistical Analysis in Psychology and Education,* McGraw-Hill Book Co., New York, 1959, pp. 179–183.

5. Stephen Landekich, "Budgeting," in H. B. Maynard (ed.), *Handbook of Business Administration,* McGraw-Hill Book Co., New York, 1967, pp. 10–37.

6. The normal probability distribution curve needs no justification here since it is a reasonable estimate of how human attributes are distributed in the population. If a large aggregate of performers were arranged along a baseline according to magnitude of performance, the vertical frequency scale would approximate the normal curve. For a thorough discussion of this see R. M. Barnes, *Motion and Time Study,* John Wiley, 1968, pp. 380–387; Clifton A. Anderson, "Performance Rating," *Industrial Engineering Handbook,* McGraw-Hill Book Co., New York, 1963, pp. 3–65; J. C. Nunnally, *Educational Measurement and Evaluation,* McGraw-Hill Book Co., New York, 1964, pp. 41–52.

7. R. M. Barnes and Clifton A. Anderson, *op. cit.* (see note 6).

5. Validating Objectives

Venture Analysis. Validating Objectives with Work Breakdown Structure. Validating Objectives with PERT. Venture Simulation. Commitment To Deliver Results. Summary. Guide Questions for the Practitioner. References and Notes.

To face the future is to face uncertainty. To set objectives, management must confront this uncertain future and make decisions about it, which means dealing with risk. The risk lies in estimating the likelihood of an event's occurring at sóme future time. Finding meaningful objectives and formalizing them into written statements, as described previously, is at best a process that leads to tentative commitments. The practitioner of managing by objectives is wise to validate these tentative commitments. The validation procedure will indicate which objectives are most likely to be reached and the associated risk. The firming up, or validation, of tentative commitments is very important in reducing the risk of abortion or defeat. This chapter describes the following methods for validating objectives: (1) venture analysis, (2) validating objectives with work breakdown structure, (3) validating objectives with PERT, and (4) venture simulation. A section is also included on the meaning of a commitment for the practitioner of managing by objectives.

VENTURE ANALYSIS

Determining objective validity may well be the most important step in the conceptual strategy of managing by objectives. Unquestionably, the confidence attributed to the results of an objective program depends on objective validity. The proof of objective validity is the burden and responsibility of the objective setters. Unless validity is shown or proved, the practitioner proceeds to implement his objectives with little confidence and high risk of not getting what he wants. The process of validating objectives requires firming up or finalizing expected end results by tracing, both forward and backward, the manner in which resources and activities have been organized. Insights into how the objective program will be implemented provide unique feedback for correction and change in the actual implementation.

Venture analysis is a systematic approach for foreseeing how well a future set of objectives will be accomplished. Virts and Garrett[1] describe this approach as determining "affordable risks." How much risk can an organization afford to take to realize a set of expected objectives? The approach includes as many variables as necessary to provide a concrete background for decision-making on the proposed venture. It results in high confidence that what is expected to happen will indeed happen. Venture analysis deals with chance, and all decisions bear risk. This is due chiefly to the randomness characteristic of events and activities in the business world. Conditions may always change in unexpected ways. The major factor in managerial decision-making is that the future is hidden.

Making a decision is more than selecting a course of action. It is foreseeing the impact and effects the decision will have on the situation to which it is directed. Venture analysis helps to anticipate faults that may occur in a proposed set of objectives before the objectives have been completely committed. Venture analysis is a systematic attempt to foresee events, degree of risk of each event, emergence of potential problems, and possible contingency actions to minimize the problems. Several approaches can be used for the analysis. Work breakdown structure[2] is a practical approach for venture analysis and will be described later in this chapter. Decision-tree simulation is still another. Recently, decision trees[3] have been used increasingly to describe and to demonstrate visually the analytical processes of decision-making relationships. The decision-tree schematic reduces abstract thinking to a logical visual pattern of cause-effect from a starting point through a series of logical possibilities. A decision tree is also known as a probability tree, which is a shorthand notation for the likelihood of a chain of events' occurring when certain decisions are made. It visually displays choices, risks, objectives, and decision criteria from one point to another. This is illustrated in Figure 5-1. The tree is made up of a series of nodes and branches. At the first node on the left, the manager is faced with setting an objective for productivity improvement. He has three choices: install new equipment, schedule overtime, or hire more workers. Each branch of the tree represents an alternative course of action or an alternative decision. At the end of each branch or alternative course is another node representing a chance event —whether sales will rise or drop. Each subsequent alternative course to the right represents an alternative outcome of this chance event. Probability assignments are made with each branch. This probability can be stated in values of a scale running from 0 (absolute impossibility) through 1.0 (absolute certainty), or in percentages ranging from 0 percent (absolute impossibility) through 100 percent (absolute certainty). Thus

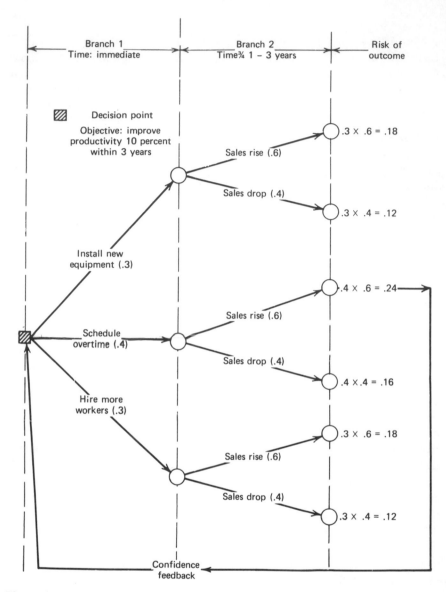

Figure 5-1. Decision-tree venture analysis.

if we assign the probability $P = 0.5$ to some event E, such as reaching the largest share of the market, this means we think the event has a 50 percent chance of actually occurring. A probability assignment is an expression of the level of confidence and risk. High probabilities mean high confidence and low risk. Low probabilities mean low confidence and high risk. Probability assignments can be made on the basis of verifiable data from the past. The weight given to past data is based on statistical extrapolations, correlations of related series, or other reliable survey information. Probability assignments can also be made on the basis of subjective judgment,—that is, personal opinion supported by the individual's experience with similar types of problems or situations. To say that a new business venture has an 80 percent chance of success, if the statement is based on previous experience or reliable data, gives us the odds of failure versus success. It identifies a level of confidence in the new venture. Risk-factor assignments are subjective probability estimates. These are simply intuitive judgments about the probabilities for a set of mutually exclusive and alternative events made by an individual possessing a general background of experience with the phenomena involved. These probability data are in contrast to those collected and used from experience and practice. In some cases, historical data are not available or are prohibitively expensive to obtain. Subjective probability estimates made by a person knowledgeable about the situation with which he is dealing can yield a high likelihood of the events' occurring. A better decision can be made on this basis than would be possible if each outcome were arbitrarily given an equal probability.

The use of a decision tree allows us to go through a trial run of likely events. A simulated feedback is obtained to check and recheck the original decision. The objective in Figure 5-1 is to improve productivity 10 percent in 3 years. The decision tree graphically and simply shows the alternatives possible after the decision is made to pursue this objective. The risk factor of 0.24 reveals the highest feedback confidence; thus, out of all the alternatives, a sales rise has the greatest chance of occurring as a result of scheduled overtime. Venture analysis using a decision tree enables management to take a more precise, confident, and direct account of the following:

1. *The impact of possible future decisions.* The network branching of a tree and its spreading chain of events can clarify potential barriers, changes, and problems. The analyst can probe a variety of effects by deliberately, on his "model" tree, imposing faults and critical conditions to foresee their impact.

2. *The impact of uncertainty on confidence.* Layout of the events in

a tree structure makes more visible the alternatives that may occur. Risk-factor assignments or probabilities give a better insight to and confidence in the future effects of a decision made in the present.

3. *The impact of varying commitments on payoff.* Trying a variety of tentative objectives in a decision tree can reveal comparative advantages and disadvantages. These can be analyzed in a payoff table for such criteria as present or future profits. This validation procedure can frequently lead to restatement of the objective or selection of a new one.

The basic point to decision-tree venture analysis is the assessment of probable outcomes of a decision to pursue an objective. The investigation gives valuable information as to the validity and appropriateness of the objective while also considering the risk involved. The possibility of building a new production facility may be structured into an objective and a decision tree may be developed to see outcomes of main, secondary, and tertiary branches, as illustrated in Figure 5-2. Expected profits over a long period can be evaluated as a result of an immediate decision. Each branch of the tree would have one criterion or several criteria to establish the likelihood of an event's occurring. A future time period makes the analysis realistic in terms of a long-term proposed commitment. Profit plans usually cover a 3- to 5-year time span. Examining the factors involved in site determination, transportation systems, and development costs for future time spans helps in determining the likelihood of profits. Feedback of risk factors strengthens or diminishes the decision to build a new production facility and may give some insight to other possible objectives to pursue.

VALIDATING OBJECTIVES WITH WORK BREAKDOWN STRUCTURE

Work breakdown structure is probably the most important single planning tool for linking objectives with resources and activities in a framework in which other planning activities can be correlated. The work breakdown structure concept[4] is a logical separation into related units of the total work required to do a job or reach an objective. The concept of work breakdown into levels with logical divisions and subdivisions is not new to the average man. It is part and parcel of his whole way of life. Many examples come to mind that illustrate this grouping into logical functions, departments, and branches. The organization chart is a graphic display of the division of labor, showing how work is grouped by specialties and hierarchy levels. A book such as this one, or a dic-

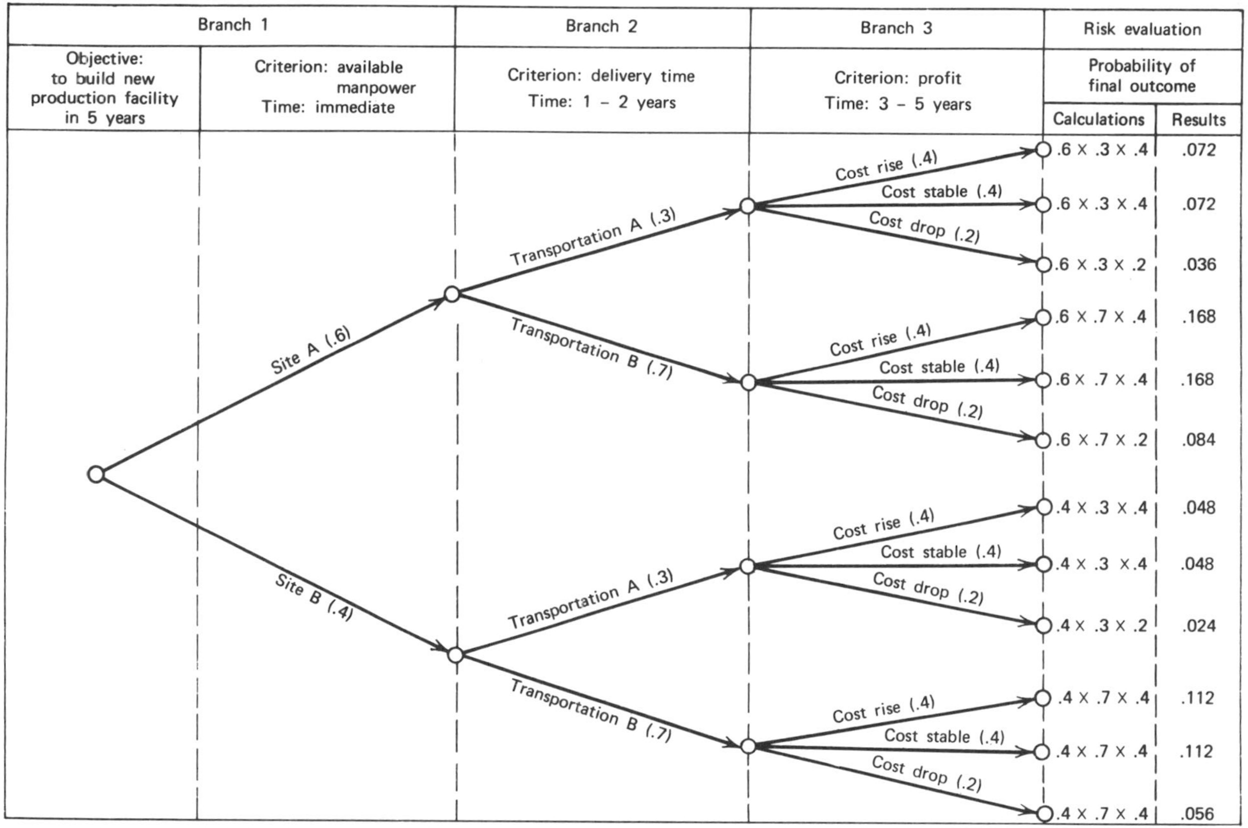

The table structure within the figure:

Branch 1	Branch 2	Branch 3	Risk evaluation	
Objective: to build new production facility in 5 years	Criterion: available manpower / Time: immediate	Criterion: delivery time / Time: 1 – 2 years	Criterion: profit / Time: 3 – 5 years	Probability of final outcome
				Calculations	Results

Tree branch labels: Site A (.6), Site B (.4); Transportation A (.3), Transportation B (.7); Cost rise (.4), Cost stable (.4), Cost drop (.2)

Calculations and Results:
.6 × .3 × .4 — .072
.6 × .3 × .4 — .072
.6 × .3 × .2 — .036
.6 × .7 × .4 — .168
.6 × .7 × .4 — .168
.6 × .7 × .2 — .084
.4 × .3 × .4 — .048
.4 × .3 × .4 — .048
.4 × .3 × .2 — .024
.4 × .7 × .4 — .112
.4 × .7 × .4 — .112
.4 × .7 × .2 — .056

Figure 5-2. Venture analysis with branch criteria.

145

tionary, or the Bible, is divided into smaller and smaller sections: chapters, sections, paragraphs, sentences, and words. These subordinate parts are tied logically into a framework to give meaning to the whole. Geographical location has the following breakdown structure: country, state, town, street, and number. The finished automobile is another illustration of work breakdown; we can trace engine level, carburetor level in the engine, float level in the carburetor, and aluminum material level of the float, each level depicting, respectively, an assembly, a subassembly, a component, a part, and a new material. The manufacturing process offers another example of grouping by levels and functions. First, concept feasibility and design level create the product. Second, development, test, and feasibility checkout assure the product concept. Third, process planning, material ordering, and production control set the stage for hardware. Fourth, implementing and operating produce the hardware. Finally, packaging, shipping, and distributing get the product into the hands of the consumer. From initial concept to consumer utilization, work breakdown provides a logical framework of divisions from system to subsystem, through task, subtask, level 1, level 2, level 3, and so on.

The use of the concept of work breakdown as a validation procedure starts with the objective to be validated. The practitioner relates all elements of the breakdown structure to this objective. He begins the breakdown by identifying the total effort required at the top level to support the objectives. The second level contains work that must be completed to support the first level. The third level contains more detail and a finer division of the work necessary to support the second level. This work breakdown continues until the last level of work that can be delegated is identified. The subdivisions of the work at each level are verified by examining the whole to be sure that the whole equals the sum of its parts. The subdivisions under a particular item must define completely all considerations making up that item. Work breakdown structure can be used to validate a company's profit objective, as illustrated in Figure 5-3. The profit objective to be reached is an increase in net earnings by 20 percent within 24 months. The work necessary to reach this objective is organized in a pyramidlike fashion from the highest to lowest level. This particular example shows the four fundamental ways[5] to improve profits in any company, namely, improvement of sales volume, improvement of price margin, reduction of capital investment, and reduction of costs. The subdivisions of the profit objective are work areas for sales volume, pricing, capital investment, and cost reduction. Further subdivisions of the total work show the requirements for meeting these four fundamental work elements. The subdivision continues until an ultimate level is reached, referred to as "end items." An end item is the smallest division of work in the work breakdown structure that can be delegated to a functional department or supervisor. The work breakdown structure of Figure 5-3 shows the work concerning sales volume broken down into several areas: introduce new products, update sales forecasts, revise sales strategies, provide sales incentives, and improve services. The work breakdown structure provides a perspective from which all the work, including the smallest functions and responsibilities, can be seen easily. This makes a matrix approach possible, so that entry information or changes can be checked from the structure. Only three levels of breakdown are illustrated in Figure 5-3, but the reader can see that several additional levels can be added easily to depict in finer detail the work necessary to complete upper-level tasks. For example, the layout for work flow under capital investment can be further divided into process flow, operational activities, material flow, and motion economy.

Work breakdown structure in the technical sciences has been largely product or hardware oriented. As applied to management activities, it encompasses several areas: hardware, software, skills, procedures, and any other element a manager needs in order to accomplish an objective. The manager's task does not usually involve hardware but leads eventually, through people, to hardware. The ability to develop a work breakdown structure depends on the practitioner's use of good judgment after he reviews all information and requirements necessary to reach an objective. Several preliminary trials will be needed before the structure emerges with all major tasks tied together. Once the structure emerges, the substance of work required to reach an objective is defined. Herein is the key to validating objectives, and it can be enunciated in the following principle:

The greater the accuracy of work breakdown definition, the greater the understanding and clarity of the actions necessary to complete objectives.

Validating objectives is defining the divisions of work necessary to reach the objectives. *If the work is understood, readily identified, and easily achievable, the confidence of reaching objectives is high!* On the other hand, if the work is hazy, highly uncertain, and not easily achievable, the confidence of reaching objectives is low. A range exists between these two extremes. The practitioner of managing by objectives proceeds to bring a level of validity to his objectives before he attempts to implement them.

Rotating a work breakdown structure 90 degrees counterclockwise and displaying end items in a matrix provides the manager with additional clarification and understanding for completing a set of objectives. Matrix cells are formed with end items at one extreme and responsibility assignments at the other, as illustrated in Figure 5-4. Each cell is regarded as a work package (WP). The total number of work packages represents

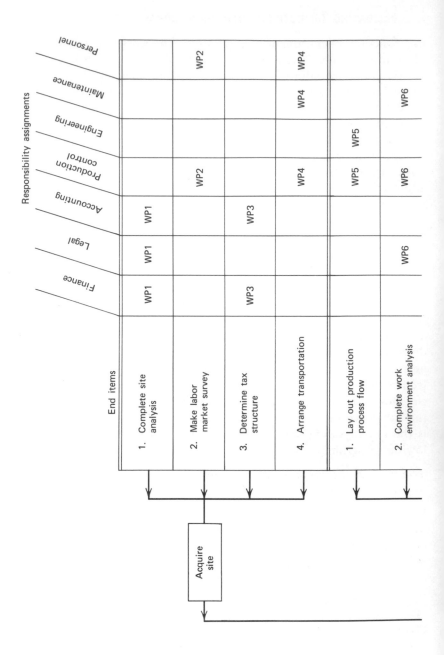

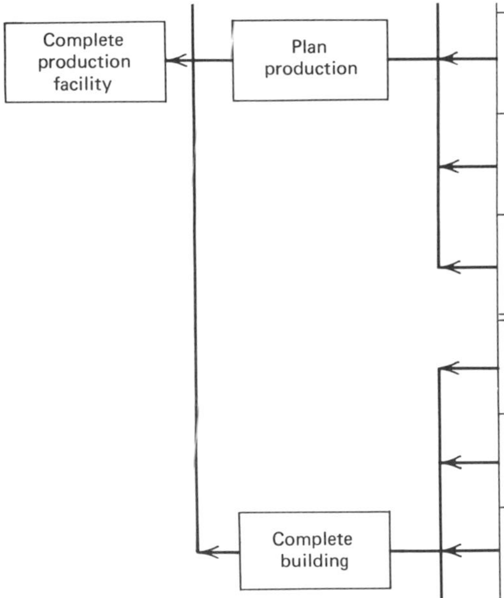

Flowchart (left side):

- Complete production facility
  - Plan production
    - 3. Complete capital investment analysis
    - 4. Determine floor-space utilization
    - 5. Organize material-handling equipment
  - Complete building
    - 1. Complete building design
    - 2. Complete plans and specifications
    - 3. Obtain bids and contracts
    - 4. Complete building construction
    - 5. Deliver and install equipment

Work breakdown matrix:

Task								
3. Complete capital investment analysis	WP7			WP7	WP7	WP7	WP7	
4. Determine floor-space utilization					WP8		WP8	
5. Organize material-handling equipment				WP9	WP9	WP9	WP9	
1. Complete building design					WP10	WP10	WP10	
2. Complete plans and specifications				WP11	WP11	WP11	WP11	
3. Obtain bids and contracts	WP12	WP12				WP12		
4. Complete building construction				WP13	WP13	WP13	WP13	
5. Deliver and install equipment			WP14	WP14	WP14		WP14	
Total work packages	4	3	4	9	9	7	9	2

Figure 5-4. Work packages within work breakdown matrix.

149

the total work necessary in a work breakdown structure to achieve an objective. A work package is a work unit or task unit to be completed and consists of several related items: an end item, an accountability assignment, a time to complete the package, a work description or a method to implement the package, a cost estimate, and a risk factor. The following is a brief description of each.

1. *End item or feeder-objective.* This is the smallest division of work that can be delegated or assigned. End items are the action links between how the work is broken down in the overall picture and how the functional areas of the organization are tied to this picture. Each end item should start with an action verb and contain the condition to be achieved. The end item relates not only the purpose of a contribution but also makes it clear to all involved in the matrix how each individual contribution is related to the whole. *End items are feeder-objectives whose end work accomplishment feeds to the upper levels.* As brought out in earlier chapters, they are the roots from which a network system of objectives is developed.

2. *Accountability.* The responsibility factor, either individual or departmental, is of prime importance in organizing and implementing work. It is the obligation to accomplish an end item on the basis of established performance standards. It is important to define the tasks that need to be done, but, if the tasks are to be achieved, it is also vital that the individual or individuals who are to perform each task be clearly designated. Clear-cut assignments of responsibilities transform the plan from a statement of intent to a statement of commitment to action.

3. *Work descriptions.* Each cell of the work breakdown matrix contains a descriptive statement of the methods and procedures that will be utilized in completing the work package. The individual or departments assigned the responsibility for completing the end item must develop and assure that the methodology, technique, facilities, and resources are available and can be deployed to complete an end item.

4. *Time allotments.* In each cell of the work breakdown matrix is not only a work description, but also a specification as to the amount of time that will be necessary to complete the individual work package. As the description of each work package is developed, the amount of time is also ascertained. The total time to complete all the work necessary to reach a specified objective is the sum of the time allotments needed to complete each work package.

5. *Cost estimates.* Each responsible individual or department assigned to complete an end item must estimate the costs that will be incurred.

Reliable and realistic cost estimates of each package, when totaled, can give a close idea of the total cost of implementing an objective. This has a high validating value for transforming tentative objectives to finalized commitments.

6. Risk factor. Each cell of the work breakdown matrix contains, in addition to the elements described previously, an assigned risk factor. As explained earlier, this is the estimated risk for completing the work package. The risk factor is a numerical value ranging from 0 to 1, similar to probabilities. A value of 1 means certainty—high likelihood of completing the job and low risk. A value of 0 means uncertainty—low likelihood of completing the job and high risk. Risk factors are assigned in the same way that probability assignments are made. The total risk factor of all work necessary to reach an objective is obtained through successive multiplications of each risk factor of each work package. A high risk factor means high confidence and high likelihood of achieving an objective. A low risk factor means low confidence and low likelihood of achieving an objective. Hence the risk factor is a measure of confidence in individuals who are about to be committed to delivering results specified in the end items. If three work packages have risk factors of 0.8, 0.9, and 0.5, the total risk factor is the successive multiplication, or 0.36.

There are many immediate benefits from use of the concept of work breakdown structure. Chiefly, it is a practical way to validate whether a tentatively stated set of objectives is achievable and to determine the risk involved. Tentative objectives can be made into permanent commitments once a high level of confidence is obtained; that is, once end items are assigned, work procedures are described, the amount of time needed is acceptable, and the likelihood of completion is high. Also, work authorizations, indications of technical information deficiencies, control sequences, and a scheduling base are other benefits provided by the matrix. The matrix array allows an insight into the critical as well as the trivial roles in each of the work packages. Priorities can be established from the difficulties, complexities, and time requirements suggested by each cell. A framework for accounting and status reporting is made easily from this matrix. This will be described in Chapter 7.

VALIDATING OBJECTIVES WITH PERT

Program Evaluation and Review Technique (PERT)[6] recently has shown itself a useful network tool for scheduling nonrecurring projects. The concept has been used to deal with a wide range of planning and control problems of a nonrepetitive nature. It permits a manager to "play the clock" in such a way that a job is accomplished in the shortest period of time with well-organized resources and activities. As a technique to handle nonrepetitive processes, it lends itself easily to validating objectives since setting and reaching for results is a nonrepetitive activity. It is a special application of network analysis for estimating and controlling the time required for activities and work packages about which little information from past experience is available. Work packages, as described in the discussion of work breakdown structure, can be interconnected to form a network of objectives; such a network traces the development of all the work necessary to reach final objectives. The network gives an overview from start to finish, clearly indicating the steps that must be taken before the end objective is reached. It shows why some events must follow others, why some cannot be done immediately, and why the total operation takes so long. The network serves to monitor or control the work program as it proceeds to its final destination. PERT network analysis consists of four steps: specifying tasks to be completed, sequencing and interrelating work packages; setting up the network; and scheduling and timing. The following is a brief description of each of these steps. Moder and Phillips[7] provide more detail and analysis than offered here.

1. *Specifying tasks to be completed (work packages).* Each task is made up of one or more events and their associated activities. The event is an end item that indicates a condition to be accomplished at a recognizable point in time. There are starting events, terminating events, interface events, and feeder events. All events are paths leading to the terminating event, which was described earlier as an end item of a work breakdown structure. An activity is the work required to complete a specific end item. Activities are the work processes and the methodology used to finish an event. Events and activities are symbolically shown in many ways. Here they are shown as circles (events) and arrows (activities). Two events are connected by one activity, as illustrated in Figure 5-5. Since events are end items, they take up no time, money, or resources in themselves. Activities, however, require time, money, and resources. Suppose a marketing research program is to be the first step in the development of a new product. Event 1 would be described as marketing research begun; event 2 would be described as marketing research finished. The arrow between these two events is described as the activity necessary to conduct marketing research. Task A is seen as two events and one activity; task B is seen as three events and two activities; task C is seen as two events and one activity, but shifted in time phase; task ABC inte-

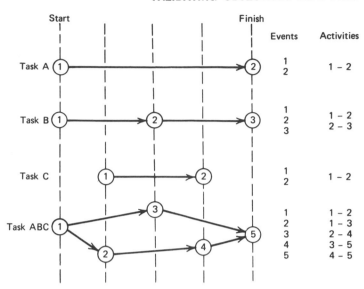

Figure 5-5. PERT sequencing of tasks.

grates all events with their time phases. Task ABC ties together all items that must reach the terminal event 5. Event sequences and priorities of the original tasks have been changed and shifted when integrated in the task ABC network. As described earlier, development of a new product in the network may now require in addition to marketing research, a production status analysis, an engineering feasibility study, and a state-of-the-art technological forecast.

2. *Sequencing and interrelating work packages.* Once the tasks or work packages have been defined along with their component end items or events, then sequencing and connecting are done by relating input-output relationships, start-stop phasing, and activities that connect one event with another. This is illustrated in Figure 5-6.

3. *Setting up the network.* The term network indicates that several events and activities are combined in such a way that input-output relationships lead to an ultimate end. There are no formulas that provide a precise and logical series of steps leading to an excellent and foolproof network. There is an art and skill to developing meaningful networks. The following are some suggested guidelines:

(a) The network should be developed by the individuals familiar with and committed to the objectives and requirements of the program.

(b) The work breakdown structure, which includes the logical se-

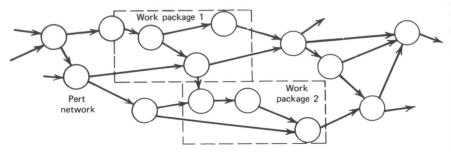

Figure 5-6.   Work packages in the PERT network.

quence of end items and activities, must be agreed upon by those developing the network.

(c) The development of the network should start with the ultimate targeted objective and proceed backward to the beginning event. The end objective is constantly and clearly in view and the network is developed in direct relation to it.

(d) As the network is developed, the question is asked about each end item, What activities must be completed before this event is completed?

(e) An activity cannot begin until an event or end item preceding it has been completed.

(f) Wherever possible, two or more end items and associated activities that can be accomplished concurrently should be set up in parallel paths. This allows a high degree of delegation because of the related parallel efforts.

(g) A critical path should be identified to discover the longest time it will take to accomplish end items and their associated activities. Increased paralleling will decrease critical path time. Increased sequencing will increase critical path time.

(h) A slack path should be identified to discover the shortest time it will take to accomplish end items and their associated activities. Decreased paralleling will increase slack path time. Decreased sequencing will decrease slack path time.

(i) When an event or an end item holds back two or more activities from starting, there is an even constraint. This event should be broken down into smaller end items.

(j) When two or more activities hold back the completion of an end item, there is an activity constraint. The activities should be combined to lead to the end item.

Work breakdown structure, as discussed earlier, made good use of work packages to reach a set of objectives. The concept of work packages can be fitted neatly into the PERT network by recognizing that one or more end items of a work package may also constitute one or more events. Similarly, descriptions, time, accountability, cost estimates, and risk factors of a work package correspond to activities of a PERT network. Thus a functional connection between the two exists, as illustrated in Figure 5-6.

4. *Scheduling and timing.* Once the tasks to be performed have been developed into a PERT network or some other related structure, it is necessary to establish some definite schedule of when each end item will be completed and the approximate date each activity will be started. By including a schedule as a part of the program for implementation, the PERT plan not only helps keep actions in proper phase, but it also sets target dates for those who are assigned the responsibility for completion. These target dates will go a long way toward ensuring that committed individuals execute their work before others commence theirs. This automatically forces coordination in starting and completing activities among several committed individuals. Time is clearly the basic variable in the PERT network since it measures how long parts of the project will take. PERT time is express in days or weeks and is estimated on a probability projection of most likely time (t_m), most optimistic time (t_o), and most pessimistic time (t_p). Most likely time is an estimate of the normal time an activity will take if the same activity were repeated an independent number of times under identical conditions. It coincides with the central interval of a probability distribution curve encompassing 68 percent of the area on each side of the arithmetic mean. This is illustrated in Figure 5-7. The most likely time is the time estimate at the mean. The most optimistic time indicates work completed under conditions better than normal. It is an estimate of the minimum time an activity will take if unusually good circumstances and favorable conditions are experienced. It coincides with the interval segment of the probability distribution curve encompassing approximately 16 percent of the area to the left of the first standard deviation. The most pessimistic time concerns work completed under conditions less favorable than normal. It is an estimate of the maximum time an activity will take if unusually bad circumstances and unfavorable conditions are experienced. It coincides with the interval segment of the probability distribution curve encompassing approximately 16 percent of the area to the right of the first standard deviation. An estimate of expected time considering, the effects of favorable and unfavorable conditions, can be calculated with the formula for expected time (t_e), as shown in Figure 5-7. Time estimates in a PERT network can now be assigned in terms of most likely time (t_m), most pessimistic

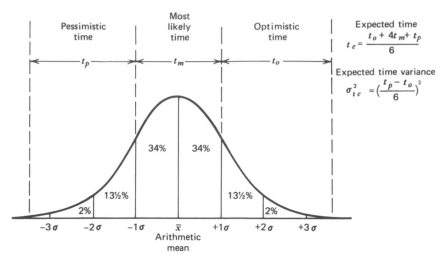

Figure 5-7.   Estimating time for PERT activities.

time (t_p), most optimistic time (t_o), expected time (t_e), and the variance (σ_{t_e}) measured in the calculation of expected time.

Once the three time estimates are obtained and assigned to activities of the PERT network, an analysis can be made of the total time requirement for the entire network to reach the terminal event. Each activity time of a specific event is cumulated along the paths of the network so that cumulated expected time and cumulated variance of expected time can be estimated for the objective to be reached. A PERT network having several paths will obviously have different cumulated time estimates. Those paths that have the longest cumulated time are called critical paths because the entire project or program will be held up because of them. Those paths that have the shortest cumulated time are called slack paths because a great deal of slack time occurs in completing their chain of events. To estimate the probability of meeting the schedule of events or work packages entailed in the completion of an objective, the critical path must be calculated. Time estimates from this path are used as a basis for entering the normal probability distribution tables. The following example will illustrate this calculation.

A company has tentatively decided to construct a new production facility. An objective has been tentatively set to complete this facility within 18 months. The management of this firm would like an estimate of the probability of completing the facility within the estimated scheduled period. After considerable analysis, a list of events was identified and tabulated (see Table 5-1).

For purposes of illustration, the events have been grossly simplified and identified with numbers. Since the events are to be structured into a flow network, sequencing and interrelating was determined and predecessor and successor events were identified, tabulated, and a network constructed. The network is simplified to portray the major events to complete the facility. For ease of explanation, network events are assigned numbers.

TABLE 5-1

Event No.	PERT Events	Successor Events	Past Estimates			Calculations				Slack Time (S_L) $(T_L - T_E)$
			t_o	t_m	t_p	t_e	$\sigma_{t_e}^2$	T_E	T_L	
1	Corporate approval	2 3	1 3	2 4	9 5	3 4	1.28 0.112	3 4	5 8	2 4
2	Production processes designed	4	2	4	6	4	0.448	7	9	2
3	Building designed	5	3	5	13	6	2.78	10	14	4
4	Layout complete equipment procured	5 6	4 1	4.5 2	8 3	5 2	0.448 0.112	12 9	14 15	4 6
5	Building complete	7	4	4	4	4	0.0	14	18	2
6	Equipment installed and operable	7	2.5	3.0	3.5	3	0.278	12	18	6
7	Production facilities completed	—	—	—	—	—	—	—	—	—

A step-by-step procedure is as follows:

STEP 1. Estimate, on the basis of past data, the time required to complete each of the events and enter these estimates in three columns: t_o, t_m, t_p.

STEP 2. Calculate, using the formula from Figure 5-7, expected time and expected time variance and enter those values in two columns: t_e, $\sigma_{t_e}^2$.

STEP 3. Calculate for each branch total earliest expected time, which is the cumulation of t_e along a path, and enter those values in the column T_E. It should be noted that this results in three paths: 1-2-4-6-7; 1-2-4-5-7; 1-3-5-7. Since the path 1-2-4-5-7 has the longest expect time for completion, it is termed the critical path. It is critical because completion of these events in the longest time can hold up the entire program. It is the path of least slack time.

STEP 4.   Calculate, using the 18-month constraint, latest allowable time (T_L) by working backward through the paths. Tabulate this under column T_L. Latest allowable time (T_L), which represents the scheduled constraint of 18 months, is the maximum allowable time in which an event can be completed without affecting the completion of the network.

STEP 5.   Calculate slack time (S_L) by getting the difference between the latest allowable time (T_L) and the earliest expected time (T_E). The slack of each event and the branches are illustrated in Figure 5-8. Critical path 1-2-4-5-7 has the least slack time because the cumulated slack time of events is at a minimum.

A probability estimate of meeting the scheduled time of 18 months should be of major concern in the completion of the production facility. Generally, it is a key concern in validating the time dimension of an objective. The validation is better when this probability is high. Low values of probability indicate that the schedule is not feasible. The calculation of this probability follows the formula[8] and procedure of Figure 5-9. The time T_L (18 months) is the latest allowable time for completing the project. The time T_E (16 months) is the earliest expected time for completing the project. The critical path only is used for this calculation.

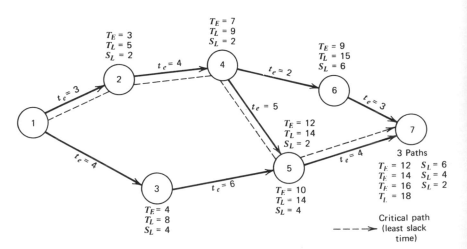

Figure 5-8.   PERTing a production facility.

Probability of Meeting Schedules

PF	.00	.01	.02	.03	.04	.05	.06	.07	.08	.09
0.0	.0000	.0040	.0080	.0120	.0160	.0199	.0239	.0279	.0319	.0359
0.1	.0398	.0438	.0478	.0517	.0557	.0596	.0636	.0675	.0714	.0753
0.2	.0793	.0832	.0871	.0910	.0948	.0987	.1026	.1064	.1103	.1141
0.3	.1179	.1217	.1255	.1293	.1331	.1368	.1406	.1443	.1480	.1517
0.4	.1554	.1591	.1628	.1664	.1700	.1736	.1772	.1808	.1844	.1879
0.5	.1915	.1950	.1985	.2019	.2054	.2088	.2123	.2157	.2190	.2224
0.6	.2257	.2291	.2324	.2357	.2389	.2422	.2454	.2486	.2518	.2549
0.7	.2580	.2612	.2642	.2673	.2704	.2734	.2764	.2794	.2823	.2852
0.8	.2881	.2910	.2939	.2967	.2995	.3023	.3051	.3078	.3106	.3133
0.9	.3159	.3186	.3212	.3238	.3264	.3289	.3315	.3340	.3365	.3389
1.0	.3413	.3438	.3461	.3485	.3508	.3531	.3554	.3577	.3599	.3621
1.1	.3643	.3665	.3686	.3708	.3729	.3749	.3770	.3790	.3810	.3830
1.2	.3849	.3869	.3888	.3907	.3925	.3944	.3962	.3980	.3997	.4015
1.3	.4032	.4049	.4066	.4082	.4099	.4115	.4131	.4147	.4162	.4177
1.4	.4192	.4207	.4222	.4236	.4251	.4265	.4279	.4292	.4306	.4319
1.5	.4332	.4345	.4357	.4370	.4382	.4394	.4406	.4418	.4429	.4441
1.6	.4452	.4463	.4474	.4484	.4495	.4505	.4515	.4525	.4535	.4545
1.7	.4554	.4564	.4573	.4582	.4591	.4599	.4608	.4616	.4625	.4633
1.8	.4641	.4649	.4656	.4664	.4671	.4678	.4686	.4693	.4699	.4706
1.9	.4713	.4719	.4726	.4732	.4738	.4744	.4750	.4756	.4761	.4767
2.0	.4772	.4778	.4783	.4788	.4793	.4798	.4803	.4808	.4812	.4817
2.1	.4821	.4826	.4830	.4834	.4838	.4842	.4846	.4850	.4854	.4857
2.2	.4861	.4864	.4868	.4871	.4875	.4878	.4881	.4884	.4887	.4890
2.3	.4893	.4896	.4898	.4901	.4904	.4906	.4909	.4911	.4913	.4916
2.4	.4918	.4920	.4922	.4925	.4927	.4929	.4931	.4932	.4934	.4936
2.5	.4938	.4940	.4941	.4943	.4945	.4946	.4948	.4949	.4951	.4952
2.6	.4953	.4955	.4956	.4957	.4959	.4960	.4961	.4962	.4963	.4964
2.7	.4965	.4966	.4967	.4968	.4969	.4970	.4971	.4972	.4973	.4974
2.8	.4974	.4975	.4976	.4977	.4977	.4978	.4979	.4979	.4980	.4981
2.9	.4981	.4982	.4982	.4983	.4984	.4984	.4985	.4985	.4986	.4986
3.0	.49865	.4987	.4987	.4988	.4988	.4989	.4989	.4989	.4990	.4990
4.0	.4999683									

Probability factor $PF = \dfrac{T_L - T_E}{\sigma_{T_E}} = \dfrac{18 - 16}{1.48} = 1.35$ (½ Normal Curve)

For $PF = 1.35$, estimated probability to meet schedule is .4115.
For full normal distribution curve: .5000 + .4115 = .9115 or 91.2%.

Figure 5-9. Estimating probability of meeting schedules.

The standard deviation of the time activities (T_E) of the critical path is 1.48. This is determined by adding the variances $\sigma_{t_e}^2$ of critical path 1-2-4-5-6 found in Figure 5-8 and extracting the square root. The probability factor (PF) 1.35 is calculated and used with the chart in Figure 5-9. From this chart, the area of the normal distribution curve is identified. This is .9115, interpreted as 91.2 percent. This means the probability of meeting the 18-months schedule for the completion of the new production facility is 91.2 percent. Thus a validation of the time dimension of an objective has been made.

VENTURE SIMULATION

The validation process in the conceptual strategy of managing by objectives may well be the step that can determine the success or failure of venturing into the future. The practitioner who gives a great deal of time and analysis to this step not only builds confidence in reaching his stated objective but also provides himself with unique insight into a future situation, enabling him to make happen what he wants to happen. How well the practitioner foresees the implications of his objectives for the implementation phases should determine the degree of his willingness to be committed to a set of results. The practitioner is wise to simulate the future situation as nearly as he can. He accomplishes this by setting up working models that provide measurements of, observations of, or insights to a coming situation. Thus far, this chapter has provided several types of models the practitioner may use to simulate some aspect for study in as great detail as he wishes. These models can approximate within certain confidence limits the real situation. How close to reality a simulated model can be is subject to several constraints, among them information, time, cost, experience, and simplicity. However, once the model is constructed, experimentation and manipulation can be done to determine consequences of changes, faults, and variances. Work breakdown structure, as described in this chapter, provides a useful model to observe and validate several aspects of an objective program. The practitioner should develop a work breakdown structural model and manipulate it in several ways to validate important considerations in an objective program. The work breakdown structure is a fundamental tool to provide the basis of analyzing and verifying a venture simulation for reaching an objective. Several steps are necessary.

1. Checklist for Work Breakdown Validity

(a) Check for totality of work needed to complete an objective.

(b) Check the "logic" of the divisions and subdivisions.

(c) Check for completeness of flow from major levels to sublevels.

(d) Check and trace all loops and paths for flow and completeness.

(e) Check the pyramidlike focus of the flow toward an objective.

(f) Check and assure that end items are feeder-objectives in the flow.

(g) Check accountability assignments of each end item to a member of management.

(h) Check number and type of work packages.

(i) Check for accuracy of time estimates of each work package.

(j) Check work descriptors for sufficient depth in detail, accuracy, and completeness.

(k) Check end items as links in the objective network.

(l) Check participation of management in feeder objectives.

(m) Check for accuracy of cost estimates of each work package.

(n) Check total cost estimate against results of the objective.

(o) Check total time allotment against results of the objective.

(p) Check reliability of risk factor assignments of each work package.

(q) Check total risk against results of the objective.

(r) Check organization chart against the total objective network.

(s) Check interlocking and coordination in the objective network.

2. Manipulate the Work Breakdown Structure

The value of any model lies in the ease with which one can manipulate its variables in such a way that he acquires a greater understanding of the real situation. Trial and error *is allowed* in model manipulation in order to observe simulated conditions. These conditions can be explored in the validation procedure offered by the model so that potential abort problems in the real situation may be uncovered. For example, the unwillingness or refusal of a supervisor to participate in the validation of a work package can be a signal as to the type of cooperation the program can expect when it is implemented. Simulating different effects of manipulating work breakdown structure can be useful in predicting success or failure of an objective. The manipulation of the work breakdown structure can take several forms. Rotation of the structure 90 degrees clockwise with the parts shifted and connected in time phase converts it to a *PERT system*. Rotation of the structure 90 degrees counterclockwise with the parts used as decision nodes and branches converts it to a *decision tree*. Rotation of the structure 90 degrees counterclockwise with end items displayed as cells develops a *work descriptor and accountability matrix*. Conversion of the structure with levels and parts simulating a management system establishes an *organization chart*. Conversion of the structure into an objective network with subobjectives and feeder-objectives assures *management coordination and interlocking*. Conversion of the structure into an objective network with cost flow levels assures *total costs in getting results*. The validation of objective setting using the work breakdown structure as a model is illustrated in Figure 5-10.

3. Trial Run Reviews and Criteria

A practitioner should submit his objective program to a series of reviews and analyses in order to give its key features a trial run for an assessment of conflicts and barriers that may arise. This will yield a confidence feedback that the plan will be implemented as intended. A procedure for submitting the proposal to a trial review must meet the following criteria:

(a) *Completeness.* A reiteration of basic questions is absolutely necessary. What is to be done? Why is it to be done? Who will do it? These questions force a review of the scope and network of interlocked end items and activities to insure that they are tied together in near-perfect phase with targeted objectivés. The plan should reveal system characteristics in which individual outputs are a result of deliberate utilization of resources. The system connecting all these outputs should reveal the stated conditions of targeted objectives. Interlocking assures this.

(b) *Attainable.* Commitments to the completed plan are made on the basis of two assumptions: that the amount and type of resources allocated are available, and that specified target dates for accomplishments have been set and aligned with other work commitments. These two assumptions should be challenged during an intense review. None of the committed managers can deliver if men, materials, and money cannot be made available within the time specified. Validating objectives assures that they will be.

(c) *Managerial support.* A basic premise for the entire strategy of managing by objectives is the assurance, backing, involvement, and support of top management. The authority necessary for the implementation of the plan must be delegated to the individuals who will work to make it a reality. Furthermore, compatibility and harmony must exist between the proposed plan and existing organizational policies. If a conflict arises, one can be sure that a group or an individual will challenge and block the entire proceedings. Prior or conflicting commitments of resources and services must be resolved so that the program has complete support all the way to completion.

(d) *Improvement.* The whole point of managing by objectives is to make a significant contribution to the entire organization. The targeted objectives, when reached, should bring about improved conditions in the organization. There must be high confidence in this expectation. Furthermore, the objective program designed to make the departments and individuals strive for higher levels of achievement should be of permanent and lasting benefit to the organization in its future work. Finally, there must be a careful evaluation of the relative value of the contribution sought to the cost expended and resources utilized. This criterion more than any other will determine the go–no-go evaluation of the proposed plan's trial run.

(e) *Visibility of events.* Foreseeing the flow of events from start to finish provides visibility; that is, management can focus on some part of the entire program or enlarge the scope of the entire plan. This visibility has a "fore" and "aft" value most useful in validating objectives. A macroview of managing a system results.

(f) *Reliability.* The whole program of effort, situational analysis, objectives, work packages, decision trees, and so on, is no better than the weakest element in the system. Forecasting occurrence and number of events in a context of priority of implementation goes a long way in improving reliability.

(g) *Interlocked.* Management by objectives is a systems approach. Input/output elements are tied together for cost flow, sales, profits, time, and so on. Interfaces are defined and managed for changes and priorities.

4. Methods of Applying Trial-Run Criteria

These criteria form important guidelines to evaluate the validity and feasibility of targeted objectives and required programming. Some suggestions on how to apply the criteria are the following:

(a) Each committed manager can make a presentation in conference with other committed managers to defend and support his role in the plan. These presentations provide a view of each part as it fits into the program as a whole. This step-by-step unfolding of the program will reveal neglected factors in the whole. Conferees will criticize each manager's presentation to uncover weak points and identify deficiencies.

(b) A "fresh" committee of noncommitted managers and supervisors can review and criticize the proposed plan. Any weaknesses or deficiencies should be explained and defended by the committed managers.

(c) A quantitative model of the plan can be developed and programmed for computer manipulation. Variables in the plan, such as time, can be forced to extremes to demonstrate the effects on the entire plan. Through this computer manipulation, the facts of the situation can be better seen and described.

(d) Management can make pilot runs of subparts of the plan under a deliberate sampling procedure, selecting a portion of the program that can be tried within the company. These pilot runs would be, in effect, controlled experiments. The results, used as a sample, might be useful in making generalizations about and assessing implications of the entire plan.

(e) Simulated runs between two competing groups can be set up—one in favor of the plan and one against it. Each group, according to its position, will work as hard as it can to implement the plan or to assure its defeat. This activity will uncover relationships between various parts of the program that may not be apparent in the original. It also allows consideration of all major variables acting simultaneously. After the simulated runs, both groups discuss the features that appear to be weak and make suggestions for their correction.

These are a few of the methods whereby a trial run can be made of the proposed plan in order to raise high the confidence that a valid plan has been organized. At this state of managing by objectives, a measure of effectiveness is established. Tentative objectives set in phase 2 have now in phase 3 been validated.

COMMITMENT TO DELIVER RESULTS

Setting objectives is deciding firmly on fixed expectations, even though objective statements can be reconsidered, renegotiated, and revised in the light of new information and needs. However, for the most part, the statement is a pledge or promise that is binding. Management is neither hoping for delivery nor gambling on it; it *will* deliver and seals its pledge with a commitment. Managers at the various levels of the organization whose effort and cooperation will be required must understand the anticipated results to be achieved and their own high accountability for delivering these results. With this understanding, all those managers involved take on a commitment to work and strive as a team. The involvement and participation of large numbers of people tend to reinforce the permanent quality of commitments since so much timing and coordination is required. Once a commitment is made, through the validation procedure, all concerned juxtapose their roles in a time sequence for a management systems operation. In some companies, it is tragic to observe the way in which lack of commitment on the part of managers tends to disrupt the activities of those who are committed. Objective-setting procedures are frequently so interrelated that a change in one area will cause an upset in other areas. Those attempting to reach production quota objectives will suffer serious disruption of their work if the sales organization does not meet the sales forecasts to which it is committed. Similarly, a profit statement of objectives will be disrupted if a new capital outlay is decided upon by the uncommitted. This reaffirms the importance of the validation process in bringing detailed planning, thinking, and understanding to a sharp point by all concerned before a commitment is made.

Commitment is a process locking all feeder-objectives together for a period of time in a prescribed direction with all management personnel. Commitment is not equivalent to support, nor is it an expression of loyalty. Both support and loyalty are desirable attributes usually found in company personnel. Commitment, however, goes beyond support and loyalty. Once a decision is made, everyone carries out the decision and makes happen what is expected to happen. Questions, disagreements, and disputes are allowed, welcomed, and aired prior to commitment. Discussions of loyalty, personal relationships, and personal likes and dislikes are brought to the surface prior to commitment. However, once a commitment is made, questions of support, loyalty, and the like become less relevant. Dissenting individuals are expected to say, "I didn't entirely agree with this decision, but I had my opportunity to influence it. Now that it is made, I'll go along with it and make it work." Release from commitment is always possible if new factors appear in a changing situation. It is distressing to observe companies still striving doggedly to fulfill their commitments when the situation has changed significantly enough to warrant redefinition and redirection. This condition constitutes one of the major difficulties in the practice of managing by objectives. It will be dealt with in greater detail in Chapter 7 in the section on troubleshooting.

SUMMARY

To set objectives is to face an uncertain future and to deal with uncertainty is to deal with risk. The practitioner of managing by objectives should engage in a validation procedure to reduce risk as much as is feasible. Determining objective validity may well be the most important step in the conceptual strategy of managing by objectives. The proof of objective validity is the burden and responsibility of the objective setter. This chapter described several methods for translating a tentative statement of objective into a validated statement of commitment.

GUIDE QUESTIONS FOR THE PRACTITIONER

1. Select your three most important objectives to be accomplished this coming year and develop a work breakdown structure for each similar to that in Figures 5-3 and 5-4.

2. Identify work packages for these objectives determining end item, accountability, work description, time, cost, and risk factor.

3. Develop a PERT network using one of the work breakdown structures developed above. Identify the critical path and calculate the probability of meeting the proposed schedule.

4. Using Figure 5-10 as a guide, make a venture simulation analysis and do the following:
   (a) Validate time and schedule
   (b) Validate managerial coordination
   (c) Validate work methods and accountability
   (d) Validate total costs
   (e) Validate the organization chart for reaching objectives
   (f) Validate risk and impact of decision-making

5. Using degrees of risk and confidence, validate how well the following criteria have been met by your venture analysis:
   (a) Completeness
   (b) Attainability
   (c) Managerial support
   (d) Improvement
   (e) Visibility
   (f) Reliability
   (g) Interlocking

6. Using the PERT network as a model, proceed deliberately to impose faults and aborts in different phases of the program and think through contingency actions to meet potential effects.

REFERENCES AND NOTES

1. John R. Virts and Richard W. Garrett, "Weighing Risks in Capacity Expansion," *Harvard Business Review*, May–June 1970, pp. 132–140.

2. Robert W. Miller, *Schedule, Cost and Profit Control with PERT*, McGraw-Hill Book Co., New York, 1963, pp. 65–67; 98–100; 152–153.

3. Two recent and thought-provoking articles on decision trees are the following: John F. Magee, "Decision Trees for Decision Making," *Harvard Business Review*, July–August 1964, p. 126; Jerome D. Wiest, "Heuristic Programs for Decision Making," *Harvard Business Review*, September–October 1966, p. 129.

4. Robert W. Miller, *op. cit.,* pp. 65–67; 98–100; 152–153.

5. Phil Carroll, *op. cit.,* pp. 10–16.

6. The network concept has developed in an evolutionary way over many years. It appears that project networking was formally defined by two research teams, one developing PERT and the other CPM. See M. R. Walker and J. S. Sayer, "Project Planning and Scheduling," *Report 6959,* E. I. duPont de Nemours and Company, Inc., Wilmington, Delaware, March 1959.

7. Joseph J. Moder and Cecil R. Phillips, *Project Management with CPM and PERT,* Reinhold, New York, 1964.

8. Readers who are statistically oriented will recognize this formula as the measure of difference between two sample values in standard error units. Those desiring further information, see Kemit O. Hanson and George J. Brabb, *Managerial Statistics,* Prentice-Hall, Englewood Cliffs, N.J., 1961, pp. 102–107.

6. Implementing Objectives

Planned Motivation. Understanding the Motivational Processes. Implementing Planned Motivation. Coaching to Implement Objectives. Persuasion Toward Objectives. Summary. Guide Questions for the Practitioner. References and Notes.

The ability to get things done on a day-to-day, program-to-program, objective-to-objective basis is no doubt one of the greatest measures of performance of men who manage. In a larger and more meaningful sense, it is also a measure of the performance of all employees in an organization. It is one thing for management and employees to have objectives logically developed, set at challenging levels, and validated to meet organizational and individual needs; it is another thing to determine the degree of competence with which committed men focus and concentrate just enough of their personal resources of time, skill, effort, and courage to initiate what has to be done, conduct the activity, and bring it to a successful end. Implementing skill is no doubt the key force behind getting the results necessary to accomplish an objective and requires infusing a spirit of willingness and drive in subordinates. One who has this implementing skill gets his subordinates to participate in objective programs successfully because they want to and not because they are driven to.

Motivation is the term used to describe the work a manager must do to inspire, encourage, and move people to perform to and beyond requirements. It involves *coaching* processes—day-to-day, face-to-face urging, directing, and helping subordinates to reach and meet their commitments. It places a heavy demand on *persuasive* skills in order to convince subordinates and gain their agreement when there are differences or disputes. Motivation, coaching, and persuasion are three vital ingredients of a manager's ability to implement the objectives he has determined to achieve. Implementing means taking action to get things done, or the practical effort necessary to carry out what is intended. It requires a determination not to be stopped. Solomon stated this idea by saying, "Whatsoever thy hand findeth to do, do it with all thy might."[1] It is completing an objective successfully.

A well-organized program designed to accomplish significant objectives is at best a document of where to go and how to get there. To make the document operational, the drive and push that can only be supplied by people must first be mustered and then infused into the plan. Like a ship whose course has been plotted and whose structure and design have made it seaworthy, it still needs the propelling power to move it forward. Motivation, coaching, and persuasion are to a valid program of managing by objectives as propelling power is to a ship on a prearranged course. Without this motive power, the ship only floats. Without skilled use of motivators in a coaching environment by a persuasive manager, a program of objectives remains only a literary document.

This chapter will introduce a methodology for implementing objectives once they have been validated. Implementing objectives was identified as the fourth step in the five-step conceptual methodology of managing by objectives. This chapter will describe several techniques and explain "how to implement" with three basic approaches: motivation, coaching, and persuasion.

PLANNED MOTIVATION

The problem of motivation continues to trouble management personnel everywhere. The search is on for the "magic formula" that will arouse within employees the wish, desire, and drive to work for company goals while meeting their own personal needs. A practical problem that must be taken into account in this search is that what motivates one man may not motivate another. The use of Herzberg's[2] motivators (satisfiers) and demotivators (dissatisfiers or hygienic factors) has variable effects on different individuals. Motivators that work well with one individual are completely useless with another. Additionally, a motivator for an individual one day is not effective with the passage of time for the same individual. What is needed is a workable scheme for relating important motivators in combinations and varying proportions to a given individual at a given time while avoiding demotivation. This scheme should be set down in an implementation schedule similar to production schedules, control schedules, and maintenance schedules. Change any one of the factors and the motivational pattern will change. Similarly, individual variations will effect the type and degree of demotivators that an individual will tolerate on the job. A recognized demotivator for one individual may not be a demotivator for another. Motivators can become demotivators with the passage of time. *Motivating is defined here as the skill of a supervisor or manager in arousing enthusiasm among subordinates for activities involved in achieving a purpose, goal, or objective.* It is the work a manager performs to inspire, encourage, persuade, and impel others to take required action. It is the process of getting subordinates to reach for company goals. Motivators are those conditions or agents within a job that cause or arouse subordinates to act. Motivators are job factors that give employees satisfaction. When these motivators relate to the work itself, they provide built-in incentives for the subordinate to complete work. When motivators are built into objectives, an intense drive to reach them results.

Ford[3] describes a series of unique experiments at the American Telephone and Telegraph Company proving that job satisfaction through the work itself can generate high levels of motivational intensity. The idea that work can be satisfying was brought out in ancient times; more recently, in 1923, Kahlil Gibran said,

> Always you have been told that work is a curse and labour a misfortune. But I say to you that when you work you fulfill a part of earth's furthest dream, assigned to you when that dream was born. And in keeping yourself with labour you are in truth loving life. And to love life through labour is to be intimate with life's inmost secret.[4]

Demotivators are those conditions or agents within a job that, if present, will give employees dissatisfaction. Demotivators are job, work, or environmental constraints that will inhibit an individual from reaching an objective. Demotivators tend to retard action toward a purpose or a goal. It would be a simple process to formulate a list of motivators and demotivators to be employed when the situation warrants. But such a list is not practical. There is a delicate balance between motivators and demotivators. Too much or too little of a motivator will turn it into a demotivator, particularly in a given labor market, a given industry, a given profession, or a given period of time. For example, challenge is now regarded as one of the most potent motivators a supervisor can use to incite action. Yet too much challenge or too little will render it a demotivator. There is an amount that is just enough.

To get a subordinate from point A to point D, the planned motivation approach utilizes the concept that multiple motivators are planned and implemented at points B and C. The concept of planning motivation is in contrast to traditional motivational practices. Planned motivation gives attention to the need for different levels of the organization since self-motivation varies from low to high as one goes up the organizational ladder. Additionally, planned motivation varies conversely from high to low. This is illustrated in Figure 6-1. In higher levels of management, because of their position of responsibility, individual managers are able to build motivators into their own work. While planning and organizing his work, a higher-level manager can arrange future commitments in such a way that his personal needs are taken care of. Very little job planning

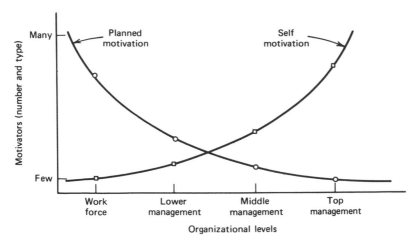

Figure 6-1.   Motivators planned by levels.

has to be done for him because he does so much for himself. For a higher-level manager, self-motivation is high and planned motivation is low.

In lower levels of management, however, an individual manager does not have the same opportunity because his job responsibilities are more restricted. On this level, job planning must fit into a strategy organized from higher levels. Thus, unlike his counterpart on higher levels, the lower-level manager cannot arrange future commitments in such a way that his personal needs are satisfied. Motivators must be planned for him and applied in a deliberate way. For a lower-level manager, self-motivation is low so planned motivation must be high.

Some motivators are common to all levels, but many are different for each level. It is unfortunate to see managers at middle levels using the same motivators for the work force that they use for lower-level managers. For example, a computer firm that employs a number of professional people in the work force tends to motivate these people and their professional supervisors with the same motivators. Recognition of position is far more potent as a motivator for first-line supervisors than for the working staff. Job enlargement is far more potent as a motivator for the working staff than it is for first-line supervisors. The computer firm ignored this differentiation and found the working force motivated but the supervisory level demotivated and dissatisfied. The firm failed to plan and use motivators for specific management levels. Management should have at its disposal a broad list of motivators. The list should be varied and at best represent potential motivators. They become actual motivators when they are applied properly at the right time to the right person on the right level.

Planned motivation is a concept for dealing with motivators and demotivators in a deliberate way. It is a *motivational strategy that finds the "best fit" among company objectives, employee needs, and the job situation.* It recognizes that effective motivation cannot be left to chance, impulse, or spontaneity. It is too complex! It must be systematic, planned, and even scheduled, in the same manner that budgets, capital outlays, new products, promotions, and so on are planned and scheduled. The planned motivation concept recognizes that multiple motivators are necessary because of the diminishing effects of motivation over time. Motivation can be either diminished or intensified, strengthened or weakened. The diminishing can result simply from conditions on the job or from unforeseen pressures. Or, the intensifying effect can be produced through a deliberate and planned situation. This means that several related motivational steps are required to arouse action in a given direction and with needed intensity of effort at the right time. A contrast of the traditional motivational practices with the planned motivational concept is as follows:

Traditional Motivational Practices	Planned Motivational Concept
a. Starts with people in jobs	a. Starts with system's objectives and feeder-objectives
b. Single or few motivators	b. Multiple sequentially related motivators
c. Through the work	c. Through the work toward objectives
d. Day-to-day chance	d. Motivators are time scheduled with hygienic factors
e. Meets the needs of employees	e. Finds "best fit" between company objectives and employee needs
f. Applies motivators in existing job classification	f. Jobs are enlarged, enriched, simplified, or standardized to meet "best fit" between company objectives and employee needs
g. Gives responsibility and control for own work	g. Fits responsibility and control within commitments of the system

Traditional Motivational Practices	Planned Motivational Concept
h. Gives job freedom and additional authority	h. Fits freedom range and authority within management system
i. Applies motivators to all levels and all groups	i. Applies motivators in a schedule by levels within an organization
j. Waits for diminishing effect before applying new motivators	j. Anticipates diminishing effects and schedules intensification with new motivators

Since the basic thesis of managing by objectives is to expect and deliver results, the motivation of this expectancy should not be left to gamble or happenstance. Motivators must be built in and demotivators must be avoided in terms of the objectives of the company and the needs of the people who are expected to implement the objectives. A planned motivational model can help a manager develop a "best fit" approach for implementing an objective program. The proper selection, proportioning, relevance, and application of motivators and demotivators suggest that planned motivation is an *eclectic* approach to creating a motivational strategy. The eclectic skill comes with experience and practice. The logic of the eclectic fit approach is illustrated in Figure 6-2.

The process starts with the objective and the motivational problem situation. From this point, the practitioner views needs of employees, potential motivators, and demotivators and fits these in with the objective to be accomplished. Practical illustrations of the model are included later in this chapter.

The use of this planned motivational model suggests that the problem in managing motivation is not managing work but managing the desire of men to work toward objectives. The work situation along with its respective variables must be identified before a motivator is selected. Working conditions such as noise, light, other workers, equipment layout, union climate, and company policies are but a few of these variables. Personal needs and motives for working must also be considered in order to identify any that might interfere with an objective program. A motivator is selected as a potential causative agent for action because it best fits three variables: the objective, the work situation, and the needs of the individual. These three variables are so closely interrelated that to assure that they are channeled in the same direction, the planned motivation concept must be scheduled, as shown in Figure 6-3.

The basic idea of managing by objectives is not only to get results but to get results within a certain amount of time. Once an objective

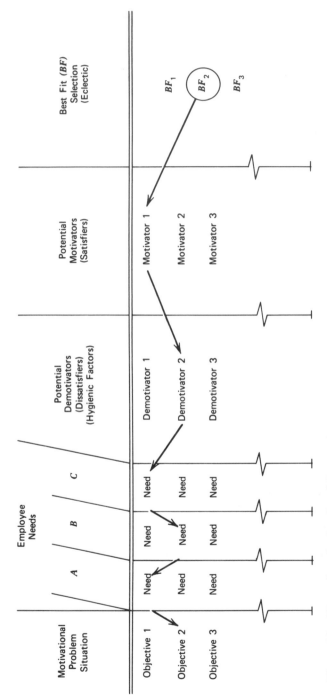

Figure 6-2. Planned motivational model concept.

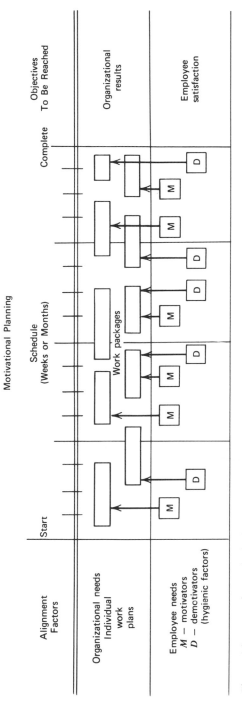

Figure 6-3. Planning and scheduling motivation.

has been committed and results requirements have been set, the practitioner must specify within individual work plans the demotivators to be avoided and motivators to be implemented within a time framework. This is accomplished under a motivation planning schedule, as suggested in Figure 6-3. Work plans, needs of employees, motivators, and demotivators are directed toward organizational results and employee satisfaction. An anticipated and planned best fit among all these elements is sought in the schedule. *Building motivators into the work and avoiding demotivators implied by the work will precede the completion date of progress points in completing an objective.* Scheduling sets the time and pace not only for the execution of work plans but also suggests when and how motivation must be infused to arrive at a completion stage. Thus planning and scheduling motivation are deliberately structured under multiple-motivator applications designed to achieve a set of expected results. The best fit process is a further explanation of the M.B.O. Rule for Aligning Divergent Objectives given in Chapter 2.

UNDERSTANDING THE MOTIVATIONAL PROCESSES

The basic drives that impel people to act to meet personal needs help explain the reasons people behave and perform as they do. Their striving after things is largely determined by their urges and needs. Each person's particular course of action has been adopted because, in some way, it provides him with satisfaction or fulfillment. Maslow's theory of needs[5] gives great insight to the levels and types of needs that drive people. It is the best explanation for the reasons that people work. A needs hierarchy exists for each individual, and his behavior is determined to a great extent by what these needs are and how they are influenced. According to an adaptation of Maslow's concept, man's needs may fall on five levels of variability, as illustrated in Figure 6-4.

First-level needs are the basic biological needs. These are the strong drives for self-survival. They pertain to the biological processes without which we could not exist as humans. Examples of these drives are hunger, thirst, breathing, sex, and sleep. These needs are instinctive and unceasing. Satisfaction of these needs can be only temporary since they occur repetitively from birth until death. They preserve the life processes of the human organism and consequently are urgent and always demand attention.

Second-level needs are the physiological needs, or the strong drives toward self-comfort. They pertain to the physiological processes that support our metabolism. Examples of these drives are exercise, shelter,

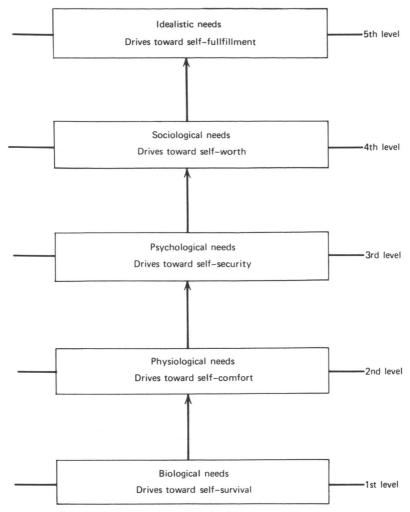

Figure 6-4. Human needs drive human behavior.

rest, transportation, clothing, and freedom of motion. These are vital in their support of the human organism's life processes. They are not as urgent as the first-level drives but become more urgent with the passage of time.

Third-level needs are the psychological needs, or the strong drives toward self-security. They pertain to the psychological processes involved in the emotional well-being of the individual. Examples of these drives are avoiding threat, danger, tension, and deprivation, and striving for job security, work satisfaction, intellectual challenges, and economic security. These are vital in their support of the mental and emotional processes of the human organism. These needs are largely acquired and culturally influenced. They appear early in life and vary in strength during different phases of life. For many people, these drives are urgent enough to demand attention; for others, they are not.

Fourth-level needs are sociological, or the strong drives for group acceptance. They pertain to man as he relates to his fellowmen or his social environment. Examples of these drives are sense of participation, variety of group membership, status, activity, and advancement. These needs are vital to man in the way he relates to other humans and to his environment. The drives toward self-worth are those that make a person wish to feel important and to be accepted by family, friends, church, and community. In an affluent society, these drives are very active. Groups, the company, and the government are highly influential on the strength and duration of these drives.

Fifth-level needs are the idealistic needs. These are the strong drives toward a sense of self-fulfillment. They pertain to the idealistic processes that support man's ideals, desires, dreams, and values. Examples of these drives are the need for beauty, wealth, humanity, fame, creativity, and religion. These needs are vital to the individual in terms of what he wants from life, or what he wishes to become. Occasionally, these needs are simply wishful thinking, as, for instance, when they involve wanting to be a great author, a painter, the president of the company, a millionaire, or to retire early. These needs are private to the individual and he is likely to share them with few others. To some individuals, these needs are strong and urgent.

Human behavior is a result of the individual's attempting to meet some felt need. These needs vary in type, level, intensity, and duration. Managers can affect the behavior of employees through blocking or supplying employee needs within the job context. Needs and behavior can be related as follows:

1.   Lower-level needs will tend to displace higher-level needs in priority when there is conflict. In a nonaffluent society such as India, the drive for food will always displace the drive for a sense of participation within a community group.

2.   The individual tends to strive to meet his idealistic needs. He moves to higher levels as he satisfies the needs of previous levels. He finally arrives at the lofty, never-ending, insatiable level at which he reaches for ideals. Since a man is always in the stages of becoming, he always reaches for his ideals and values as his fulfillment in life. Other need levels are stepping stones to the idealistic level.

3. A man's response to being motivated is dominated by the level of need in which he finds himself. Examine a man's behavior or performance and it is quite possible to determine the need he is trying to meet. Conversely, to know a man's need helps one predict what his future behavior and performance will be.

4. Man is insatiable in his appetites. Theoretically, once a need is satisfied, there will be no further motivation toward behavior; however, since a man never gives up wanting some kind of fulfillment, he will move up and down the various levels. In the drives of unionism one can see the insatiability of men's wants.

5. Deprivation of need fulfillment by a supervisor, a company, or the government will generate behavioral consequences. In a nonaffluent culture, the lower the level, the more serious and violent the reaction. The higher the level, the less serious and less violent the reaction. To block the drive for food in the Indian culture is to generate a serious rebellion. In an affluent culture where the basic needs such as food and water are readily met, lower-level needs in conflict with higher levels will not generate a serious reaction. In affluent cultures, it is the blocking of higher-level needs that generates strong reactions. Highly rebellious political behavior may result when these higher-level needs are thwarted or frustrated. Youth demonstrations in the United States over the issues of Vietnam and minority oppression are examples of this.

6. Intensity of striving will be greatest at that level to which each individual assigns a high priority. It appears that all humans have needs on all levels. Yet each individual places a priority on the level and type of need he wishes to fulfill. Since each individual will assign a different priority, a very complex set of priority patterns will emerge. To complicate matters, since a man is by nature insatiable, his needs and priorities will change with time.

The striving to meet wants and needs is motivation. Behavior or performance is directed and determined by needs. This provides a fundamental clue in the management of people from the standpoint of managing by objectives. If the manager assesses the needs of people as carefully as he does their goals and can align them with company objectives, strong motivation will result. The reader is reminded of the disparity angle described in Figures 2-5 and 2-6 of Chapter 2, which explains this alignment. The individual sees himself as meeting his own needs first and those of the company second. It was mentioned earlier that the needs hierarchy provides a clue to a man's behavior. This is about all we can expect. The motivational processes are so complex that a man seems to be striving to meet several needs simultaneously. They become even more complex when we note that some needs have short time spans while others are of longer duration. A complex fluctuation pattern may be conceptualized for each individual as he meets his needs on the five levels over a period of time. This is illustrated in Figure 6-5. Since motivators are causative agents that help an individual identify and meet a need, the practitioner of managing by objectives would do well to acquire an insight into the needs of his subordinates and identify motivators that aid in fulfilling them. Similarly, the practitioner would do well to recognize demotivators as causative agents that keep a subordinate from satisfying a need. Avoiding practices that demotivate will go a long way toward removing dissatisfaction.

IMPLEMENTING PLANNED MOTIVATION

Today, there are many good motivational concepts and principles[6] useful in increasing employee commitment to company objectives and goals. These concepts and principles often fail in actual practice, however, not so much because they are faulty in themselves, but because management lacks the ability to translate and implement them in a manner consistent with the overall structure and needs of the particular organization. The complexity of motivational problems combines the effects of a whole

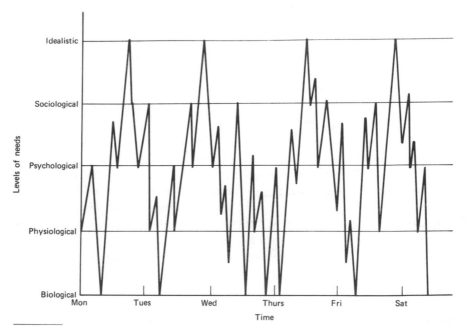

Figure 6-5. Fluctuating nature of human needs.

array of factors demanding optimization. Solutions require that no one factor be entirely neglected or left to chance or considered singly. Rather, a planned, combined, and select fit approach should be used in a progressive manner. In order to discover how management can implement motivational principles, several related processes must be undertaken. Management must do the following:

1. Be able to analyze company objectives, task assignments, work packages, or problem situations as to their technical, financial, and human relations requirements.

2. Recognize the disparity that exists between company expectations and employee expectations.

3. Acquire an insight into the "whys" of employee behavior and needs and work toward developing the skills to narrow the disparity. Use the M.B.O. Rule for Aligning Divergent Objectives.

4. Plan the selection, use, and application of motivators to work assignments or problem situations.

The manager's choice of approach and skill in implementing these processes in a useful strategy determine to a large extent the type of motivational response he gets from his subordinate. Planned and scheduled motivation was introduced earlier as a deliberate strategy of building a motivational climate through the work toward objectives. This was illustrated in the planned motivational model concepts of Figures 6-2 and 6-3. The following are the specific steps a practitioner should take to institute and implement planned motivation: (1) build motivators into statements of objectives; (2) examine existing jobs for feasibility of reaching objectives; (3) acquire insights into subordinate needs; (4) develop a list of potential motivators; and (5) apply motivators as a "best fit" toward objectives.

1. Build Motivators into Statement of Objectives

Planned motivation begins with the structuring of a formal statement of commitment. The whole motivational strategy begins with objective setting. Getting participation and involvement of those to be committed is a process of relating people meaningfully to their future. The give and take during this phase is an expression of subordinates' reaching for both company and individual future needs. It is during this phase that the disparity between the company and the individual is lessened and goals are brought into greater alignment. The objective network approach and the feeder-objective concept create a system of expectations that the subordinate not only understands but helped to formulate.

Direct employee participation and involvement in decision-making about company objectives or feeder-objectives provide a strong base for applying additional motivators. The objective to be formulated must be analyzed for its human relations requirements and motivators must be built in wherever possible.

2. Examine Existing Jobs for Feasibility of Reaching Objectives

With objectives clearly in view, jobs and job groupings must be examined to determine where additional motivators can be inserted and applied meaningfully. An attempt should be made to avoid demotivators or dissatisfiers even if job changes must be made. It is inconceivable for a company to pursue a set of new objectives, new commitments, and new directions and still hang on to old jobs, old positions, or old duties. Herein lies a great difficulty. A company that embarks on an objective program must be prepared to make job changes to reach its objectives. The creation of a management system requires that jobs and job elements align themselves with the expectations set up by objectives. There are four basic and systematic ways to change a job for motivational purposes, and the practitioner must be prepared to carry them through. These are illustrated in Figure 6-6.

(a) *Job enrichment.*[7] This is restructuring an existing job by including a number of projects, tasks, or duties that the subordinate finds personally rewarding because they meet many of his higher-level needs. Duties and responsibilities of higher management, when delegated or assigned to subordinates, fall in the enriching category. These are found by allowing the subordinates themselves to identify the enriching elements. In order to fulfill his need, the subordinate must be convinced that he is doing the work of higher management. This process is known as *vertical job loading* and can be practiced in a practical way. As an example of job enrichment, a supervisor might allow his subordinate to help him prepare the annual budget for submission to higher management.

(b) *Job enlargement.*[8] This is restructuring an existing job by expanding it to include task elements from other subordinates' jobs to make it more interesting, more varied, and more meaningful. It meets the employee's needs by eliminating monotony and repetition. This process is known as *horizontal job loading* because it attempts to interchange tasks among a peer group. Horizontal job enlargement tends to counteract oversimplification and gives the worker a whole natural unit of work.

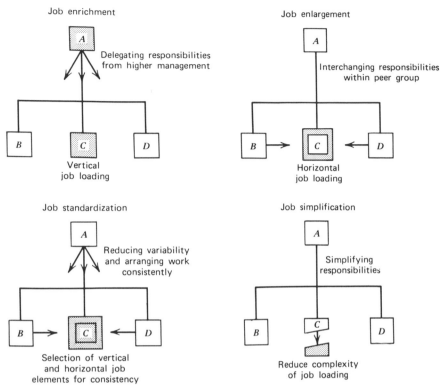

Figure 6-6. Ways to restructure jobs to meet objectives.

As an example of job enlargement, a supervisor might allow his drill press operator to run the miller and sanding machines in addition to the drill press.

(c) *Job standardization.*[9] This is the restructuring of an entire job by reducing variety and establishing consistent routines, work elements, and duties to meet the commitment demands of a feeder-objective. Job standardization may be carried out through combinations selected from both vertical and horizontal loading, that is, on the basis of "standardized" tasks from the higher management level as well as "standardized" tasks from the employee's own level. Job standardization requires a complete change in job content from the original position. The machine operator who runs many different types of machines with varying degrees of skill and productivity provides an example of this. He is also required to perform a variety of operations with each machine, the particular type of operation changing from day to day. The supervisor standardizes this operator's job content by limiting the number of machines and operations he performs from day to day. The supervisor establishes a consistent routine for the operator's day-to-day work.

(d) *Job simplification*.[10] This involves reducing a number of task elements or duties within his job that the subordinate finds personally annoying, complex, or difficult. Many subordinates favor job simplification since it gives them a high degree of specialization and meets their need to be an "expert." Subordinates less capable are not given work that overwhelms them. This reduces the amount of support they need from their supervisor and promotes independent action. An example of this is the personnel administrator who is expected to perform a number of jobs within the personnel function, such as recruit, interview, train, test, counsel, discipline, and discharge. The supervisor simplifies his job by reducing the number of duties he is expected to perform in the personnel department. He may have the personnel administrator specialize in recruiting, interviewing, and hiring.

The manner, method, and time for changing jobs for motivational purposes must be carefully chosen. Several criteria must be used to justify the change. For example, cost of the change must be weighed against increased value of performance. Demotivator effects on group attitudes must be considered before one individual job is altered. Job change must mean greater productivity to a planned and stated objective.

3. Acquire Insights into Subordinate Needs

Motivating subordinates starts with real insight to and understanding of their needs. The identification of apparent needs is a part of the planned motivation approach. Having a general list of these needs, such as the following, is helpful. The practitioner should develop his own list for each individual as well as for his entire group.

A. Self-survival needs (biological)
    (1) Needs minimum wage sufficient for biological requirements
    (2) Needs food during working hours
    (3) Needs protection from dangerous working conditions such as noise, temperature, fumes, dust, and chemicals.
    (4) Needs water during working hours
    (5) Needs rest periods during arduous work
    (6) Needs shelter against the weather
    (7) Needs to work in an unpolluted environment
    (8) Needs regular and sufficient sleep
    (9) Needs periodic examinations to assure his survivability
    (10) Needs clothing for protection of the body

B. Self-comfort needs (physiological)
    (1) Needs freedom of motion to relieve muscular fatigue
    (2) Needs transportation aids to avoid fatigue
    (3) Needs facilities to arrange for working conveniences
    (4) Needs clean surroundings
    (5) Needs an optimum length of working hours
    (6) Needs additional wages to make life outside work comfortable
    (7) Needs working conditions that will not place undue strain on health
    (8) Needs to have work station arranged for ease in carrying out work
    (9) Needs exercise to feel healthy
    (10) Needs periodic relaxers like coffee and doughnuts
    (11) Needs a work atmosphere in which work can be carried on for some time
    (12) Needs facilities and equipment for personal habits
    (13) Needs housing for opportunity to make a home

C. Self-security needs (psychological)
    (1) Needs security of employment and income
    (2) Needs to have supervisor periodically assure him he is needed
    (3) Needs to feel protected against unknown future with all types of insurance and a pension
    (4) Needs a safe work station
    (5) Needs additional wages to provide for bank balance to handle any emergencies
    (6) Needs to feel his opportunities do not lead to a dead-end street
    (7) Needs to feel he is learning and growing on the job in terms of job requirements and job security
    (8) Needs to feel his company is putting into effect quickly his acquired skills in education and training
    (9) Needs work that fascinates and generates intense interest
    (10) Needs to have his ideas, suggestions, and proposals heard and discussed
    (11) Needs to feel his company is growing in capability to secure his future
    (12) Needs to feel he has a chance to find his own niche
    (13) Needs to feel his company pays as good or better salaries than other companies
    (14) Needs to learn for himself
    (15) Needs to know and to be assured periodically where he stands with his supervisor and his company

(16) Needs help to recall or remember facts and procedures not frequently practiced

(17) Needs level of training to achieve what is expected of him

(18) Needs to feel fairness of wages, promotion, and task assignments

(19) Needs clear understanding of the requirements of the job

(20) Needs impartial treatment from supervisor

(21) Needs to know what is going on and why

(22) Needs to know how outside conditions may affect his job

(23) Needs to avoid boring and monotonous routines

(24) Needs to understand company policies as they relate to him and his job

(25) Needs to feel there is justice in management

D. Self-worth needs (sociological)

(1) Needs to engage in responsibilities that family, relatives, friends, peers, and community think important, significant, and complex

(2) Needs to feel he can do things others cannot

(3) Needs a high salary to feel his "worth" (money is a score-keeper)

(4) Needs to win among those who are trying to win

(5) Needs to feel he is a future management prospect

(6) Needs to feel the location of the company is valuable for recreation, sports, cultural activities, and friends

(7) Needs to feel the image and reputation of the company are accepted by friends and the community

(8) Needs to talk to people to feel his own individuality

(9) Needs some freedom for individual judgment in doing work

(10) Needs to display company-wide status symbols that convey accomplishment and value

(11) Needs recognition of an individual contribution

(12) Needs to have his ideas, suggestions, and proposals accepted and implemented

(13) Needs opportunity to participate in group activities

(14) Needs to have everyone know that he is steadily progressing and developing

(15) Needs acceptance by his group of peers in intellectual and work activities

(16) Needs to have his opinion treated with respect

(17) Needs to be identified by name

(18) Needs to be involved and participating in decisions affecting his job or other jobs with which he is connected

(19) Needs to know relationship of the job to the finished product

(20) Needs to know relationship of the job to the supervisor's job

(21) Needs to know relationship of his job to those of others in the group

(22) Needs to feel and understand that job change is change upward

E. Self-fulfillment (idealistic)

(1) Needs to have life goals respected and accepted in such areas as religion, art, fame, beauty, and humanity

(2) Needs to feel he is a counselor with plenty of available good advice

(3) Needs to feel great rewards await him as recognition of his achievements and contributions

(4) Needs to feel more important than his supervisor

(5) Needs to do increasingly more different work toward great achievements

(6) Needs to feel his experiences are broadening; that is, while in production, he deals with personnel problems; while in engineering, he deals with finances; while in marketing, he deals with manufacturing

(7) Needs to feel that job assignments are meaningful milestones of progress in a great career

(8) Needs to feel someday he can be president of the company

(9) Needs to feel that if he wishes, he can be a consultant to many companies

(10) Needs to have plans for and confidence in a bright future

(11) Needs a sense of outstanding citizenship in the community

(12) Needs to be recognized for religious values

(13) Needs to feel there is a future life and that death does not end all

(14) Needs to display company status symbols among his peers, to show them that he is rising in the organization

(15) Needs to feel he can retire in a manner that meets his retirement needs

4. Develop a List of Potential Motivators

The practitioner of the planned motivation concept not only acquires an insight into why people work and the effects of needs on behavior and performance, but also he formulates a list of motivators that are potentially capable of connecting the needs of employees with the needs of the company. Having a list of these motivators is helpful. The practitioner should be aware, however, that they will not work all the time with all people. They are rather potential sources of motivation that may work if the conditions are right and if they are applied skillfully. It should be kept in mind they could become demotivators if improperly used under unfavorable conditions. The list is broken up into two parts: nonfinancial motivators and financial motivators.

A. Nonfinancial motivators

(1) Arrange work for performance stretch. The most effective effort is put forth by subordinates when they attempt tasks that fall in the range of challenge—that is, not too easy and not too hard—where success seems quite possible but not certain. High performance can never be achieved without high standards. The very process of determining what constitutes challenge and setting objectives accordingly, if done with the subordinate and not for him, is a potent motivator for getting him to act. Possible challenges lie in increasing the number of assignments performed by any one subordinate and shortening the time in which a set of assignments is to be completed.

(2) Acknowledge performance accomplishments toward objectives. Good job performance in pursuit of objectives that is recognized and rewarded (reinforced) is more likely to recur. The type of performance most likely to emerge in any situation is that which the subordinate found successful or satisfying previously in a similar situation. The supervisor who plans and provides for a steady, cumulative sequence of successful performance experiences toward attainable objectives will bring the worker to a high level of motivation. Such a supervisor will see that subordinates get recognition for those accomplishments that both he and the employee consider important or substantial. He will give a feedback to the individual on what he has or has not accomplished, both positive and negative.

(3) Allow participation in the job itself. Subordinates are more apt to throw themselves whole-heartedly into a work assignment if they themselves have participated in the selection, planning, and decision-making involved in the work packages. A subordinate should become involved and make as many decisions as necessary about the work he is to do. He should be given as much responsibility he can and will take. Genuine participation, not pretended sharing, has been found to increase the desire to produce, learn, and excel.

(4) Arrange and give promotional opportunities. Avenues of advancement should be provided for all subordinates regardless of sex, age, and length of service. Paramount in the minds of subordinates is the question, How can I get ahead? A supervisor who provides these opportunities for

advancement immediately after a good job done will find that they have more influence on the subordinate than any big promotion that comes much later. In fact, promotion, to be most effective to a subordinate or to his on-looking peers, should follow almost immediately a desired performance and be clearly connected with that performance in the minds of all subordinates.

(5) Enlarge, enrich, simplify or standardize jobs. Monotonous, mechanical effort reduces and deactivates most employees, causing them to become dullards on the job. Opportunity for fresh, novel, and stimulating experiences is a kind of reward quite effective in motivating. Job enlargement and enrichment with variety or interesting and innovative experiences provide a stimulus to the employee. Complicated work tasks should be made simpler and easier to understand. Special projects, unusual assignments, and working with other groups on new responsibilities are some of the ways to do this. Job changes must be legitimate changes in the minds of subordinates, which often means rewriting position descriptions.

(6) Develop and train subordinates. When a subordinate experiences discouragement and failure in his work assignments, his self-confidence, level of aspiration, and sense of worth are likely to be damaged. The subordinate who sees himself at his worst at work is liable to place little value on his job. Conversely, a subordinate who sees his supervisor take a personal interest in his acquiring new skills and knowledge is likely to spur his performance to greater levels.

(7) A supervisor must be a "motivational example." Subordinates learn much from seeing and observing their supervisor and fellow workers accomplishing their tasks. Subordinates' attitudes are heavily influenced by interest, preferences, prejudices, likes, and lislikes of their group and supervisor. There is nothing quite so effective as for the supervisor to be an example of what he requires. The supervisor-subordinate relationship is a powerfully binding one. The subordinate senses, sees, and feels the performance of a supervisor and assimilates far more impressions and effects for motivation than one realizes.

(8) Provide better than minimum working conditions. A worker's reaction to such things as poor working conditions—noise, faulty equipment, or distractive conversations, for example—is likely to be apathetic conformity, defiance, scapegoating, or escape. The existence of working conditions below what is regarded as minimum for doing a job provides the basis of dissatisfaction. The supervisor should help the subordinate in his day-to-day accomplishment by controlling unfavorable working surroundings. This will remove demotivators or dissatisfiers.

(9) Invite inventiveness and creativity on the job. Subordinates' reac-

tions to excessive direction and autocratic demands lower the stimulation to think, learn, suggest, and produce ideas. A subordinate who has been working at a job for a period of time will often find better ways to do it. The supervisor should be receptive at all times to ideas and suggestions for working more efficiently and productively. He should ask subordinates for their opinions and suggestions.

(10) Show subordinates' contribution to the "big picture." Every subordinate wants to know where he fits into the organization. The supervisor should explain to him why his job is important in relation to the entire enterprise. There is a great transfer value to an individual situation through collecting and seeing other situations. A supervisor should share with subordinates the exciting plans and programs for the future whenever possible and keep them informed where necessary.

(11) Other motivators:

(a) Give knowledge of progress performance in getting results.
(b) Arrange periodic face-to-face meetings for open discussion (president–supervisors; supervisor–his group).
(c) Show subordinates what other employees can do and are doing.
(d) Set up a "pride" system for meeting targets.
(e) Delegate responsibility early and encourage rapid promotion.
(f) Show personal interest in the employee's knowledge, skills, and progress on the job.
(g) Provide informal coaching and teaching on the "whys" of the job.
(h) Allow some freedom for individual judgment when making work assignments.
(i) Provide for competition with others through self-determined standards.
(j) Involve employee in broad-range goal setting for company.
(k) Provide access to information as related to job requirements and needs.
(l) Create an atmosphere of positive attitudes and approval.
(m) Assign employee to influential group of workers with positive attitudes and high standards.

B. Financial motivators

(1) Relate wages and salaries to M.B.O. productivity. Annual salaries established at levels on a par with similar positions in the industry and the labor market can no longer be considered effective for motivational purposes. An accountant working in an insurance company and making $12,000 a year will not be motivated financially to transfer to an advertis-

ing agency at the same rate of pay. To use wages and salaries as a motivator, the level of dispensation must be higher than that available in the labor market. When the advertising agency offers $15,000 a year, the accountant may have the incentive to transfer. Additionally, to use increases in wages and salaries as a motivator, the increases must relate to results the employee obtained on the job. Rewards and remuneration should be clearly granted on M.B.O. productivity. The whole process of relating M.B.O. productivity and financial rewards is accomplished with the formal commitment of performance against objectives, as worked out and validated between a supervisor and his subordinate for a specified time period.

(2) Fringe benefit program must have favorable edge. Standard fringe benefit packages that are widely accepted in competitive positions can no longer be regarded as important for motivational purposes. Such items as vacations, life insurance, travel benefits, and accident, hospitalization and retirement insurance are now expected norms in many jobs. Unless there is a favorable edge, these can only be dissatisfiers if they do not reach a minimum level. A company must provide an unusual or exceptional benefit in its fringe package, a benefit offered by no other company in the same labor market. Some examples of outstanding fringe benefits that support M.B.O. productivity are bonus vacations for increased productivity; educational tuition abatement for favorable performance review; company-sponsored travel for reaching and exceeding targeted objectives; and use of company facilities and equipment when results and performance have reached specified levels.

(3) Make effective use of financial incentives. Financial incentives intended to improve the manager's or subordinate's economic status and give tangible recognition of his effort can be potent motivators. Incentives falling within this category include expense account allowances, use of company automobiles, attendance at industry or trade conventions and professional meetings, annual bonuses based upon operating results, and use of company owned or leased resort facilities. These incentives require immediate outlay of cash by a company and generally create ordinary income for the worker. Adding these incentives toward achieving objectives tends to improve M.B.O. productivity.

(4) Set up attractive "deferred" compensation programs. Compensation programs that contain provisions creating deferred compensation for the individual while immediate ordinary tax deductions can be taken by the company are as follows: pension plans, profit-sharing plans, stock-option plans, retirement plans, production profit plans, phantom stock plans, and thrift plans. The decision as to their use will depend upon conditions specific to the company and comparable costs of the programs. Plans that

provide opportunities for ownership, such as the stock option, create a sense of partnership and are most potent as motivators. Deferred compensation rewards should be set up to fall within short periods for younger employees and longer periods for older employees.

(5) Use new financial benefits as motivators. Additional forms of benefits could be incorporated in a total compensation program to develop incentive by directly improving the economic status of a subordinate, giving him tangible appreciation of his effort. Some of these are medical expense reimbursements, educational tuition refunds for dependents, low-interest loans, annual physical examinations, and special royalties on inventions and publications. Financial incentives should be set in steps with levels and amounts given on the basis of results. Merit pay increases must be clearly and unmistakably connected to an unusual work contribution to the company. Compensation rewards should be allocated and distributed in terms of desires and needs of employees, such as those relating to Christmas time, vacations, time off, illness, special events, and outstanding family needs.

5. Apply Motivators as Best Fit toward Objectives

The basic problem in motivation of subordinates is neither the lack of a framework for thinking about motivation nor the lack of insight for understanding people and their needs. The "deep secret" of motivating employees toward accomplishing company objectives lies in the *skill of aligning the needs of subordinates with company goals in such a way that both are accomplished within an expected time!* When a subordinate sees that his work performance for the company also meets his personal needs, his drive becomes intense. When there is little or no conflict between the two and a subordinate gains satisfaction in meeting both, his motivation is high. The skill of the practitioner in fitting the needs of employees into the needs of the company with an implementation schedule is the key skill for motivation. The planned motivation concept is the eclectic approach for getting the best fit between the two. Motivators are the connecting line between the two. The planned and scheduled motivation model described in Figures 6-2 and 6-3 is a logical framework for this connection and alignment. The following case examples, Figures 6-7 to 6-11, illustrate the use of this concept.

COACHING TO IMPLEMENT OBJECTIVES

Coaching has been generally recognized as an important factor whereby supervisors can help subordinates reach objectives. It could also be an

Motivational Problem Situation	Employee Needs — Emp. A / Emp. B / Emp. C / Emp. D				Potential Demotivators (Dissatisfiers)	Potential Motivators (Satisfiers)	Best Fit Application (Avoiding Demotivators Instituting Motivators)
Problem: unable to get and keep employees working in the foundry	Foundry Workers				Foundry hot, dirty, smelly place to work	Make work desirable and safer	Install fans, safety devices, showers, and lockers
	Needs protection from dangerous working conditions				Many safety hazards exist	Keep environment clean	Automate foundry processes where possible; encourage foundry workers to operate foundry equipment
Objective: reduce foundry turnover 10% within 12 months	Needs to work in an unpolluted environment				Low company image to work in foundry	Raise value of job equal to or better than other job classifications	Allow shower time within working day
	Needs job with good image to family, peers, and community				Low community image to be foundry worker	Provide automated working conditions where possible	Redesign job in order to raise wages to other job classifications
	Needs facility aids for working conveniences				Lowest wage classification in company	Provide privilege for foundry workers not found in other jobs	Match workers' attitudes and temperament to job requirements
	Needs to be respectable in appearance before children and family				Dead-end job no transfers in or out	Build up image of foundry jobs in the community	Build up image and importance of jobs in foundry throughout company
	Needs to see value and importance of foundry work					Encourage transfers to other jobs for qualified individuals	

Figure 6-7. Planned Motivation Model: case example 1.

Motivational Problem Situation	Employee Needs				Potential Demotivators (Dissatisfiers)	Potential Motivators (Satisfiers)	Best Fit Application (Avoiding Demotivators Instituting Motivators)
	Emp. A	Emp. B	Emp. C	Emp. D			
Problem: low productivity	Jerry Daniels				Work routine and boring	Enrich job for variety and interest	Provide face-to-face discussions on how to improve productivity
Objective: increase productive output 15% within next 4 operating quarters	Needs and wants job security since loyalty to family strong				Indifferent climate prevails: high performance not recognized, low performance not corrected	Arrange some challenges for performance stretches	Discuss possible job transfer to an area of low productivity requirements
	Needs to do quality work; takes pride in finished product				Supervision pushes quantity at the sacrifice of quality	Assure family-connected deferred compensation normal	Enrich job with responsibility to conduct informal on-the-job training and indoctrination of new employees
	Needs no accumulation of money				Work simple and task elements few in number per employee	Recognize performance for both quality and quantity	Set up "pride" system of meeting targets of both quantity and quality
	Needs to be involved because of high capacity and ability				Work situation stifles human individualizing	Allow participation in parts of job planning	
	Needs to feel he is a counselor with plenty of available good advice						

Figure 6-8. Planned Motivation Model: case example 2.

Motivational Problem Situation	Employee Needs Emp./Emp./Emp./Emp. A / B / C / D				Potential Demotivators (Dissatisfiers)	Potential Motivators (Satisfiers)	Best Fit Application (Avoiding Demotivators Instituting Motivators)
	Peter Kyle						
Problem: employee at the top of pay scale and unable to get merit increases	Needs to accumulate money				Company's principal method of getting and holding employees has been with financial motivators	Arrange training and development experiences for higher classifications	Enrich job with leadership and supervisory responsibilities
Objective: to retain in employment ambitious and outstanding employee	Needs opportunities for growth and advancement				Company's wage structure has fixed limits to wage levels	Enrich job with additional responsibilities	Enroll in presupervisory training and development
	Needs to feel his company is growing				Limited participation in departmental planning and decision making	Involve in broad-range goal setting of department	Redesign job to enlarge tasks from peers and obtain new classification
	Needs work challenges					Assure merit-rating limit. Explore adjusting merit structure upward	Allow some freedom to set self-determined standards
	Needs to learn new things on the job						Encourage ideas for improvement of company or department
	Needs to feel his job does not lead to a dead-end street						

Figure 6-9. Planned Motivation Model: case example 3.

195

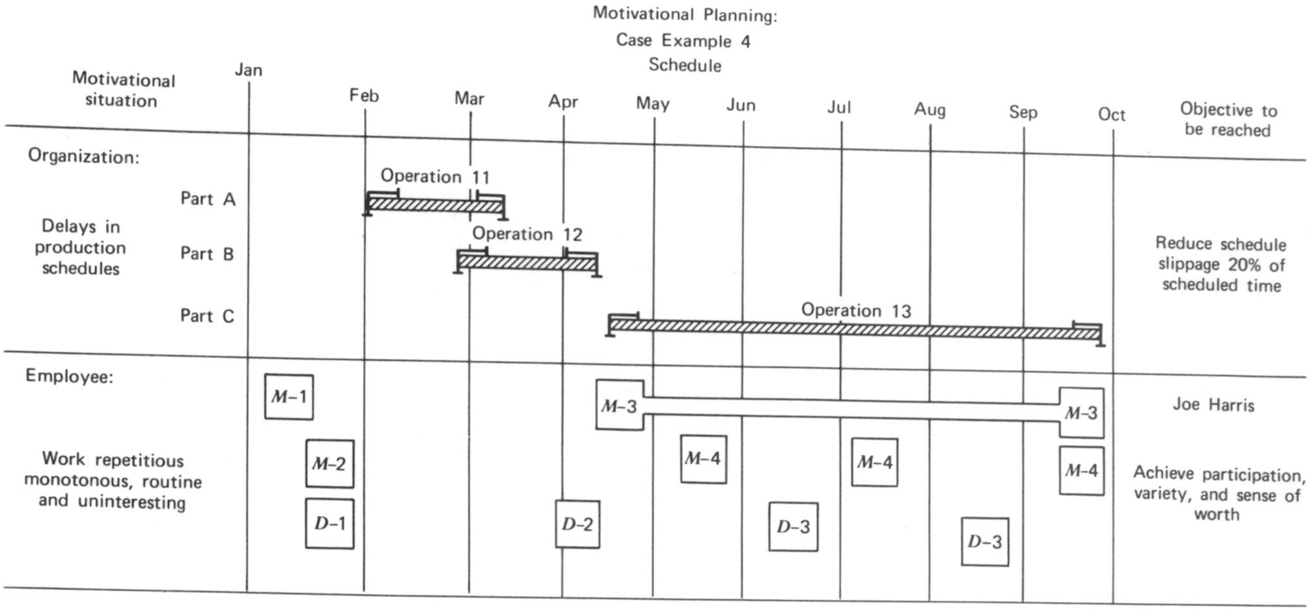

Motivational Planning:
Case Example 4
Schedule

Motivational situation	Jan	Feb	Mar	Apr	May	Jun	Jul	Aug	Sep	Oct	Objective to be reached
Organization:											
Part A Delays in production schedules			Operation 11								Reduce schedule slippage 20% of scheduled time
Part B			Operation 12								
Part C					Operation 13						
Employee:											Joe Harris
Work repetitious monotonous, routine and uninteresting	M-1				M-3					M-3	Achieve participation, variety, and sense of worth
	M-2			D-2	M-4		M-4		M-4		
	D-1					D-3		D-3		M-4	

M-1 Arrange face-to-face discussion to collect ideas on how to avoid delays
M-2 Allow Harris to suggest ideas on how to handle customer changes
D-1 Avoid schedules "mysteriously" set by outside person
D-2 Avoid unsatisfactory working conditions
M-3 Enlarge job to include dispatching responsibilites conditional to completing operation 13
M-4 Show performance progress toward targeted dates
D-3 Allow Harris to suggest ideas for automating repetitive routines

Figure 6-10.

Motivational Training.

Case Example 5

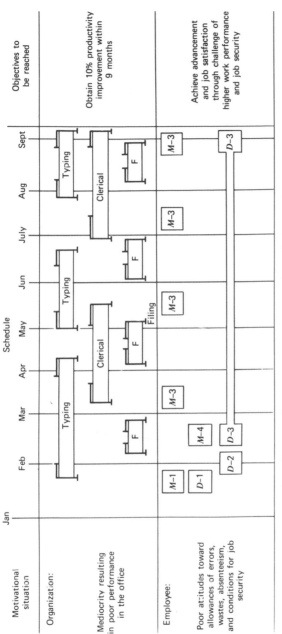

D–1 Provide conference and group discussion on factors for job security
M–1 Institute standards of performance in wastes, absenteeism, errors, and connect to income progression
D–2 Identify and control causes of poor attitudes and interruptions
D–3 Create climate of improvement through supervisory and employee examples
M–3 Show periodic high personal interest in performance improvement, provide coaching and training
M–4 Institute rotational scheme or transfers among employees in similar jobs to avoid job mismatch

Figure 6-11.

important developmental tool for converting potential performance to actual performance. Marion Kellogg[11] speaks of this idea of coaching as reinforcing on-the-job development, putting development into the work itself. In helping subordinates to reach these objectives through development, some very useful lessons can be learned by once again studying the parallel with a football game. The football coach learns to observe his men in action from the sidelines in order to detect their strengths and weaknesses for winning a game. A coach never directly participates in the execution of the play. He has assisted each player in practice and has helped him develop so that he is ready to achieve goals. He urges, prompts, leads, helps, instructs, corrects, disciplines, and trains subordinates to prepare themselves not only for the expected developments of the game but also for the unexpected. Coaching is the art of making the poor performer better, the better performer best, and the best performer superlative. The coach instills within his team not only the strength to play but also the will and desire to win. The football coach knows his coaching job is never done. When he thinks a man performs the way he should, he still continues to observe him from time to time to prevent him from slipping into bad habits. When necessary, he repeats his coaching. He develops his players to their fullest potential.

In industry and business, as on the football field, winning results can be accomplished by this potent relationship between supervisor-coach and subordinate-player. The supervisor who practices the strategy of managing by objectives must set up coaching practices in order to get employees to want to put forth their best efforts to win. The supervisor's central and prime responsibility is to get things done through people.

The supervisor has examined his own coaching skills to assure himself that he can cause each of his subordinates not only to intensify his desire to do his best, but also to release the potential locked within him by stretching for results as never before. Coaching is the vital ingredient that releases individual capacity toward maximum performance. The coaching process used by the supervisor is potentially the most direct and effective way he can influence his subordinates. It provides daily guidance and help to subordinates in meeting their commitments. This help comes out in many forms. It can assist the subordinates in their knowledge and ability as they relate to current commitments, or it can be the encouragement and stimulation that is often needed when the going gets rough.

There is no single best technique for coaching. Kellogg[12] has listed a series of do's and don't's for effective coaching. Effective techniques will vary with the objectives to be reached, the jobs that are involved, and the relationship between the supervisor and the subordinate. If coaching is viewed as guidance, help, and encouragement to implement objectives, then the best technique is the one that fits the situation. Viewed in this way, coaching is an on-going process and not a periodic event. It is a part of the superior's day-to-day work activity and not a once-a-year task. Coaching cannot be delegated or shifted to another superior since the leadership component is part and parcel of the coaching process. The leader must be easily available to his followers if the followers will go to him for leadership. Coaching that is effective is also time consuming. Counseling, which usually refers to improvement of shortcomings, requires analysis of the problems and suggested remedies and solutions. This analysis may take the form of observations or interviews, which will make demands on the coach's time. The tendency of some supervisors is to shift or delegate coaching responsibilities to another because of these time demands. Such a shift results in an inferior and ineffective coaching process. The supervisor who takes time to consult with his subordinates and to help them overcome problems instills in the subordinates his own confidence that the work will be completed. Almost every organization can identify one or more managers who have been quite effective in guiding and stimulating subordinates to complete their objectives. An examination of each of these effective coaches reveals that they use different techniques to deal with different situations. However, some suggestions can be drawn from observing these managers and their methods. The following principles and guidelines are but a few that one may glean. They are useful in guiding the coaching process to get individuals to implement objectives. They are useful in releasing individual capacity toward maximum performance.

1. A supervisor must have daily face-to-face, two-way interactions with his subordinates on work progress and individual growth.

2. A supervisor must use good timing in offering correction and suggesting improvement in performance.

3. A supervisor must not excessively criticize or discipline so that a subordinate is fearful of moving ahead.

4. A supervisor must recognize the expenditure of effort that yields good results for the firm immediately following the expenditure of the effort.

5. A supervisor must set up and control the situation to allow a subordinate to perform without excessive interference.

6. A supervisor will limit his coaching aims to a specific few but important areas needing change or improvements.

7. A supervisor must confine his coaching to the work and the subordinate's ability to accomplish it.

8. A supervisor must make subordinates feel responsible and accountable for bringing work to a successful end.

9. A supervisor must show a keen and sincere personal interest in a subordinate to help him with his difficulties.

10. A supervisor must allow a subordinate to express his individuality in his work by letting him do the job in his own way.

Coaching has been generally recognized as a most important factor in assisting those committed to a program or specified objectives to achieve them within the designated period of time. Improvement in coaching practices by managers and supervisors will go a long way in operating the objective plan effectively. In addition to following the principles described above, a manager or supervisor can improve his coaching practice by recognizing the most common reasons for failure.

1. *Excessive activities.* The failure to set priorities and assign weights to the many activities required in day-to-day work for reaching objectives will eventually cause scheduled deadlines in the objective plan to be missed. In fact, a tough attitude must be maintained to postpone or discard the many trivial activities that drain valuable time. A good coach will not delegate to subordinates or allow himself to be victimized by time-robbing trivialities on the job. A good coach must help his subordinates separate essentials from nonessentials and be able to cut corners where possible. Practicing managing by exception,[13] where attention is given to the extraordinary rather than to the ordinary, might be very useful here. Some of the time-robbing activities are too many meetings; inefficient and drawn-out conferences; unspecialized memo distribution; social conversations; reading long reports; indecision; poor information retrieval methods; attention to recurring problems; excessive company time given to personal matters; and noncooperation.

2. *Restricted climate.* A climate that does not allow individual ingenuity to solve problems as they develop will bring the objective plan to a halt. Policies, directives, and attitudes that set undue constraints and excessive limitations will eventually force personnel into apathetic conformity. A good coach develops open-mindedness and encourages a spirit of creativity in discovering new and better ways of coping with responsibilities. A good coach will examine existing policies and other regulatory rules to determine their stifling effects on the performance of individuals. This open-mindedness also allows an "open door" policy for subordinates to consult with the boss when and if they need to for work clarification and counsel.

3. *Uncoordinated activities.* The strategy of managing by objectives requires a high degree of cooperation in undertakings in order to mesh

into a coordinated program. Poor human relationships and faulty communication patterns will tend to cause wide differences and disruptions among the multiple and diversified activities required to get things done. A good coach will seek out, uncover, and correct feelings of dissatisfaction. He will uncover focal points of trouble. He will reconcile differences among the various individuals and groups through repeated emphasis on the value and prime importance of the whole plan, in comparison with the subvalue or secondary importance of each component of the plan.

4. *Unsolved problems.* Half-solved problems will tend to crop up repeatedly to harass the efforts channeled for completing the objective plan. Problems that have not been solved will flare up, creating a never-ending series of crises. A good coach solves problems so that they stay solved. He is careful of writing off or discarding small problems that can grow into larger and more complex ones through neglect. He practices with his subordinates a sensitivity for prevention of unexpected incidents and events that block and drain the efforts to operate the plan.

5. *Performance variability.* Neglect in approaching and dealing with company politics, grapevine rumors, unethical behavior, job obsolescence, and work conflicts can cause variabilities in performance that make completion of the objective plan a chance occurrence. A good coach has the courage and the grit to get the job done under any condition of stress. He has the managerial backbone to hold back the forces that threaten to distort, distract, or deviate his planned course of action.

6. *Poor timing.* The coach must time his coaching activities carefully; this is very important. The coach of a football team must know when to call a huddle with his team and when not to. Too much coaching can be as damaging as too little. Nothing is more annoying to a subordinate than to get coaching and a run-down of errors long after the fact. On the other hand, a subordinate will not appreciate being alerted to traps too far in advance. Warnings about possible errors and guidance around the traps are most effective just before the performance is to be executed. This is the basic reason that coaching is a day-to-day process.

The absolute necessity of assuring that the coaching process of urging, prompting, leading, and helping subordinates operates the plan without following chance factors requires a system of reminders and checks.

A coach's log is a very useful device for providing a system of regular reminders of what has occurred in relation to objectives and what corrective actions must be taken. In this log are recorded deviations or difficulties experienced by subordinates as well as proposed remedial actions. If the log is regularly and faithfully utilized, the coaching process is assured a major day-to-day role in the activities of a supervisor. The log structure for each subordinate should be developed to fit the situation of each manager. Generally, it should contain log entries of work to be done in relation to objectives committed, work now in progress and under schedule, and work completed as part of the work package of a feeder-objective. The log is useful as a source of information if it contains supervisory notes on critical performance incidents, both favorable and unfavorable; past verified accomplishments in the objective program; evaluation notes on subordinates' ability to perform the work in the period ahead with caution and pitfalls identified; a list of supervisory actions that are likely to pay off in improved employee performance; and a personal sketch of each member of the coaching team in terms of skills, background, past assignments, personal history, strengths, and weaknesses. The coach's log is not only a document for improving the performance of subordinates; it can also be the basis for setting future objectives with the same group of people.

PERSUASION TOWARD OBJECTIVES

Implementing skill has been identified as the chief ability of a manager in getting work done toward reaching an objective. Planned motivation and coaching are two ingredients in this skill. A third ingredient that pays great dividends for accomplishments is the ability to articulate instructions, information, ideas, task requirements, and system's needs with persuasiveness and conviction. Force and threats of force in a managing by objectives program are open denials of the essence of the entire program. In its broadest philosophical view, managing by objectives is a motivational strategy whereby people work because it is satisfying. Heavy compliance and authoritative decisions are signs that the program is faulty and misapplied. On the other hand, there are some human tendencies that emerge from time to time that pull subordinates away from commitments they have readily accepted. These human tendencies are so ingrained that subordinates may not even be aware of them. They form barriers and obstacles to getting a job done. When he becomes aware of them, the practitioner is wise to employ a series of skillful persuasive maneuvers to keep the subordinate on the right track. Here are a few of these emerging barriers that interfere with an objective program.

1. *Effects of prior habits.* One reason that many individuals in an objective program tend to function less than required or differently from what is expected is that they are victimized by habits formed on the basis of previous experience. Prior experience and previous training tend to

force the mind into set patterns of thought. Bellows[14] refers to these sets of mind as regulators of behavior. They are habits that incline the person to act according to comfortable grooves developed in the past. These habits breed repetition. They stifle innovation and change in new directions. Since objective setting is formulating new directions, the danger of individuals' following habitual grooves in old directions is very real. To offset these habits, management can use the objective-setting participative processes and the coaching given by the supervisor. A spirit of group activity usually prevails in an objective program, and this spirit encourages and sustains an individual in ignoring habits of the past and in relating new work methods to the demands of the objectives. The coach often finds himself persuading the subordinate to decondition himself, to root out the restricting effects of habits.

2. *Negative reactions to the future.* The future is always uncertain and often strange. It is not unusual for individuals, in spite of their verbalized commitments, to adopt a frame of mind that holds that objectives cannot be reached. These people can often supply proof that is so convincing that one is often tempted to discard any further work toward objectives. When the purveyor of this negative attitude supports it with high intelligence, he can denigrate, immediately and logically, any proposed objective that means moving in new directions. Some of these negative attitudes are illustrated by the following: "I just know we can't make it"; "We've never done it that way before"; "It's too late to start"; "It won't work in my area." Clark[15] refers to these attitudes as "killer phrases." The practitioner of managing by objectives must exercise the art of persuasion to think up and to show all the reasons that an objective will work and why it is good for a section or department. He must recognize that environmental prejudices will always emerge to oppose an active enthusiasm for implementing objectives. He must work at replacing negativism with positive attitudes through examples, confidence, and success.

3. *Effects of failure.* A coach knows that self-discouragement can undermine any effort toward reaching goals. Failures in reaching goals in the past will always breed discouragement toward trying for future goals. Many of these failures in an objective program have resulted from the tendencies of some managers to overchallenge subordinates. For example, a subordinate who proposes to reduce costs 10 percent finds that his supervisor is not only receptive to the idea, but that he even encourages him to go for 20 percent, a figure that may not be realistic. The failure of the subordinate to attain the overchallenging target creates a self-discouragement that undermines future initiatives on his part. Self-confidence is developed when the practitioner keeps the objective in the

challenge region and is there to help his subordinate when he fumbles, stumbles, and experiences a series of starts and stops. Persuasively, he develops a sense of trust and confidence within the subordinate that the fear of failure is only a resistance to change from the known to the unknown. He instills the idea that progress is made only when there is a performance stretch.

4. *The "silent" bosses.* There is nothing that spurs subordinates on to implement their objectives so much as when top management gives help, praise, and recognition on a face-to-face basis. It is a mystery to me why managers are quite active and involved with subordinates in setting objectives, only to withdraw from the scene once these objectives are finalized. The discouragement that hurts most in subordinates' efforts to get the job done is that which comes from the "bosses." When they withdraw from a personal position to the impersonal one of reviewing the scoreboard without reviewing those who are making the scores, encouragement to get the job done is lost. Managers should still be active on a face-to-face basis with their sections and departments during the long and arduous period of implementation.

5. *Doubting conversations.* A person is highly influenced by the thoughts, feelings, and responses that come from conversations among members of a group. Doubts often emerge for a subordinate when he hears the irritations, worries, and criticisms of others. A subordinate's response will be a composite reaction to all these influences both around and within him. Persuasion consists of instilling and strengthening a positive response toward an objective to counter the negative responses acquired from others. Implanting such a response is important in making the person's activities purposeful and in raising his confidence about getting the job done. The persuasive skills are many and varied. Developing receptivity, or readiness to get the job done, is one. This requires the orientation of the individual toward an objective through information, facts, examples, and cases. Asking a thought-provoking question is another persuasive skill. Questions can expose positions, arguments, and faulty attitudes. When the subordinate sees all the facets of a problem openly, he takes a more objective view of the matter. Still another skill is the ability to explore thoroughly the spectrum of possibilities and to lead the subordinate to recognize the soundness of certain alternatives and the weakness of others. Doubts can be reduced when alternatives are compared as to strengths and weaknesses.

Persuasion covers a whole gamut of activities, permeating attitudes, conversations, communications, and even results. The ability to foresee the barriers that may inhibit the implementation processes of an objective program forms the basis for the practitioner to understand why he must be active day to day, face to face with his subordinates. The persuasive skills he uses to counteract these barriers and to keep subordinates heading in the committed direction is important in getting the job done. The practitioner of managing by objectives would do well to improve his persuasive skills. The following are some useful guidelines from Abelson's research[16] on how opinions and attitudes are changed.

1. *How to deal with arguments in implementing objectives?*

(a) Are more subordinates persuaded by hearing both sides of an argument or one side only? *Answer:* When group members are generally friendly, when your position is the only one that is being considered, or when you want immediate, though temporary, change, one side of an argument should be considered. However, when the group starts out disagreeing or when it is probable that the group will hear another argument from someone else, it is better to bring out several sides to the argument in a manner most favorable to your position. Do it your way.

(b) When both sides of an argument are to be considered, which should be considered first? *Answer:* When opposite views or arguments are considered one after another, the one considered last will probably be more effective, remembered better, and more persuasive.

(c) In arranging a series of arguments, should the more important ones be considered first or last? *Answer:* If the group is initially not very interested in the issues, the important arguments should be presented first. Where interest is high, save the most important for last.

(d) Will a subordinate's opinion be changed to agree with your own if you state your conclusions or if you let your subordinate draw his own? *Answer:* If you want the subordinate to change his opinion, lead him up to the desired change, but let him take the last step himself. People seem to be more easily convinced if they think they make up their own minds.

2. *How to allow groups to influence and change individuals?*

(a) Are subordinates in a section persuaded more by the section they are in or by an individual supporting an issue? *Answer:* A subordinate's opinions and attitudes are strongly influenced by the groups to which he belongs and wants to belong.

(b) What control does a section exercise over its members' opinions when the supervisor wants those opinions changed? *Answer:* The subordinate is rewarded for conforming to the standards informally set up by the section but often punished for deviating from them.

(c) Which member of a section or group is easiest to persuade? *Answer:* Subordinates who are most attached to a group are probably least influenced by the supervisor or company if its views conflict with the established group norms.

(d) Is it easier to change an attitude that has been stated publicly or one that is held privately? *Answer:* Attitudes that subordinates make known to others are harder to change than attitudes that subordinates hold privately.

(e) Can you increase persuasion by getting subordinates involved in issues of an argument? *Answer:* Subordinate participation helps to overcome resistance to change. Receptivity is developed since ideas, alternatives, facts, and other information help to expose the strengths and weaknesses of an argument.

3. *What is the persistence of an opinion?*

(a) How long does an existing opinion last? *Answer:* An opinion can remain long after a communication has been forgotten. Almost anyone worth his prejudices can marshal, on short notice, any number of sound arguments to support his convictions. A newly adopted attitude remains with its host as long as it continues to provide satisfaction for him. It is probably fair to say that an attitude is adopted in the first place because it answers to some need, such as making a subordinate acceptable to the group he works with.

(b) Does repeating a communication make it more effective? *Answer:* Repeating a communication tends to prolong its influence. Frequent reminders of an original commitment tend to keep alive the commitment in the subordinate's mind.

(c) Is opinion change at its highest point right after the persuasive communication has ended or sometime later? *Answer:* Desired opinion change may be more measurable sometime after exposure to the communication than right after exposure.

4. *How to appeal to individuals?*

(a) What programs and instructions do subordinates tend to look for from supervisors? *Answer:* A great amount of evidence can be cited to show that subordinates look for the programs, instructions, and directives that support their attitudes and beliefs, and that they tend not to expose themselves to communications that conflict with their own viewpoints.

(b) Is it best to tailor your appeals to the intelligence levels of your subordinates? *Answer:* Subordinates with high intelligence will tend—because of their ability to draw valid inferences—to be *more* influenced than those with low intellectual ability when exposed to persuasive communications that rely primarily on impressive logical arguments. Subordinates with high intelligence will tend—because of their superior critical ability—to be *less* influenced than those with low intelligence when exposed to persuasive communications that rely primarily on unsupported generalities or false, illogical, irrelevant argumentation.

(c) In order to change a subordinate's opinion, what do you have to know about why he has that opinion? *Answer:* When the factors underlying attitudes are taken into account, persuasion is more likely to be successful. Successful persuasion depends on an understanding of why a subordinate should accept your point of view, buy your argument, or reach for stated goals.

(d) What characteristics of subordinates make them more easily influenced by persuasive communications? *Answer:* There seems to be no general susceptibility to persuasion. Rather, subordinates with certain specified personality traits are likely to be more readily persuaded by certain appeals and modes of involvement.

5. *How to make a supervisor a persuader?*

(a) Does a subordinate have to believe in the persuader before he accepts his arguments? *Answer:* There will be more opinion change as a result of persuasion in the desired direction if the supervisor has high credibility than if he has low credibility.

(b) When is belief in the persuader less important in changing opinions? *Answer:* High credibility sources may be important if the persuasion attempt is designed to get immediate results (signing a document, starting resistance, taking a vote). However, if the aim of persuasion is long term, then the believability of the supervisor may not be such a crucial issue.

(c) Do the persuader's reasons for wanting to change opinions have an effect on how successful he will be? *Answer:* The motives attributed to a supervisor may affect his success in influencing subordinates. If a supervisor does not believe and accept his own argument, his persuasive skill will be weak.

(d) Is what a group of subordinates thinks of a supervisor interrelated and influenced by his message? *Answer:* A supervisor's persuasiveness is increased if he expresses some views that are also held by his subordinates.

(e) Should a persuading supervisor try for a maximum of opinion change or a minimum of opinion change at a specific time? *Answer:* The greater the opinion change desired, the less likely the change will occur.

SUMMARY

The implementing skill required to get things done on a day-to-day, program-to-program, objective-to-objective basis is the heart and core of successfully practicing managing by objectives. It is the true mark of the M.B.O. practitioner. This implementing skill gets subordinates to participate in objective programs because they want to and not because they are driven to. Motivation, coaching, and persuasion are three vital ingredients of a manager's skill in implementing stated and committed objectives. This chapter provided several approaches and techniques for completing the fourth step of the practice of managing by objectives.

GUIDE QUESTIONS FOR THE PRACTITIONER

1. What are the three basic ingredients of implementing skills?
2. How does the concept of planned motivation differ from the traditional forms of motivational strategy? How are they similar?
3. Explain process of aligning the needs of employees with the needs of the company.
4. What is a motivator?
5. What is a demotivator?
6. Name four ways to change jobs for motivating toward objectives.
7. Describe the eclectic fit approach in the planned motivational model.
8. Explain the needs hierarchy as a basis of the motivational processes.
9. Which motivators are practiced in your company? List the demotivators.
10. Select two significant objectives in your company and, using the eclectic fit approach of the planned motivational model, identify the fit strategy needed to reach your objectives.
11. How does the coaching principle improve implementing skill?
12. Identify conditions or reasons for coaching ineffectiveness in your company and suggest remedial actions.
13. Make a list of motivators used in your company and rate each one as to its effectiveness.
14. How does persuasion improve implementing skills?
15. Identify conditions in your company that suggest persuasive skills are needed.
16. Supervisors have used the following as ways to motivate people. Rate each one:

Motivator Demotivator Neither Either

(a) Demonstrate that you can do all the jobs performed by the people you supervise.   _____   _____   _____   ____

	Motivator	Demotivator	Neither	Either
(b) Pay wages that compare with those paid for similar work by outside industry.	_____	_____	_____	_____
(c) Set up a top-flight program of fringe benefits (vacations, pensions, health and accident insurance, etc.).	_____	_____	_____	_____
(d) Take every opportunity to be personally friendly with subordinates.	_____	_____	_____	_____
(e) Provide first-class technical assistance for subordinates who run into problems.	_____	_____	_____	_____
(f) Encourage subordinates by praising a good job done, even to the point of being lavish.	_____	_____	_____	_____
(g) Acknowledge and praise those accomplishments of a subordinate that both you and he consider important.	_____	_____	_____	_____
(h) See that subordinates get recognition or praise occasionally, even if no specific reason exists for it	_____	_____	_____	_____
(i) As a subordinate becomes more proficient, give him several similar tasks to perform.	_____	_____	_____	_____
(j) Help the individual find the work that he wants to do.	_____	_____	_____	_____

	Motivator	Demotivator	Neither	Either
(k) Let the subordinate make as many decisions as possible about the work he is to do.	_____	_____	_____	_____
(l) Give each subordinate every possible responsibility, resolving doubtful matters or delegations in his favor.	_____	_____	_____	_____
(m) Arrange for the equal distribution of unpleasant tasks among all subordinates.	_____	_____	_____	_____
(n) Strive to provide avenues of advancement for all subordinates regardless of sex, age, length of service, etc.	_____	_____	_____	_____
(o) Set goals with a subordinate, nor for him.	_____	_____	_____	_____

REFERENCES AND NOTES

1. *The Holy Bible,* Ecclesiastes 9:10.

2. Frederick Herzberg, "One More Time: How Do You Motivate Employees?" *Harvard Business Review,* January–February 1968, pp. 53–62.

3. Robert M. Ford, *Motivation through the Work Itself,* American Management Association, 1969, pp. 20–41.

4. Kahlil Gibran, *The Prophet,* Alfred Knopf, New York, 1923, 1951, pp. 25–26.

5. Abraham H. Maslow, *Motivation and Personality,* Harper and Brothers, 1954.

6. Many perceptions of the motivational processes are available in the literature since the literature is voluminous. The reader interested in pursuing these ideas is reminded of several references, such as the following: S. W. Gullerman, *Management by Motivation,* American Management Association, New York, 1968; F. Herzberg, B. Mausner, and B. B. Snyderman, *The Motivation To Work,* John Wiley, New York, 1965; D. McGregor, *Human Side of Enterprise,* McGraw-Hill Book Co., New York, 1960; V. H. Vroom, *Work and Motivation,* John Wiley, New York, 1964.

7. Frederick Herzberg, William J. Paul, and Keith B. Robertson, "Job Enrichment Pays Off," *Harvard Business Review,* March–April 1969, pp. 61–78.

8. *Ibid.*, pp. 61–78.

9. Benjamin W. Niebel, *Motion and Time Study*, Richard D. Irwin, Homewood, Ill., 1967, pp. 348–371.

10. Gerald Nadler, *Work Simplification*, McGraw-Hill Book Co., New York, 1957, pp. 124–141.

11. Marion S. Kellogg, *Closing the Performance Gap*, American Management Association, New York, 1967, pp. 124–130.

12. *Ibid.*, pp. 126–127.

13. Lester R. Bittel, *Management by Exception*, McGraw-Hill Book Co., New York, 1964, pp. 3–32.

14. Roger Bellows, *Creative Leadership*, Prentice-Hall, Englewood Cliffs, N.J., 1959, p. 178.

15. This whole subject of negative attitudes and killer phrases as related to creativity is more fully discussed in Charles H. Clark's *Brainstorming*, Doubleday, New York, 1958, pp. 90–91.

16. Herbert I. Abelson, *Persuasion*, Springer, New York, 1959.

7. Controlling and Reporting Status of Objectives

Controlled Targeting. Status Reporting. Status Control Performance Indicators. Trouble Spots and Remedies. Performance Appraisals. Summary. Guide Questions for the Practitioner. References and Notes.

The purpose of control is to keep activities and effort on a prescribed and planned course. The practitioner is informed on progress that is being made and what action he must take to accomplish his objectives. The entire process of control starts with the objective-setting process. Gathering of information, making improvement forecasts, collecting alternatives, deciding on tentative commitments, validating the commitments, and deciding on objectives to pursue are steps in which control points and measurements are built into the program.

Controlling and reporting the status of objectives is the fifth and last step of the five steps in the practice of managing by objectives. This chapter will describe how this step is executed as a follow-up of implementing objectives. The discussion covers the following: (1) controlled targeting, (2) status reporting, (3) status control performance indicators, (4) trouble spots and remedies, and (5) performance appraisals.

CONTROLLED TARGETING

On the other side of the planning coin is control. On the other side of the objective program coin is a control program. Planning and controlling are inseparable. Control begins with planning by building into the objective program points for control purposes. The practitioner assesses and regulates work in progress with these points to make sure that what is happening is what he wants to happen. Control should not be treated as a separate function but as part of the total objective-setting and implementation process. As Lindberg states it, "Controls are future-shaping devices and as such operate according to views of what tomorrow can and should bring."[1] The lines between control and the other phases in the strategy of managing by objectives are not sharp. Controlling is in the nature of follow-up to the other phases of the strategy. It helps to ensure that what is intended to be accomplished is accomplished within defined boundaries or standards. The boundaries are many, but four[2] are most essential:

1. Quantity (How much?)
2. Quality (How good?)
3. Time (When accomplished?)
4. Cost (What expense?)

Controlling consists of keeping work activities within specified performance standards designed to reach objectives. The standards guide the individuals and activities toward the objectives. Comparing actual performance with predetermined standards and ascertaining the difference, if any, is the heart and core of keeping the implementation processes on course toward targets. Sometimes there is overshooting of the standards; sometimes there is undershooting. This overshoot or undershoot can make the difference between the successful and the unsuccessful practice of managing by objectives. The overshoot or undershoot concept, illustrated in Figure 7-1, will waste time, money, effort, and material. Controlled targeting is controlling performance with regard to both content and time. There can be too much or too little. The quality of performance can be too high or too low. The costs, too, can be too high or too low. And finally, the performance must be on time, without slippage in either direction. The following are some guidelines to executing controlled targeting:

1. *Assure that a control system exists.* Controlled targeting must be a system if it is truly to control a management system. Key elements of the system must be identified for a total affect, not just partial effects. The problem of coordination really emerges in this phase of managing by objectives. Unless the total management system is acting in unison, overshooting and undershooting become common occurrences. Control points or standards should be identified and ranked for importance in keeping the objective program on course. Greatest control effort, as suggested by Allen,[3] should be concentrated at the points of action and decision-making. The further away from the point of action the control effort is made, the less effective the control and the more the time lags that are introduced. Control should be focused where problems are generated since nipping the problems in the bud will eliminate a host of secondary and tertiary effects. Controlled targeting recognizes the danger of chain reaction. Herein lies a disadvantage of the objective system concept. An unrecognized problem, if it gets out of control, can

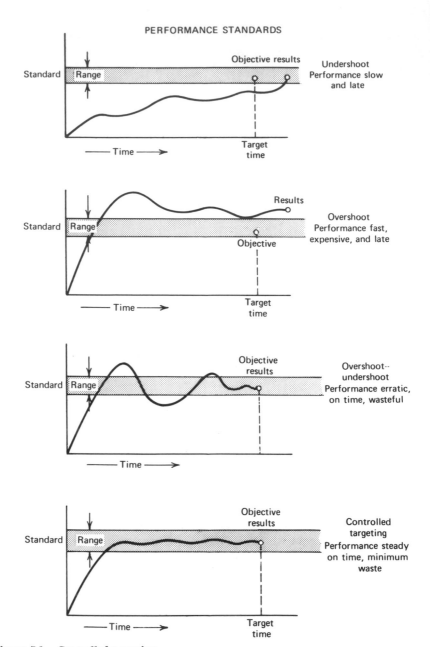

Figure 7-1. Controlled targeting.

conceivably create a series of chain reactions that will bring the entire objective program to a halt or at least cause serious delay. This represents a "potential cost" or a disadvantage to be weighed against the attractive advantages offered by creating a unified system for getting quantum jumps in results. The practitioner should be alerted to this phenomenon and set his control priorities where they count most.

2. Put control system on real-time basis. The importance of timing cannot be overstressed. After-the-fact information only helps in future actions; it cannot control present activities. The practitioner must set his pace in such a way that target time will not be missed. Some objective programs can be computerized, thereby providing variance returns within the time period to effect a correction for targeted time. Noncomputer timing techniques[4] such as control charts, Gantt charts, PERT networks and other schedules are very useful for handling performance measurement with regard to target time while maintaining standards. Real-time control as suggested here is not intended to mean expensive day-to-day feedback of returns. Real-time control means that performance variances must be identified and given to the practitioner in sufficient time for him to make a useful correction before the targeted date. In some cases, it may indicate day-to-day surveillance and control. In other cases, it may mean week-to-week or month-to-month. The vitality and criticality of the control point set the basis for real-time reporting and correcting for the practitioner.

3. Use performance standards. Setting a performance standard gives workers a guideline for differentiating good and acceptable intensity of work from poor and unacceptable intensity of work. It provides a test of performance as it is executed toward meeting an objective. It even serves as a springboard to higher standards for the future. Rowland calls this idea "managing for direction."[5] The standard defines a range of output from minimum level to maximum level that will eventually lead to a targeted objective, as illustrated in Figure 7-1. The reader will note the inclusion of a maximum level since controlled targeting emphasizes both excess and deficiency: too much or too little. For example, the practitioner must assure quality to a minimum level or run costs beyond those expected in the commitment. The range between these two levels has to be defined as the intensity of performance just right to meet the requirements of the feeder-objective module or the ultimate objectives of the enterprise. A performance standard gives the criteria by which progress can be measured and evaluated. If the standards are understood and accepted by both supervisor and subordinate, then both need only concern themselves with variances from the standard. These variances give an idea of the corrective action that needs to be taken to get results on a short-range, day-to-day basis on the right course toward objectives. Programs, schedules, budgets, procedures, policies, techniques, and activities should be arranged and defined in terms of the intensity of work required to achieve ultimate results.

4. *Set up performance measures.* Performance measuring is the work a practitioner does in recording and reporting work in progress and work completed. Recording and reporting involve evaluating and checking the performance against planned action and conveying this information to all concerned. No matter whether the variance is over or under what was intended, measurement is the means for determining it. Measurements are made to answer such questions as, How long will it take? Are we doing the work that is needed? Do we need more manpower? Can we interchange work tasks among two groups? In order to make measurements, suitable units of measure must be built into standards or objectives. When we ask how long will it take, we expect an answer that will tell us how many days, weeks, or hours. Similarly, when we ask whether we need more manpower, we must use units of measure to give us answers in terms of more or less manpower. When units of performance measurement are carefully identified and built into plans of actions, standards, and procedures, all that is needed is careful reading and reporting. Later in this chapter, an extensive list of performance measures for the practitioner is suggested. Evaluating work performance in progress requires comparing actual performance with expected performance. This evaluation cannot take place unless performance measures are used in such a way that variances are collected and conveyed to those who can execute a correction.

5. *Provide audit and inspection of system.* The practitioner should be on the alert, always observing, reviewing, and inspecting to see that the control system is functioning as intended. Periodic audits are one way to assure that the system is operating as intended. The audit inquires into the accuracy of the records and the results reported. It goes into the adequacy of the management system as well. A good audit should be carried through all phases of the strategy of managing by objectives. The baselines described in Chapter 1 are documentation points for collecting information and making decisions. Changes are made to and from this point. The audit very often can use these decision modes to verify practice and performance against what was agreed upon in the baselines. Unsatisfactory items in the audit are referred to the responsible members of the organization for immediate action. The reader can readily see that auditing should start with the individuals involved in

the work. It should be an act of self-evaluation and self-correction. It is also a good idea to allow an outside group with an objective view of matters to analyze the program to be sure it is moving in the directions expected.

STATUS REPORTING

An effective status reporting system is a system designed to keep all levels of management completely informed on developments and status of the implementation results that affect them. Status reporting must be an integral part of the total information flow in the enterprise with emphasis on reporting in time for decision-making, correcting, and adjusting. Record keeping, follow-up reports, and status information on results should be working tools for the practitioner in order to effect the best possible action at the best possible time with the responsible functional and operational personnel. Status reporting must convey information in such a way that fast corrective action can be taken when necessary. Status reporting is not simply giving information but organizing and arranging it so that it reveals corrections or changes that are needed to remove barriers to reaching an objective. Giving too much, too little, or the wrong kind of information must be guarded against. Every effort must be made to remove from the practitioner the intolerable burden of having to wade through data to extract meaningful information. Status reporting must be a system for measuring and correcting progress along a path of milestones of progress toward reaching objectives, as illustrated in Figure 7-2. The concept of deviation- or error-detecting with feedback control has been borrowed from engineering systems. It has traditionally been known as servomechanisms, or self-regulating control systems. Kepner and Tregoe[6] have adapted this to a systematic approach for problem solving.

Status control of objectives requires an approach and set of procedures that provide continuous feedback to the manager. There is no reason why accounting information and reports that already exist in a company cannot be used for this purpose. These documents need to be placed in a status reporting format that is, above everything else, aimed at stimulating needed action to keep progress trends moving in the direction of accomplishing objectives. A good objective status control system focuses on deviations from objectives set for each manager for a particular period. It is the examination of results for that period. A status report for that period would be sent to the responsible practitioner, outlining the progress and status of his activities. For many reasons,

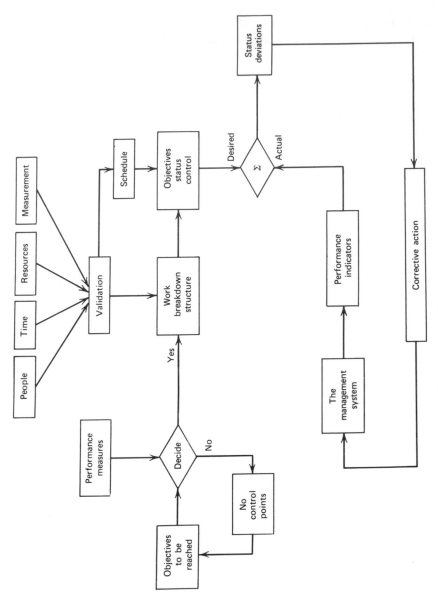

Figure 7.2. Systems concept of objective status control.

perfect progress should not be expected in any status reporting system. The most one can realistically aim for is a minimum number of status deviations and a minimum number of corrective actions. That perfection is not achievable is largely due to the conflicts that arise between individuals' interests and the company's requirements. The status control system must sense the deviations of targeted progress from actual progress and assure that these fluctuations remain within acceptable limits. A "down" in one period must be compensated for by an "up" in the next period.

Ordinarily, an objective status control system is a total system in the sense that it embraces all aspects of company commitments and activities. It needs to be a total system to ensure that all sub-objectives and programmed activities are operating as intended and are in balance with each other. With this total view, management can review the manner in which each part is progressing in relation to the whole. For this reason, the objective status system must be integrated and interlocked. All data, information, performance indicators, and progress measurements must be related and structured into this system. On the other hand, there is no reason that each manager cannot set up his own objective status system in order to have fingertip control of his program and his progress. With this system, he can "tailor fit" its structure to meet the needs of his group and section. However, he must be sure that his individual status control system is compatible with the total company. This compatibility is assured through a control structure and measurement indicators.

The objective status control system has two essentials: a definite logical action pattern and a feedback reporting time matrix. In the logical action pattern, certain steps are taken in a prescribed sequence so that status deviations are easily revealed and corrective action indicated. The feedback reporting time matrix relates the expected activities on a time scale with appropriate dates. A PERT network system is a natural means for measuring actual time against expected or estimated time. The following outline of a status control structure is suggested in Figure 7-3.

Column A. List of targeted events or end items found in the work breakdown structure that require critical control. Each manager must analyze the network to determine the critical events that require careful surveillance and status reporting, particularly in critical paths and related paths to other networks.

Column B. Measurement presupposes a series of key points or performance indicators to collect information and data on expected progress against actual performance. Quantitative standards or judgmental statements that are indicators of performance are identified for each of the

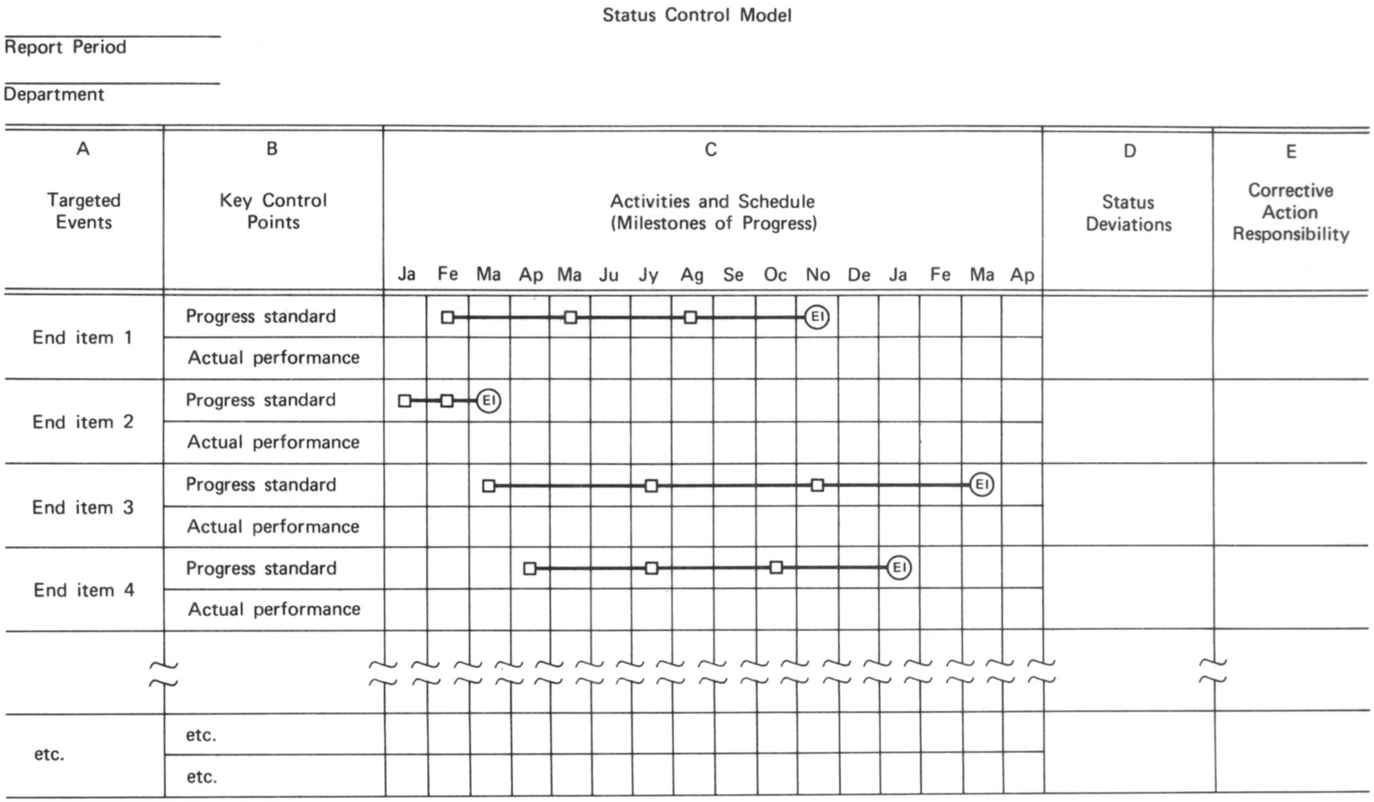

Figure 7-3. Status control model.

major events. A sample listing of quantitative measures that can be used as performance indicators are listed in the next section.

Column C. On the principle that time is the essential dimension for comparing expected activities with actual activities, a schedule is utilized in the comparison. On the schedule, one can readily contrast progress of work.

Column D. Status deviations are immediately apparent at the control point. Status deviations are identified as failures or deficiencies in terms of what is expected within the status reporting period.

Column E. Corrective action responsibility is the identification of the individual or section that will be responsible for following up measured deviations with plans for corrective action to eliminate or minimize the deviations.

In the practice of managing by objectives, it has become more and more apparent that managers are increasingly operating their objective programs out of sight of their superiors and other managers. An overview of the entire program is thus difficult to obtain. Even traditional forms of status reporting are being overworked in the attempt to supply this total overview. The growth of information management is a symptom of this. The larger the company practicing management by objectives, the greater its need for managers to be knowledgeable and effective in areas beyond their direct observation. Operations auditing,[7] a new management technique, has come into existence because of the need to manage from a distance and out of sight. Operations auditing is particularly critical for top management personnel who are involved initially in the objective-setting and validation processes but who withdraw during the implementation and control phases. Status reporting, which is a form of operations auditing, should give top management an overview of progress at a glance. An instrument that provides such a view of the total objective program on a time basis is the matrix status report for initiating and instituting corrective action. The concept of system matrix status reporting, which displays three dimensions—results (r), time (t), and performance appraisal (σ), can be a useful way to make decisions. This is illustrated in Figure 7-4.

Since performance results are tabulated in the matrix on a time spectrum, a glance at the whole enables easy selection of the variances from expected results that have been flagged as requiring special attention. Information on cost, schedule, quality, manpower, and other factors are distilled, summarized, and analyzed on the matrix array. *To give an individual manager or top management the whole picture at a glance*

Expected Results		Time				
	t_1	t_2	•	•	•	t_m
r_1	σ_{11}	σ_{12}	•	•	•	σ_{1m}
r_2	σ_{21}	σ_{22}	•	•	•	σ_{2m}
•	•	•	•	•	•	•
•	•	•	•	•	•	•
•	•	•	•	•	•	•
r_n	σ_{n1}	σ_{n2}	•	•	•	σ_{nm}

r = expected results by each manager
t = time periods (past, present, future)
σ = performance variance ($\pm$)

$$\sigma = \frac{\text{performance}}{\text{performance standards}} = \pm \frac{P}{PS}$$

$$\sigma = \text{performance} - \text{performance standards} = \pm (P - PS)$$

Figure 7-4. Matrix status reporting concept.

Objectives Matrix System Report

Date _____

Manager _____

Expected Results	Time Past Period April—June	Current Period July	Trend August	September
Reduction of spoilage and defective work	+10	+6	−1	−4
Reduction of engineering services costs	+5	+4	+6	+5
Manning level schedule adherence	−22	−8	+2	+4
Reach new level of machine output	+5	+4	+3	−1
Improve material utilization	+10	+8	+7	+9
Reach new level of sales volume	−7	−3	+1	+5

Figure 7-5. Objectives matrix system report.

at the entire company's variances from expected results on a real-time basis is to put them in control. That is, appraising variances on the basis of time so that actions can effect changes in time for final results puts management in control. To control, top management must be able to observe actual progress toward achieving the company's vital expected results. The matrix reporting concept is extended into trends in order to determine expectations in a future period. This is illustrated in Figure 7-5.

Variance numbers are percentage completion points from expected milestones of progress. Variances tabulated with positive values are variances meeting or bettering performance standard requirements. The larger the numbers, the better the performance. Variances tabulated with negative values are variances falling below performance standard requirements. At one glance and on one instrument, the practitioner can see those results targeted for a future period that are working out of trouble as well as those that will shortly fall into trouble. With this overview, the practitioner may take appropriate action where needed to effect correction and adjustment.

STATUS CONTROL PERFORMANCE INDICATORS

Since control consists primarily of measurement, it is necessary to adopt a basis of measurement that will disclose qualitatively and quantitatively progress being made in relation to progress expected in the program. It must be remembered that the basic purpose of the strategy of managing by objectives is to yield results, to get things done. In spite of a host of activities programmed to reach key events, it is still the results that justify all activities. The practicing manager must identify performance indices that are useful in giving feedback on his progress toward getting these results. Ratios and index numbers can be the basis for making comparisons of actual performance with expected performance. These ratios can be plotted on a graph, diagrammed on a control chart, or tabulated on a matrix, all of which provide an idea of the progress being made toward completion of objectives. Ratios can also be specially grouped to evaluate the group's progress separately and distinctly from that of other groups. Ratios, indices, and percentages, however, should be used with care because they can be deceptive; numbers often convey an accuracy and precision that does not exist. The problem posed by absolute and relative figures lead to making assumptions that may yield spurious results. Nonetheless, ratios and index numbers, handled carefully, can be extremely useful tools for a skillful practitioner. The following is a suggested list of performance indicators a practitioner can use to get an idea of his progress toward implementing his objectives.

1. *Profit*
   - Sales growth rates and profiles
   - Customer complaint profiles and rates
   - Overhead cost levels and drift ratios
   - Net profit as a percentage of sales
   - Percentage of increase in dividends
   - Sales cost proportion trends and levels
   - Frequency and size of sales orders
   - Cost of transportation as a percentage of sales level and order
   - Mean deviations from standard costs
   - Variable cost rates and levels for sales orders and levels
   - Percentage of return on investments
   - Percentage of share of actual and potential markets
   - Current assets to current liabilities ratios
   - Accounts receivable trends, rates, and collectibility ratios
   - Cost of employer recruitment and placements
   - Direct to indirect labor ratios
   - Marginal cost trends and ratios
   - Profit to total assets
   - Ratio of debt to equity funds
   - Sales per employee ratios
   - Net operating income
   - Debt to total assets ratio

2. *Productivity and schedules*
   - Inventory correlates with sales levels
   - Back order profiles and rates
   - Back order correlates with inventory levels
   - Frequency and range of missed delivery dates
   - Percentage of deadlines met
   - Percentage of performance variance against budgets
   - Set-up time rates and profiles
   - Machine hours per product correlates with process types
   - Percentage of utilization of labor capacity
   - Output/input correlates between equipment utilization and labor capacity
   - Percentage of projects completed against forecasts
   - Equipment depreciation and obsolescence trends

- Percentage of time in raw materials availability
- Ratio of experienced production personnel to new personnel hires
- Ratio of farmed-out work to in-company production
- Output per unit of labor input
- Aging of work behind schedule
- Frequency rates for rescheduling

3. *Efficiency*

- Percentage of error in filling orders
- Defect correction ratios
- Percentage of scrap and waste
- Mean and range of equipment downtime
- Damage claims as a percentage of sales levels and orders
- Percentage of unit cost in material handling
- Overshipment and undershipment ratios
- Percentage of utilization of capital equipment
- Percentage of utilization of available floor space
- Ratio of inventory to assets
- Traffic intensity ratios
- Task-time completion rates
- Percentage of hand motions
- Queue ratios
- Percentage of items delivered as promised
- Inventory turnover
- Percentage of rework
- Percentage of set-up and preparation time
- Frequency of depletion of safety stock
- Demand time to supply time ratios
- Minimum lead time reorder levels
- Net sales to inventory ratio
- Stockouts to desired service levels

4. *Manpower management*

- Quits and mobility flow rates
- Before and after training scores
- Absenteeism time ratios
- Weed-out and screening profile rates
- Percentage of implementation of performance appraisal recommendations
- Percentage implemented with placement planning charts

- Accident frequency profiles and rates
- Supervisory appointment rate from presupervisory selection and training
- Health profile trends and rates
- Total suggestions submitted and percentage implemented
- Employee transfer requests profiles and rates
- Grievance generation and settlement ratios
- Average tardiness trends and rates
- Number and settlement of disciplinary cases
- Percentage of time allowances for personal needs
- Number of promotions within
- Overtime deterioration ratios
- Recruitment and placement costs
- Percentage of completed development experiences
- Percentage of error
- Additions of staff per repetitive program

TROUBLE SPOTS AND SUGGESTED REMEDIES

Managing by objectives has been adopted by many progressive profit-making companies that have invested considerable time and resources in order to gain the benefits from this managerial way of life. Some have even gone through painful policy and organizational changes to ensure existing organizational conditions compatible with objective implementation. Many companies employing this strategy are reporting great results for both company and employees, with ever-widening claims.[8] Experiencing successful results in these companies has, in turn, stimulated greater interest in refining and sharpening this tool for getting even better results. Some users of this strategy not only extol its merits in application but also claim improvements in and often complete elimination of long-term troublesome organizational conditions. A list of the benefits reported by these companies was described in Chapter 1 under the heading "Benefits from the M.B.O. System." These benefits can be summarized as follows:

1. Increases profits through results-oriented employees
2. Brings clarity and precision to jobs, programs, and planning
3. Heightens motivation to make performance stretches
4. Brings organizational clarity through elimination of misfits and redundancy
5. Promotes coordination through interlocking and alignment
6. Makes compensation allocations easier with results evaluations

7. Encourages management development through performance stretches and objective performance evaluation

8. Improves supervisor-subordinate communication relationships

9. Provides definition and clarification of problem areas

10. Builds confidence and certainty in commitments

In spite of all its reported benefits, management by objectives is not without its problems and troubles.[9] Many can be summed up under the headings of hard work and persistent effort. In fact, the work required is so hard that only a long-term commitment to the practice justifies its adoption. It takes several years to develop the proficiency and skill to make it work. Although complaints vary from company to company, trouble spots do appear for most of those that try it. Following are some of the trouble spots that have been identified and some suggested remedies for these problems.

Trouble Spots	Remedies
1. Persistent pursuit of targeted objectives when a change or desist is indicated.	1. Cease implementing objectives when unexpected changes render objectives unfeasible, irrelevant, or impossible. Select alternatives or contingencies from a situation action model and set up a desist time schedule. Revalidate. Communicate change to all participants. Select objective with highest payoff.
2. Persistent pursuit of targeted objectives when an unexpected opportunity arises.	2. Reanalyze payoff of existing objectives in light of the new opportunity. Permit new targets to be set in lieu of prior commitment if utility and value are substantially greater. Shorten time-span commitment if new opportunities arise frequently.
3. Overemphasis on achieving targeted objectives at the expense of results not specified.	3. Targeted objectives must be significant, critical, and high in priority. Keep the number of these objectives at a minimum

Trouble Spots	Remedies
	and make it clear that unanticipated routine work must be completed. Routine work can be set up and written in terms of maintenance objectives or can be handled in a traditional way.
4. Unfair acceleration of targeted objectives even to the point of unattainability.	4. Hold frequent progress conferences to clarify difficulties and reset levels of challenge. Hold frequent meetings for the purpose of removing obstacles hindering accomplishment. The M.B.O. Rules for Stretching Performance and Performance Distribution within a Group should guide setting the challenge level for attainability.
5. Philosophy and understanding of managing by objectives only on the lower levels of management. Top management gives lip service only to the effort.	5. Bring in an outside consultant to do an internal selling job. Distribute among top managers articles, studies, and books that deal with the systems approach to the strategy and the need for total management involvement and support.
6. Writing objectives in terms of work activities rather than in terms of work results.	6. Set up training programs and workshop seminars for practice in writing objectives as results rather than as activities. Develop a manual that illustrates sample objectives similar to company needs. Show how validation procedure can evaluate the wording of an objective.
7. Gearing compensation strictly to results regardless of outside influences.	7. Develop checklist of probable influences that may keep an individual from reaching results. Set up a policy for changing or

Trouble Spots	Remedies
	modifying objectives if circumstances beyond anyone's control occur. Otherwise compensation should be geared closely to results.
8. Difficulty of setting measurable goals for staff personnel who assist line people to get their results.	8. Use two-way or three-way joint feeder-objectives. Objectives set for staff personnel should be set in a "line context," and the score of results should be shared by both. Use M.B.O. Rule for Interlocking Functions.
9. Juggling challenge level to justify pay increases.	9. Use past records to validate performance stretch. Document performance history for comparison with similar jobs in the future to assure the mission of improvement. The 5 to 15 percent progressive performance stretch should apply.
10. Individual's or department's objectives are not interlocked with the whole enterprise.	10. Use concept of feeder-objectives and develop an objective network to show input and output contributions in the total system. Clarify within the system for an interlocked fit. Follow M.B.O. Rule for Interlocking Functions.
11. Objectives are not attained owing to circumstances beyond everyone's control.	11. Failure to attain objectives can provide useful experience factors and guidelines for the next round of objective setting. Greater emphasis should be put on level of attainability and the probability of occurrence. Experience with risk factors should provide future guidance. Greater emphasis

Trouble Spots	Remedies
	should be placed on the validation phase (step 3) if a firm is plagued with circumstances beyond everyone's control.
12. Employee participation is meaningless and not a real commitment.	12. Allow employee to take an active role in the preliminary phases of decision-making. Identify and clarify for him areas of accountability between the objectives set and the responsibilities of his job. Build motivators into areas of accountability.
13. Unable to get tough management with die-hard traditional approaches to managing to try to experiment with managing by objectives.	13. Carefully select a project that can be set up as an objective program. Get agreement from management to implement the project using the M.B.O. approach. Report the results of the project and contrast the advantages and disadvantages with the traditional way. Allow the completion of the project to be a point of influence to persuade others.
14. M.B.O. involves substantial paper work and red tape.	14. Some paperwork must be tolerated. By keeping the number of objectives to the critical few necessary for performance stretches and quantum jumps, the paperwork requirements will be kept to a minimum. Paperwork short-cuts will develop with experience and knowledge of the system. Follow M.B.O. Rule for Focus.
15. Objective performance evaluation will threaten the use and value of the conventional merit	15. Objective performance evaluation and merit evaluation serve the same purpose. The former

Trouble Spots	Remedies
rating system or managerial trait technique.	emphasizes results, the latter emphasizes activities or traits. The merit system will be changed if not eliminated entirely. Some trait evaluation will be retained where it is clearly relevant to a manager's ability to get results. The practice of managing by objectives as a new strategy will cause an impact leading to change in existing practices. A company must be prepared to make these changes.
16. Difficulty in quantifying targeted objectives; targets are written as traits or duties that merely sound like targets.	16. Writing good objectives is a skill developed through training and practice. *Performance in every job can and must be measured!* Skill can be developed in training programs, workshop seminars, and staff coaching. Special examples can be formulated as a guide for those needing special help. A guide manual can help.
17. Objective setting does not fit in with highly specialized and technical work.	17. Objective setting fits into any kind of work where a "package" of results is expected from work activities. The claims that a specialized situation cannot be results-oriented is not true; the situation needs to be reorganized and redefined in terms of getting results. Often this redefinition should be shifted to an individual rather than a department or, conversely, shifted from an individual to a team or project.
18. Unable to get feedback of	18. Feedback under M.B.O. takes

Trouble Spots	Remedies
contributions and measurement of progress.	three forms. First, the individual observes and knows his own performance in relation to what is expected of him. Second, the individual gets periodic reports with evaluations of his overall performance. Third, the individual gets coaching, counseling, and appraisal reviews from his superiors who have first-hand knowledge from which to assess the work.
19. Objective-setting processes are time consuming and must be done after hours.	19. Objective setting is not extra work. It is part of the person's job to plan ahead, make improvements, and set deadlines. Time must be found during regular hours. Lack of time may be the result of the practitioner's setting objectives over too wide a range of job responsibilities. The chief value of managing by objectives is focus and concentration on the three or four areas most critical to the company. The beginner at using the strategy should "crawl before he runs."
20. Difficulty in determining priority with a multiplicity of possible objectives.	20. Use decision matrix in the situation action model and payoff analysis to optimize alternatives.
21. Unable to get total management involvement owing to the fluidity and scattered nature of the organization.	21. Select task force to create a large matrix of alternatives and criteria. Allow individuals unable to involve themselves in the development of the matrix to select alternatives and

Trouble Spots	Remedies
	optimize in terms of their needs and position. In this way involvement is through the matrix.
22. Difficulty in deciding on entry points from which to begin the objective-setting process.	22. First enumerate clearly the many entry points possible for the organization: (a) Five-year profit plan (b) Top-down, bottom-up system (c) Budgetary approach (d) Common objective approach (e) Appraisal by results approach (f) Job descriptions approach Carefully assess which entry points, either singly or in combination, are most likely to set down roots for the objective-setting process. An outside consultant can help.
23. Unable to implement M.B.O. at lower organizational levels.	23. A philosophy and understanding of the concept of managing by objectives must be provided to first-line supervisors before strategy and technique. They must see and understand M.B.O. as a managerial way of life. Training programs, seminars, and managerial coaching for first-line supervisors are an absolute must.
24. Management people too overloaded with day-to-day production necessities to take the time to coordinate with other sections.	24. Setting objectives is a fundamental act of managing. Second to it is establishing the necessary confidence that reaching for objectives will not abort. Crisis managing devel-

Trouble Spots	Remedies
	ops when coordination with and confidence in other sections does not exist. The M.B.O. Rules for Focus, Balancing Organizations, and Interlocking Functions should be followed. Assure that joint feeder-objectives exist in every department.
25. Objectives set so low that the benefits do not justify the expenditure of effort and resources.	25. Estimate cost of reaching objectives and compare with benefits accrued. If benefits are not greater than cost, objective level must be raised for better results. Managing by objectives must exact a performance stretch from all employees in its generic mission of improvement.
26. An objective statement does not have a risk value; the uncertainty or confidence of delivering results has not yet been determined.	26. Risk is high when uncertainty and low confidence prevail. Collect needed and relevant information and set up a decision tree to reduce uncertainty and raise confidence. Use past histories or information from other prior sources when nothing else is available.
27. Difficulty in equating compensation increments to basis of achievement.	27. Objectives having greatest payoff or utility should be given greatest weight for rewards, both financial and nonfinancial. Subordinates must have in advance a clear understanding of the weight various job aspects will have in a final evaluation. It should be noted that financial compensation for achievement of objectives is only one form of reward.

Trouble Spots	Remedies
28. The time span in which objectives are to be achieved is too long to give a feeling of progress.	28. Using the feeder-objective approach, bridge long-range objectives by creating short-range milestones of progress. Each feeder-objective meets a target date that contributes toward an ultimate set of results. Follow M.B.O. guidelines for long-range, short-range, and immediate-range forecasting for setting time span.
29. Action toward reaching objectives is at a low level and not intensive enough.	29. Subordinates probably were not involved in the objective-setting process and are most likely pursuing a manager's personal set of objectives. Get a subordinate to feel that a commitment of the company is partly his doing, a result of his thinking and his decision. This goes a long way in getting him to deliver necessary results.
30. Meeting originally set objectives but unable to meet the changes that affect the objectives during the time intervals.	30. Set objectives for shorter periods of time. Forecast the changes that will occur during the time interval and build these into objective requirements as contingencies.
31. Independent setting of objectives by different departments results in objectives that are overlapping, conflicting, and out of sequence.	31. Use the validation procedure suggested in Chapter 5 to bring about alignment, interlocking, and network connection. The work breakdown structure serves as a guide for varying levels to achieve coordination.
32. Getting older persons who have been disillusioned in the past by new programs to become involved, participate in, and ac-	32. Reduce resistance and reluctance to participate by: (a) Developing the climate. Circulate M.B.O. literature,

Trouble Spots	Remedies
cept the objective-setting processes.	books, magazines; use the company newspaper; circulate successful company cases; hold special presentations on M.B.O. (b) Provide knowledge and understanding of M.B.O. through training programs, seminars, consultants, a company M.B.O. manual, and books. (c) Use certain people to set examples. Have president teach approach to others; hire experienced M.B.O. practitioners as advisors; use managers who show leadership qualities for coaching and persuading. (d) Involve personnel. Allow experimentation and trial of M.B.O. with special projects that pose no great difficulty; allow personnel to try it alone with good coaching.
33. Objective-setting process only practical for certain sections or functions of the company. It is not applicable to R & D purely creative work.	33. The objective-setting process is applicable to areas of responsible creativity. Any R & D effort is intended to support a company-wide effort to gain new or improved products and services for consumer markets. Responsible creativity is the only justification for R & D organizations. Objective-setting processes are attainable under these conditions.
34. Objectives based on a performance appraisal program	34. Most appraisal programs are staff-conceived, corporate-wide,

Trouble Spots	Remedies
achieve neither expected results nor management involvement.	and personnel-oriented. As such, they never become a significant part of the line managerial process or a managerial way of life. Instead of administrating the M.B.O. program from a staff department, decentralize its administration among the various line departments.

The companies that have had successful results with the strategy of managing by objectives and have overcome trouble spots have done so because their supervisors and managers were not only familiar with the strategy's rationale and procedure, but also were willing to put forth the effort and time needed to make it work.

PERFORMANCE APPRAISALS[10]

Commitments to objectives not only serve as a meaningful basis for evaluating company performance but also give significant advantages to individual performance appraisals. The strategy of managing by objectives, when used in an accurate and meaningful way, can provide an enlightened basis for the periodic review of an individual manager's or employee's performance. A rater enjoys the opportunity to use the resultant accurate data as the basis for his appraisal. The ratee enjoys participation in and commitment to those performance requirements in which he is involved. A strong and impartial attitude toward the appraisal process generally prevails between the two.

The technique of individual performance appraisals using the management by objectives approach has significant advantages over the many other appraisal methods currently employed. The following are some of these advantages:

1. *Appraisals relate more closely to the job.* Appraisal is oriented toward job requirements and work results rather than toward personality traits or general descriptors. Specified objectives are highly related to results needed and expected by the company. Evaluation is tailored to and already well-structured situation. Job clarification and responsibility definition from the practice of managing by objectives make appraising more accurate.

2. *Appraisals are more objective.* Supervisors are usually reluctant to cite deficiencies without outstanding evidence. Having reliable and accurate information on performance helps the supervisor to be less subjective. The role of the appraiser changes. He does not have to defend his position. The supervisor is on solid ground during a confrontation with employees. He is armed with information which the employee is acquainted with and understands.

3. *Appraisals are active and positive.* The appraisal involves both the supervisor and the subordinate and thus is not passive. Each is active in a positive way in assessing job performance. There are no unilateral actions, as found in other appraisal systems. This enhances a meeting of the minds, communications, job expectations, and motivation.

4. *Appraisals are opportunistic.* Appraisals do not have to follow past practices or procedures. New opportunities or new challenges are easily handled within the objective-setting process. The performance appraisal approach avoids slavishly following preconceived ideas and methods. It encourages an employee to innovate because it is future-oriented.

5. *Appraisals encourage performance stretches.* There are many purposes to appraisals. Chief among them is the stimulation it gives to improving individual performance. The mission of improvement is generic to the practice of managing by objectives. Level and consistency of effort can be readily evaluated for individuals in the system.

These advantages are not only feasible but are currently enjoyed by companies using performance objectives methods. In companies that have reported use of this technique, there is conviction that exceptional results are experienced in terms of improved performance.

The ways in which individual companies are using performance objectives as appraisal systems vary. This lack of uniformity is the result of the companies' various reasons for using the system. Some use an appraisal system to determine annual salary increases; this is commonly known as "merit rating." Others use appraisal systems to identify and develop promotable managers. Still others use appraisal systems to stimulate, motivate, and encourage improved performance. In actuality, the appraisal system can combine all these reasons since each relates to concerns and accountability of managers. Performance appraisals are part and parcel of the entire managing process and can include virtually all elements of managing: organizational planning, delegation, evaluation, control, communications, development, motivation, and coordination. Managing by objectives as a performance appraisal system provides results-oriented job descriptions and clear-cut company objectives from which accountability and measurability are clarified. From this standpoint, *a performance appraisal program using managing by objectives is both a "rating" device for evaluating individual performance and a "managing" procedure to ensure the processes of management.* Previous chapters in this book have centered on the latter but a few words need to be said about the former.

A performance appraisal system using the managing by objectives approach should be tailored to meet unique requirements of the company, department, or individual. As a rating device for individual performance, the following steps need to be taken:

1. *Prepare commitments.* The individual prepares a *preliminary* list of the three to five most important objectives he hopes to achieve in a given year. He does this by following Phases 1, 2, 3, and 4 of the conceptual strategy of managing by objectives. He carefully regards and analyzes his responsibilities, opportunities, and commitments with his superior. These commitments are written as objectives and not as activities. It will take practice and skill to set these in the right nomenclature. Areas of responsibility that give rise to objectives might be the following: volume output, quality level, cost performance, methods improvement, housekeeping, sales, skills development, and time control. The objectives developed from these areas form the basis for discussion and subsequent joint agreement between subordinate and supervisor. Each objective must be written according to the guidelines suggested in Phase 2. A most important guideline is building the performance measurement or indicator into the statement of objective. Without this quantitative indicator, progress toward results becomes merely a matter of interpretation. Performance standards for the activities are developed to indicate the level or intensity of effort that is needed to achieve the objectives. Prior agreement is obtained on these performance standards and evaluation is made on this basis. The job or position descriptions can be useful if they are written to incorporate both objectives and standards. If not, new appraisal forms should be developed. Samples of new forms are illustrated in Figures 7-6, 7-7, and 7-8.

2. *Plan and schedule activities.* Both supervisor and subordinate reach a common agreement on the methods and activities necessary to reach stated objectives. Outside departments and personnel may be involved as resources to pull together all necessary work for the objective program. There must be a meeting of the minds between a supervisor and a subordinate in this step in order to acquire confidence in reaching stated

Performance Objectives Appraisal

Name				Date
Position		Dept		Division

		List	Start	Complete	Give
STEP 1.	Priority	Objectives	Date	Date	Performance Standards

STEP 2.   Comment on results achieved for each objective listed in step 1:

STEP 3. Improve individual's performance: Where performance is strongest	Where performance is weakest

STEP 4.   Specific plans to improve:
Actions and Activities   Responsibilities   Dates

Supervisor Date	Next higher supervisor Date

Figure 7-6.   Sample performance objective appraisal.

objectives. The value of working toward a targeted date has already been discussed. Feeder-objectives can be set into a time schedule that both supervisor and subordinate agree upon.

3. Implementing scheduled activities. The subordinate proceeds to implement his planned objectives. The individual applies his skill, ingenuity, effort, time, and energy in getting done what has to be done. The supervisor provides day-to-day coaching and help to the individual. Managing by exception is not the rule in this case. The supervisor does

Results Planning and Appraisal Report

Name _____ Department _____ Date _____

Results expected:	Performance standards:
1. _____	1. _____
2. _____	2. _____
3. _____	3. _____

Approved: _____ Date _____   Coordinated with _____ Date ____

Planned activities: Schedule:

1. _____   Start   Complete

2. _____

3. _____

4. _____

Evaluation of results:	Tentative objectives for next year:

Evaluation approved:

_____ _____   _____ _____
Reporting Manager   Date   Coordinating Manager   Date

Figure 7-7. Sample performance objective appraisal.

not sit back and wait for exceptions to arise before he acts. Instead, he looks for progress in implementation, both positive and negative, and wishes to be informed of not only what is wrong but also what is right.

4. *Progress reviews.* Periodically, during the ensuing months, there should be formal discussions relating to the objectives that were set. These could be quarterly progress reviews. The purpose of such reviews is to keep a greater proportion of management informed of progress in order that objectives may be revised if necessary. New objectives may be

Cost Reduction
Performance Appraisal

Objective:_____

_____

_____

_____

_____

Target: $_____

Activities:_____

_____

_____

_____

_____

_____

Results:_____

_____

_____

_____

_____

Percent of Objective	Jan	Feb	Mar		Apr	May	Jun		Jul	Aug	Sep		Oct	Nov	Dec	
150%																
125%																
100%																
80%																
60%																
40%																
20%																
0%																

Figure 7-8. Sample performance objective appraisal.

introduced, some eliminated, and priorities reorganized. These reviews are not intended to be performance appraisals with formal interviews to discover individual performance. The aim is to determine work progression toward meeting targeted objectives. The atmosphere is one of mutual help, progress assessment, and problem solving.

   5. *Annual review.* The underlying value of annual performance review is the opportunity it affords to gain feedback about results achieved and

information about progress toward results expected. The annual cycle is convenient because of other annual instruments such as budgets, profit statements, and forecasts. The manager prepares, in advance, this annual review summarizing individual achievements and suggesting ways to improve in subsequent years. The principal purpose of the formal annual performance review is to determine what was actually accomplished and what improvements can be made. Causes for lack of progress or lack of achievement are brought out at this time. There is a meaningful exchange between supervisor and subordinate.

SUMMARY

On the other side of planning is control. On the other side of an objective program is a control program. The purpose of control is to keep activities and efforts on a prescribed course of action. Control should not be treated as a separate function but as part of the total objective-setting and implementation processes. Controlling is in the nature of follow-up to the other phases of the strategy. Comparing actual performance with prescribed standards and ascertaining the difference, if any, is heart and core of control.

This chapter provided a description of the fifth and last phase in the strategy of managing by objectives. Several techniques were presented to keep status reporting an integral part of the total objective program of an enterprise. Trouble spots do exist in the practice of managing by objectives. This chapter presented a troubleshooting chart that suggested some remedies for typical problems encountered by firms introducing the strategy. Hard work, new policies, and organizational changes will be required to create a management system ready to produce the type of results for which the system has been created.

GUIDE QUESTIONS FOR THE PRACTITIONER

1. Explain how overshooting or undershooting will hamper performance in reaching a set of objectives.
2. List and describe the guidelines for controlled targeting.
3. What is meant by status reporting?
4. Using the status control model, develop a work breakdown structure of end items necessary in working toward an objective and write performance indicators into the end items. Schedule the performance indicators in a spectrum of milestones of progress.

5. Develop a status reporting matrix for your company for viewing total objectives at a glance.

6. List performance indicators presently used in your company.

7. Formulate a list of potential trouble spots for implementing a system of managing by objectives and collect possible remedies for overcoming these trouble spots.

REFERENCES AND NOTES

1. Roy A. Lindberg, "The Unfamiliar Art of Controlling," *Management Review*, August 1969, pp. 49–54.

2. It would be wrong to leave the impression that these four are the most critical. It is doubtful that any two organizations will be plagued with the same concerns in exactly the same manner. The practitioner needs to find his critical few.

3. Louis A. Allen, *The Management Profession*, McGraw-Hill Book Co., New York, 1964, p. 319.

4. James J. O'Brien, *Scheduling Handbook*, McGraw-Hill Book Co., New York, 1969.

5. Virgil K. Rowland, *Managerial Performance Standards*, American Management Association, New York, 1960, pp. 19–20.

6. J. F. Van Valkenburgh, T. B. Nooger, and K. P. Neville, *Basic Synchros and Servomechanisms*, vol. 2, John F. Rider, New York, 1955, pp. 1–13, and Charles H. Kepner and Benjamin B. Tregoe, *The Rational Manager*, McGraw-Hill Book Co., New York, 1965, pp. 54–55.

7. Roy A. Lindberg, "Operations Auditing: What It Is? What It Isn't?" *Management Review*, December 1959, pp. 2–10.

8. See Chapter 1.

9. Henry L. Tosi, and Stephen J. Carroll, "Managerial Reaction to Management by Objectives," *Journal of the Academy of Management*, vol. 11, no. 4, December 1968, p. 415.

10. Marion S. Kellogg, *What To Do about Performance Appraisals*, American Management Association, 1965.

8. Training and Developing Men To Manage by Objectives

Development through Doing. Skills for Managing by Objectives. Development Through Workshop Seminars. Reference Reading. Summary. Guide Questions for the Practitioner. References and Notes.

Managing by objectives is not self-teaching. Although the strategy seems basically clear and easy to implement, learning a new skill can be harder than the work itself.[1] For example, interlocking feeder-objectives into a network of mutually supporting and coordinating efforts requires adopting a whole new outlook oneself as well as persuading others of its validity. It is harder to get men to set targets for results, as opposed to activities, since most managers have always conducted their managerial approaches using the latter.[2] Companies have experienced difficulty in conveying to managers how to set and apply measurements to objectives. Intuitively, a manager senses that his goal has been set correctly but he cannot express it in measures that are appropriate and precise. Experience has shown that this difficulty can be overcome by continual practice and application on the job. A manager or supervisor must experience this difficulty in order to learn how to develop precise, appropriate, and quantitative measures that serve to define results for goals and control. This skill comes with continual applications over a period of time.

This chapter will describe concepts and techniques most useful for training and developing practitioners in the strategy of managing by objectives. The sections included are (1) "Development through Doing," (2) "Skills for Managing by Objectives," (3) "Development through Workshop Seminars," and (4) "Reference Reading."

DEVELOPMENT THROUGH DOING

Training men to manage by objectives must focus on the work a manager must perform on the job. There may be programs and helpful procedures that contribute to turning out top-flight managers who can use the

M.B.O. strategy skillfully. At best, these programs guide and give direction in the development of this unusual and unique skill. A down-to-earth practical approach must be well structured and must focus on responsibilities carried out from day to day. The individual who is to be trained must practice the strategy in his own job without external pressures and influences. He can be encouraged to develop himself through his absorption in the strategy and its challenge that calls forth his best effort.

Top management, of course, must encourage this approach by their participation and use of the skill in their own work. The emphasis in this approach is on the individual rather than on a group, as it is in a formal training context. It must be kept in mind that, basically, management toward objectives is intended to get improvements on the job. On-the-job development and training thus should be the focus. Marion Kellogg considers this idea as building development into the work itself.[3] Individuals should be given the latitude to restructure delegated assignments in an objective approach. In other words, the individual, when first asked to complete a project, should be allowed to set the project in target fashion, relate the targeted results to existing commitments, and proceed to validate and organize precisely for implementation. This process enables careful analysis of activities, authority, and the work situation to predict accomplishment of the assignment within a specified period of time.

A perfect solution for training men to manage by objectives has not yet been found and probably never will be. Success in many companies, however, seems to result from the following general pattern:

1. Find the way in which managing by objectives works in your company and do more of it! Focus the strategy in the areas of greatest importance. Bring it to bear on the area of the company's greatest need. Share with others your knowledge of how managing by objectives will fill this need.

2. Give on-the-job training in the skill with the focus on practicing the strategy at all times to get results. Men learn best by doing work and getting results. Methods employed should involve the trainee's doing as much of the work himself as possible.

3. Develop a guideline manual that sets forth the procedures for a systematic approach to the strategy. Specific examples from within the organization should be included. Policy guidelines and proven practices should also be included.

4. Do not allow training to be formalized as only a behavioral activity. The soundest approach is to put managing toward objectives in a line

context for a balanced way of managing. Some departments tend to emphasize the behavioral and human dimensions of the strategy at the expense of the technical, economic, and functional requirements.

5. Establish through policies and examples that managing toward objectives is a way of life. Each manager and supervisor develops confidence toward its use when he sees his supervisor as well as the company's president performing in the same fashion.

6. Select and hire individuals who have practiced the strategy in other companies successfully and who can wield influence and provide information within the natural work setting. These individuals can be demonstrators of the technique and coaches for those who need help.

7. Key the training of men for managing toward objectives on an individual basis. This means the individual must want to develop the skill. He will ask for the assistance he needs because he sees the value of it for himself and for the company. External pressures and influences should not force him into it.

There is no doubt that the most effective training is built into daily on-the-job experience—experience that has been varied in type and level to stretch the individual to new levels of achievement. Some type of training program should exist to complement the critical on-the-job implementing experience. Training programs, however, are most useful in the areas of providing stimulation, influencing attitudes, and imparting knowledge. Open resistance and antagonism toward M.B.O. can be brought out into an open forum with experts and peers. Real understanding of the philosophy of managing by objectives can be acquired in a situation where there is give and take in dialogue and discussion. Trainees would be informed as to the potential benefits of using M.B.O., the problems associated with its use, how to overcome these problems, and the techniques for applying the strategy. Through discussion of difficulties, training programs can avoid getting off on the wrong foot. Specific skills can be acquired in training programs or workshop seminars. The first and most obvious of these skills is the ability to write a formal statement of objectives.

It was pointed out in an earlier chapter that considerable skill is required to set formal statements of objectives that have undergone several processes, the last of which is validation. A considerable investment in time is necessary to obtain commitments of people, resources, and money. Although this investment is necessary and advantageous in terms of the potential benefits that can be derived from it, some will not accept the investment that is required. These same individuals will attempt to practice managing by objectives informally and individually, thus eliminating the total management approach and management system that need to be created. *Managing by objectives cannot be carried on in an informal way! In order to provide the best results and the greatest benefits, it must be carried out with formalized processes of relating, involvement, and commitment.* Extensive training designed to provide practitioners with a thorough knowledge of these processes and aligned with on-the-job development and practice will truly give subordinates the specific skills necessary to practice managing by objectives as a managerial way of life.

SKILLS FOR MANAGING BY OBJECTIVES

The function of any skill is to make possible the application of knowledge and understanding to innovate or solve problems. Skill is the ability to apply knowledge effectively and readily in the performance of a particular physical or mental task. Knowledge alone does not make the skill but rather the ability and ingenuity with which the knowledge is used in a variety of complex applications. The M.B.O. practitioner will exercise this ability with varying degrees of competency and proficiency. Use of the skill is in many ways a measurement of the use of knowledge. For the M.B.O. practitioner, this means that the acquisition of knowledge and understanding of M.B.O. is essential if he is to develop the skills appropriate to a given situation. Knowledge is defined here as stockpiles of valid information organized from past experiences to specific problems. The following six general categories of skills appear to be the basis from which specific and specialized skills of managing by objectives emerge:

1. ***Technical skill.*** This skill involves the proficient use of knowledge in specific disciplines. This is the specialized information, methods, processes, procedures, and techniques involved in the technology of the product or services of the company or industry.

2. ***Behavioral skill.*** This skill is primarily the utilization of knowledge and understanding of people as they conduct themselves with others. Such understanding promotes working with others cooperatively and effectively as a natural and continuous activity. It requires an awareness of attitudes and beliefs held by individuals and groups and how these govern their goal-reaching processes.

3. ***Conceptual skill.*** This skill is the ability to utilize existing knowledge in order to perceive additional knowledge. It is purposeful risk taking for creating new conditions. Exploration, questioning, and probing

are some of the tools that cut across established areas of a business. Conceptual skill is interdisciplinary since it involves the ways in which various functions of systems depend on other systems as well as the way changes in any one part affect all the others.

4. *Implementing skill.* This skill involves the ability to get work done on a day-to-day, program-to-program basis, or the ability to concentrate just enough resources of time, money, and effort to initiate what has to be done, conduct the activity, and bring it to a successful end. Achievement and accomplishments are the principal dimensions for employing this skill.

5. *Economic-business skill.* This skill is the utilization of knowledge and understanding of the business enterprise as a firm operating in a market for the sale of goods and services. It involves the manner in which an enterprise uses scarce and limited resources to meet changing and unpredictable demands. It involves the strategy of production, distribution, and consumption of goods and services with maximization of output and minimization of input.

6. *Managerial skill.* This skill is the effective utilization of general management information, specific knowledge, and proven practices in the planning, directing, and controlling of a business enterprise toward profit and perpetuation. It involves the organization and strategies of people, facilities, resources, and money for selling products and services within the limits of costs, quality, and time.

The separation of these six broad skill areas is only useful for purposes of analysis and discussion. In practice, these areas are so closely interrelated that it is difficult to determine where one ends and another begins. We receive some benefit from examining each of them separately in spite of their interrelatedness. The capable practitioner of managing by objectives is more a generalist than a specialist since he deals with segments of the skills from each of the six broad areas, as illustrated in Figure 8-1. The practitioner cannot know everything contained in each of the six areas, yet he must have the insight and perception to extract from each the degree of the skill that is needed to achieve results in his program. As defined earlier, a skill is the effective utilization of knowledge. The practitioner must be alert to the generation of new knowledge in each of the six categories and assess the manner in which he can exploit it to improve the specific nature of his practice.

Identifying specific skills of successful M.B.O. practitioners has been difficult because of the extreme complexity of the strategy as a managerial

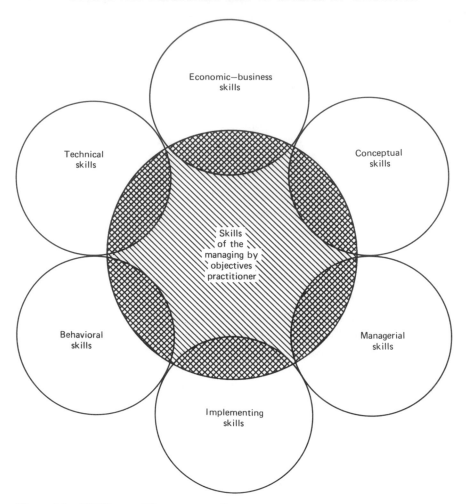

Figure 8-1.   M.B.O. practitioner a generalist.

way of life. Tests and measuring techniques have proved inadequate. Different situations call for different managerial life styles, which, in turn, require different skills and characteristics. No single set of specific skills exists, since some situations require one set of skills while other situations require another. Thus we cannot expect to generalize from one situation to another. On the other hand, there appears to be a core or common body of specific skills extracted from the six broad areas that, once acquired and developed, can lead to successful practice of managing by objectives. These specific skills are as follows:

1. *Objective-setting skills*
   (a) Ability to generate alternatives or improvements from present and past experiences
   (b) Ability to estimate likelihoods from present experiences
   (c) Ability to predict and project concerns and desires
   (d) Ability to sense and forecast trends
   (e) Ability to perceive where improvements can be made in everyday experiences even where it is not normally in one's province of thinking
   (f) Ability to predict ends from certain beginning even without orientation
   (g) Ability to see the whole from given constituent parts
   (h) Ability to sense and make use of pace, sequence, and time
   (i) Ability to sense, predict, and forecast an accomplishment at a point in time
   (j) Ability to sift simple patterns from complex ones
   (k) Ability to focus on the critical and separate the trivial

2. *Implementing objectives skills*
   (a) Ability to work a task to completion with intensified drive
   (b) Ability to sense people's needs and drives and relate them to planned accomplishments
   (c) Ability to foresee barriers and pursue circumventing steps
   (d) Ability to fit people into proper work assignments
   (e) Ability to gain rapport and response from people
   (f) Ability to compromise and gain consensus
   (g) Ability to articulate and persuade hostile and competing groups
   (h) Ability to empathize with company life styles
   (i) Ability to convey information with clarity
   (j) Ability to coordinate various "power" groups
   (k) Ability to move ahead in the face of risk, uncertainty, and unknowns
   (l) Ability to align, dovetail, and connect two or more directions

3. *Measuring and correcting skills*
   (a) Ability to measure parts as progression toward wholes
   (b) Ability to analyze a complex mass of information into numerics and quantification
   (c) Ability to find measures of central tendencies
   (d) Ability to measure deviation, variation, and drift from prescribed directions
   (e) Ability to sense progress with sampling indicators on a time spectrum

   (f) Ability to initiate feedback corrections or reduce variance
   (g) Ability to break down a complex situation into its component parts
   (h) Ability to collect relevant information from probing, questioning, and observing
   (i) Ability to schedule interwoven and simultaneous projects
   (j) Ability to form judgments and determine trends from statistical data

Formal education is neither an exclusive nor a completely sufficient method for providing these specific skills to the practitioner of managing by objectives. Neither completion of some level of formal education nor work within a specific discipline signify preparation for the practice of managing by objectives. At best, this sort of education signifies a breadth and depth of knowledge acquired during a preparatory stage. This forms the basis from which skills can develop. Historically, skills have been acquired and developed through experience on the job. Formal education provides a basis for efficient transmittal of information and knowledge. On-the-job experience is the skill's development process for utilizing knowledge in problem applications.

DEVELOPMENT THROUGH WORKSHOP SEMINARS

Learning by doing can be augmented by a number of valuable off-the-job training methods. Several institutions now specializing in management education offer workshop experience in management by objectives that few companies can equal. Of course, a company does not have control over the course or seminar content and must rely on the participating individual to relate and transfer as much as possible to his on-the-job needs. Outside programs make available valuable experience and discussion that can be very beneficial. Getting away from the immediate job to see things from a distance with others who are doing the same thing has a healthy impact on clarity and definition. Questions raised by other participants often enable one to study a point of view that otherwise would go unrecognized. When these two advantages are combined— the exposure to other viewpoints and a perspective on one's own company—an individual can get some meaningful guidance for his own development.

Company resources may prove quite effective for training individuals in the strategy of managing by objectives. Firms that can provide in-plant programs, while also taking advantage of outside professional assistance, can provide a more meaningful experience than can outside seminars and

TABLE 8-1 SEMINAR OUTLINE MANAGING BY OBJECTIVES

I. Preliminary (2 weeks before seminar)
   1. Study *Manual for Developing Individual Objectives*
   2. Study definitions of all terms
   3. Read two books from list suggested in Reference Reading
   4. Prepare solution to company case

II. First day
   1. Managing by objectives
      (a) Concept of getting results
      (b) Traditional methods of managing compared
      (c) Organizational barriers to getting results
      (d) Company purpose and philosophy of M.B.O.
   2. Finding the objectives
      (a) Trends, errors, forecasting disruptions
      (b) The mission of improvement
      (c) Situation analysis and the action model
      (d) Assessing managerial performance stretches
   3. Objective setting processes
      (a) Establishing and writing performance objectives
      (b) Objective networks and feeder-objective modules
      (c) Organizational entry point
      (d) Interlocking and weighting objectives for optimum results
   4. Workshop: Participants make a situation analysis and write a statement of objectives for their respective departments. Critiques and analyses will be offered by participants to improve the skill of setting objectives. (Personal plan for practicing managing by objectives is initiated.)

III. Second day
   1. Work breakdown structure
      (a) Organizing programs to deliver results
      (b) Work breakdown matrix
      (c) Networks and project systems
      (d) Interlocking through objective networks
   2. Validating objectives
      (a) Work packages and risk factors
      (b) Decision trees and PERT networks
      (c) Trial run of programs
      (d) Venture analysis and simulation
   3. Workshop: Participants will continue with personal plans to validate their anticipated objectives by organizing and developing resources. Potential problems analyses and trial run of programs will be conducted.

IV. Third day
   1. Techniques for implementing objectives
      (a) Planned motivators and the motivational process
      (b) Releasing individual potential through coaching
      (c) Techniques of persuasion
      (d) Completing work packages

TABLE 8-1   (Continued)

---

   2. Objective status control systems
     (a) Status control model
     (b) Appraisal systems and performance indicators
     (c) Diagnosing troubles and suggesting remedies
     (d) Personal performance appraisal
   3. Workshop: Participants will analyze a developed plan for implementation to detect trouble spots and problem areas. Remedies and contingency actions are proposed and analyzed. A personal plan for managing by objectives is completed.
   4. Summary and conclusions
     (a) Strategies to obtain performance improvement
     (b) Competitive edge
     (c) Objective-oriented companies and individuals
     (d) Management practices of the future

---

workshops. Particularly useful is the participation of line managers in presenting the program to subordinates. This has a twofold advantage. First, it forces the line manager to analyze his own philosophy and understanding of managing by objectives in preparation for conducting the program. Second, it places the line manager in the true position of a coach—teaching, explaining, guiding, directing, and helping. This reinforces the subordinate's relationship with and respect for his supervisor. To assist a company that wishes to set up an in-plant training program for managing by objectives, a seminar workshop has been organized and suggested outlines are given in Tables 8-1 and 8-2.

TABLE 8-2   GUIDELINE MANUAL FOR DEVELOPING INDIVIDUAL OBJECTIVES

   I. Company purpose for managing by objectives
  II. Brief theory of the management concept
 III. Summary of objectives procedure in company
 IV. Procedure in detail
    1. Finding the objectives
    2. Setting objectives
    3. Validating objectives
    4. Implementing objectives
    5. Status reporting and progress reviews
  V. Questions and answers
 VI. Company case history
VII. Personal plan
VIII. Additional reading

REFERENCE READING

Additional reading resources for the development of skills for practicing the strategy of managing by objectives are given below.

Batten, J. D., *Beyond Management by Objectives,* American Management Association, New York, 1966, 140 pp. Drawing on his knowledge of management methods and practices, the author claims that many objective programs lack one vital element, one intrinsic power that makes things happen: motivation. Without motivation, or personal involvement, a management by objective program may never pay off. The author shows how many managers install a so-called management by objective program with its apparatus of goals and required results, and then they sit back and wait for great things to happen. But merely establishing the machinery is not enough: it is only when employees from top to bottom are motivated and see the importance of an all-out effort both to themselves and to their companies that objectives are reached and organizations come alive.

Drucker, Peter F., *Managing for Results,* Harper and Row, New York, 1964, 240 pp. The effective business, the author observes, focuses on opportunities rather than on problems. How this focus is achieved in order to make the organization prosper and grow is the concern of this book. Drucker takes a hard look at products and services to see how many qualify as tomorrow's breadwinners. Only when an executive has an accurate picture of realities is he able to make his business effective. The book combines specific economic analysis with entrepreneurial forces for business prosperity.

Hughes, Charles L., *Goal Setting,* American Management Association, 1965, 157 pp. This book explains in meaningful practical language how to recognize the needs for self-fulfillment and job satisfaction and how to stimulate goal-seeking behavior in all employees—how, in short, to make management by objectives a reality. The author describes how overall objectives can be broken down into subgoals that managers and employees at all levels can readily grasp, associate themselves with, and contribute toward their achievement, creating both individual and company success. Effective performance and company survival and growth depend on the validity of the goals themselves and the goal-setting processes.

Howell, Robert A., *Management by Objectives—Should It Be Applied?* Doctoral Dissertation, Harvard University, Cambridge, Mass., June 1966, 269 pp. This is a research report of the findings of nearly a year's organizational study aimed at determining how the application of an actual management by objectives system compares with a theoretical model structured after a budgetary system. The organization studied is a large U.S. corporation that has utilized management by objectives for all its supervisory personnel for about 5 years. The study shows the strong correlation that exists between managing by objectives and organizational structure, activity usage, and activity morale.

McConkey, Dale D., *How To Manage by Results,* American Management Association, New York, 1965, 144 pp. This book is for those executives who are vitally concerned with profits and the day-to-day realities of obtaining tangible results. The author provides a thorough explanation of what is meant by management by results. He summarizes the whole approach in a few guidelines and pertinent facts for developing and initiating a results program. The author provides useful charts to help implement a company's program and includes case studies from United Air Lines, Monsanto Company, State Farm Insurance, and other leading organizations.

McGregor, Douglas, *The Human Side of Enterprise,* McGraw-Hill Book Co., New York, 1960, 244 pp. In formulating Theory X and Theory Y, the author opened up new vistas for others to reflect upon. Theory X and Theory Y are essentially ways of describing how a manager feels about people and their normal reaction to work. They are two extreme ends of a management point of view and in a practical way, a manager may fall somewhere in between. The author identifies the assumptions each of these theories contain and how these assumptions determine how well managers handle people. This book has significant implications for getting results through understanding and motivating employees.

Killian, Ray A., *Managing by Design,* American Management Association, 1968, 369 pp. Effective management performance is no accident. It is the result of a calculated plan for achievement formulated by the executive who aims for success and gets it. The author offers practical guidelines to get favorable results in the job. He gives techniques for setting up plans and following through, for keeping operations moving with problem solving, for channeling company resources in directions offering greatest benefits, and for finding ways to communicate with subordinates.

National Industrial Conference Board, *Managing by and with Objectives,* Study No. 212, National Industrial Conference Board, New York, 1968, 77 pp. This report deals with the concept of management by objectives and the practices followed by companies to implement the concept. It concentrates upon the experience of firms that use management by objectives as a general approach to the task of managing the business rather than for some other more limited purpose. The report discusses the procedures used to determine objectives, the degree to which objectives are quantified, and the mechanisms used to ensure that the objectives of one manager do not conflict with those of others. It examines the case of objectives in controlling business operations and in appraising managerial performance. Five case studies of companies using this approach to management illustrate the key elements of the technique.

Odiorne, George S., *Management by Objectives,* Pitman Publishing Corp., New York, Toronto, and London, 1965, 196 pp. The author shows that only the precise definition of both corporate and personal goals can produce effective management today. He describes a system of management that defines individual executive responsibilities in terms of corporate objectives. He shows how managers jointly identify organizational goals and define major responsibilities in terms of the results expected of them. With management by objectives, account-ability is established and a team effort, which does not eliminate individual risk taking, becomes possible.

Odiorne, George S., *Management Decisions by Objectives,* Prentice-Hall, Engle-wood Cliffs, N.J., 1969, 252 pp. The author provides working managers with tested scientific methods that will dramatically improve their decision-making and problem solving ability. Emphasis is placed on making sophisticated mathe-matical and behavioral techniques intelligible and useful. These are also brought to bear on crucial areas of costing, sales, production, and planning. He presents models of every type of decision facing management. Models are analytically treated for input, action, output, and feedback in the objective approach.

Schleh, Edward C., *Management by Results,* McGraw-Hill Book Co., New York, 1961, 251 pp. The unique results system developed successfully used by the author for more than 20 years gives a fresh practical insight into solving manage-ment problems. The author shows how his technique is applicable to every level of responsibility—how judgment, ingenuity, and initiative are maximized. Broad in scope, the book carries the reader through all types of management problems from the simplest type of delegation from one man to another through the application of results management.

Steward, Nathaniel, *Strategies of Managing for Results,* Parker Publishing, West Nyack, N.Y., 1966, 213 pp. The author uses examples from actual experiences to show exactly where things went wrong in many companies and how executives took steps to correct them. He points up blind spots of middle management and how these can impair the future. These blind spots concern people, ideas, values, handling of problems, realities, and so forth. He indicates symptoms of these blind spots and countermeasures that overcome them. The author shows how to indoctrinate people in the art of diagnosing and reports on some of the managerial morale situations growing out of troubleshooting experience.

Valentine, Raymond F., *Performance Objectives for Managers,* American Man-agement Association, New York, 1966, 208 pp. The author characterizes the concept of managing by objectives as a style of thinking and demonstrates how managerial efficiency can be increased by following logical techniques. The author explains the use of a quantitative approach that deals with actual re-sults rather than with traditional behavior ratings, and shows the advantages of a performance objectives program in upgrading the capability of the man-agerial force. He shows how many current methods of measuring managerial performance are neither fair nor objective. He describes practical methods for performance appraisals and tells how performance objectives are meaningful in appraisal systems.

SUMMARY

Managing by objectives is not self-teaching. Companies experiencing difficulty in practicing the technique must set up formal training and development programs to impart the understanding and skills needed for implementing the strategy. This chapter shows that a perfect solution for training men to manage by objectives has not been found since different situations demand different approaches. However, on-the-job experience gained through day-to-day work responsibilities is the most effective way to develop proficiency. This chapter also identifies general and specific skills needed for successful practice of the strategy.

GUIDE QUESTIONS FOR THE PRACTITIONER

1. Is the practice of managing by objectives self-teaching?
2. Why is it necessary to formalize the practice of managing by objectives?
3. Explain developing skills through on-the-job experience.
4. How is a skill acquired?
5. Why is it necessary to identify areas of skills development for the practice of managing by objectives?
6. What is meant by the eclectic approach to skills acquisition?
7. List specific skills that separate the successful practitioners of managing by objectives from the unsuccessful ones.
8. Outline a formal workshop seminar that can be used within a company to train and develop personnel in the practice of managing by objectives.
9. List additional reading resources available to help in developing the strategy of managing by objectives.

REFERENCES AND NOTES

1. Douglas H. Fryer, Mortimer R. Feinberg, and Sheldon S. Zalkind, *Developing People in Industry,* Harper Brothers, New York, 1956, p. 80.
2. George S. Odiorne, *op. cit.*
3. Marion S. Kellogg, *Closing the Performance Gap,* American Management Association, New York, 1967, pp. 124–130.

9. Improvement Applications

Profit Improvement. Sales Improvement. Cost Improvement. Management Time Improvement. Communications Improvement. Methods Improvement. Training Improvement. Summary. Guide Questions for the Practitioner. References and Notes.

The mission of improvement is generic to the managerial function. Managers should never be content with the state of affairs. They should never rest on their laurels but rather search for new plateaus of accomplishment. Elemental to any business looking for new directions or setting objectives is the mission of improvement. It must be the very foundation of any planning effort. It recognizes *a simple truth: even though the future of a company is uncertain, the company must act and react to make itself better than it has been in the past.* The illusive competitive edge that every business attempts to maintain can be thought of in terms of the mission of improvement. The continuous performance stretch for more and better results is the competitive edge a company has. As long as a company embarks on hard-hitting aggressive improvement programs, competitors will find it difficult to keep up unless they make the same performance stretches. The practitioner of managing by objectives must assume primary responsibility for the mission of improvement to provide this competitive edge. The practitioner must develop the skills and competence to embark upon and achieve improvements for the enterprise. These improvements permeate and interlock the entire organization so that the "leap forward" is natural and expected. As a beginner, the practitioner experiences results that are minimal. With time, growth, and experience, results are increased with repeated thrusts so that improvement becomes a way of life. This is illustrated in Figure 9-1. The critical point of any business is usually at the end of the introduction, growth, and saturation phases. The practitioner has three alternatives to choose from: do nothing and experience, before very long, an abort or bankruptcy;[1] put out a minimum of effort and experience a general decline or obsolescence; or execute repeated thrusts in performance as required by the practice of managing by objectives.

This chapter deals with a selected few of the many areas of an enterprise that can undergo improvement. These areas are (1) profits, (2) sales,

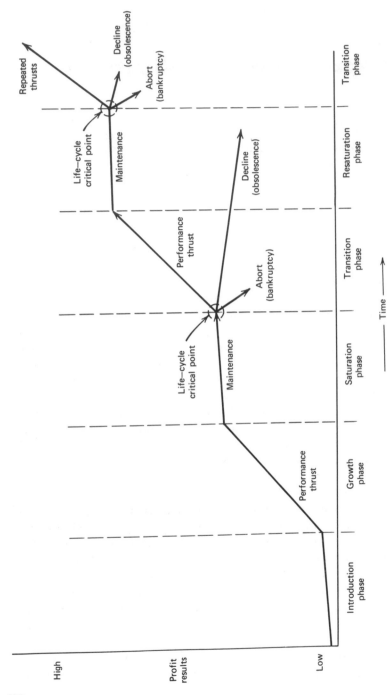

Figure 9-1. Improvement requires repeated thrusts in performance.

(3) costs, (4) management time, (5) communications, (6) methods, and (7) training.

PROFIT IMPROVEMENT[2]

Successful managers hit profit targets more often than their unsuccessful colleagues because they plan their profits and keep their operations and activities pointed in that direction. They never lose sight of their prime objective—to finish the year with a profit. They recognize that profits do not just happen; they are caused. Profit improvement is establishing profit objectives in a profit plan and organizing all efforts to reach these objectives. The objective-setting processes of the strategy of managing by objectives make the planning and organizing for profit systematic and deliberate. The following are four ways to improve profits:

1. Increase sales volume
2. Increase price margin
3. Reduce capital investments
4. Reduce costs of operating

The profit improvement plan should be organized around these four major objectives rather than, as traditionally, around company functions. The 5-year profit plan described in an earlier chapter is a progressive forecast and connects both long-range and short-range targets. The progressive forecast was described in Chapter 3. Each part of the plan includes a forecast, objectives, means for reaching the objectives, and provisions for making adjustments when changes occur. The annual profit plan contributes to the long-term future of the enterprise as the individual manager's objectives contribute to the company's annual plan. The future commitment of a firm is balanced with a present need, and the company meets that need in the light of its future commitment. An outline of the more important aspects of an annual profit improvement plan is given in Table 9-1.

A profit plan is an active, viable strategy for obtaining profits with contributions from all segments of the organization. When sales and profits are below the expected level in a fiscal period, an intense effort is organized to make up for these losses in the succeeding period. Measuring, correcting, improving, and ultimately achieving are the essence of the profit plan. A company must experience profit since it is only through profits that incentives, benefits, equipment, services, and growth can be obtained. Failure to make a profit starts a set of reactions that eventually cause failure of the enterprise. A profit and loss (P. & L.) statement is a

TABLE 9-1   ANYONE'S COMPANY: PROFIT PLAN, 19XX

A. Profit objective
   1. Total capital to be used
   2. Return-on-investment objective after taxes
   3. Profit objective for 19XX

B. Sales improvement
   1. Marketing forecast, planning, and strategy
   2. Requirements and alternatives for sales volume
   3. Sales volume objective contributed by:
      (a) Sales and contracts feeder-objective plan
      (b) Engineering feeder-objective plan
      (c) Research feeder-objective plan
      (d) Public relations feeder-objective plan
      (e) Quality control feeder-objective plan

C. Price margin improvement
   1. Competitive analysis, pricing review, and discounting practices
   2. Requirements and alternatives for percentage of market share
   3. Price margin objective contributed by:
      (a) Sales feeder-objective plan
      (b) Finance feeder-objective plan
      (c) Production feeder-objective plan
      (d) Accounting feeder-objective plan
      (e) Legal feeder-objective plan

D. Capital investment improvement
   1. Facilities analysis, cash flow, equipment utilization
   2. Requirements and alternatives for capital additions
   3. Capital improvement objective contributed by:
      (a) Production feeder-objective plan
      (b) Finance feeder-objective plan
      (c) Accounting feeder-objective plan
      (d) Research feeder-objective plan
      (e) Legal feeder-objective plan

E. Cost improvement
   1. Cost effectiveness, cost control, cost avoidance
   2. Requirements and alternatives for cost reduction
   3. Cost improvement objective contributed by:
      (a) Production feeder-objective plan
      (b) Purchasing feeder-objective plan
      (c) Quality control feeder-objective plan
      (d) Personnel feeder-objective plan
      (e) Accounting feeder-objective plan

F. Changes in annual profit plan
   1. Authority for initiating and approving changes
   2. Procedure for effecting changes

vital indicator of the health and position of the enterprise. The statement not only pinpoints the profit and loss for each product line as well as for the entire operation; it also breaks down profit and loss on each item for the current period as well as cumulatively to date. Comparing the P. & L. statement with those of other periods and other companies provides a form of measurement to determine the action necessary to handle variances. The P. & L. statement offers a way to discover trends. From a single month's profit picture of what has happened and what is likely to happen should emerge certain trends. Thus a downward trend can be controlled and redirected before it gets out of hand. Records of sales and costs over past months and years can provide a useful measure for making improvement forecasts for coming months and years. This was described earlier in the discussion of improvement forecasts. The most reliable and meaningful way to predict the future is to extrapolate the past.

Profit squeezes suggest pressures from many directions. The customer presses for lower prices. The employees demand higher wages. Vendors and suppliers cut into company profits through the high costs of their materials. And last but not least are the high costs of overhead, benefits, services, and facilities. These opposing pressures have escalated profit shrinkage. An active management must oppose these pressures with an equal force to hold overhead down, stop profit leaks, protect profit margins, and grant wages only when there is a proportional increase in productivity. Profit improvement must focus on two general areas: generating sales and regulating costs for meeting these sales. Instead of trusting to luck and happenstance, the practitioner must concentrate his limited resources and facilities on improving his sales volume while simultaneously decreasing his costs. Profit is the difference between total sales and total costs. The practitioner must strive each year to get a larger and larger difference between the two. He must reach for higher sales volume at lower cost. He sets objectives and plans accordingly to get a percentage increase in sales volume from the previous year. Similarly, he sets objectives and plans accordingly to reduce his operating costs by getting a percentage decrease in operating costs from the previous year. If a practitioner has not systematically, deliberately, and skillfully planned his targets for profit, total sales, and total costs, then it is not likely that he has done the planning necessary for the work, services, manpower, methods, and schedules to reach these targets. It is useful to organize one's thinking about profit improvements in a logical form. Comparisons made from year to year yield a profit improvement analysis, as illustrated in Figure 9-2. Profit planning is sensing the rates of increase and decrease that may be occurring in a trend. Trend effects are a guide to the percentage amounts to include in improvement objectives. There is

Comparing Fiscal Years

Objectives	19__	% Change	19__	% Change	19__	% Change	19__	% Change
Sales volume								
Returns & allowances								
Cash discounts								
Net sales								
Total costs								
Direct labor								
Direct material								
Overhead								
Taxes								
Profit amount								
Profit percentage								
Return on net worth								

Figure 9-2. Trend analysis for profit improvement.

always a certain amount of risk inherent in setting future targets. A feel for changes over the years, months, or weeks helps minimize the risks one should take. It builds confidence that the objectives set for the coming period will be reached. For example, a profile trend of how payroll is increasing or decreasing in relation to total sales helps the practitioner intuit the percentage level that should be targeted for the next period. Or he might make his judgment on the basis of an examination of the total number of payroll hours worked by all employees against total sales. To the practitioner, the foremost question should be, How does the most recent fiscal period compare with the period before and the period before that?

In summary, profit improvement begins by targeting percentage increases in sales volume and price margin and percentage decreases in capital outlay and operating costs. A strategy is set up that involves all members of the enterprise and focuses their activities, efforts, and resources to these ends. Through the performance and implementation stages, the targets that must be hit are never lost sight of, and day-to-day operations are pointed in that direction. The objective network concept described in an earlier chapter not only structures the involvement and contributions but suggests the alignment and orientation that must be maintained, as illustrated in Figure 9-3.

SALES IMPROVEMENT[3]

Sales improvement planning is nothing more than planning to increase the number of customer orders, size of orders, and frequency of repeat orders. To effect sales improvement, there must be a deliberate and systematic marketing strategy. A managing by objectives practitioner trying to get sales improvement using the M.B.O. approach must know where he has been, where he is going, and how the marketing effort relates to the total organization. With this strategy, he sets his sales volume targets, validates them, organizes his work packages, and proceeds to implement them. If he runs into problems, he has contingencies, information, and experience to reformulate a new plan to enable him to move ahead, even if at a slower pace.

The amount of gross sales in any business is a chief indicator of the health and growth of the business. Costs are important and so is cash position, but sales volume is a measure of the number of customers coming to the enterprise or the amount of customer satisfaction given by the enterprise. To examine sales volume with regard to level, amount, and rate is to examine the number of customers, the amount of their pur-

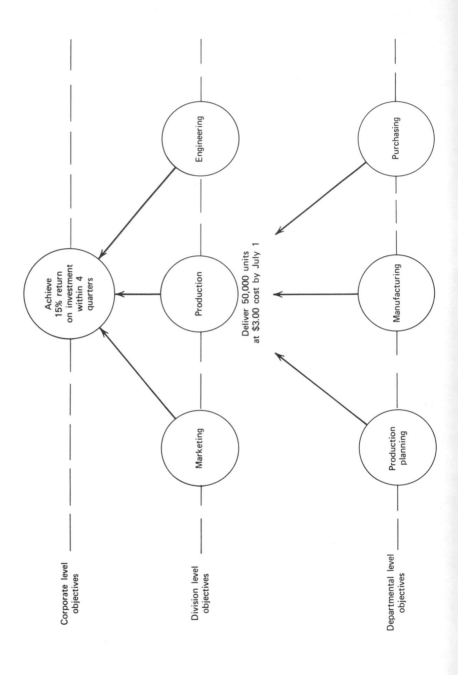

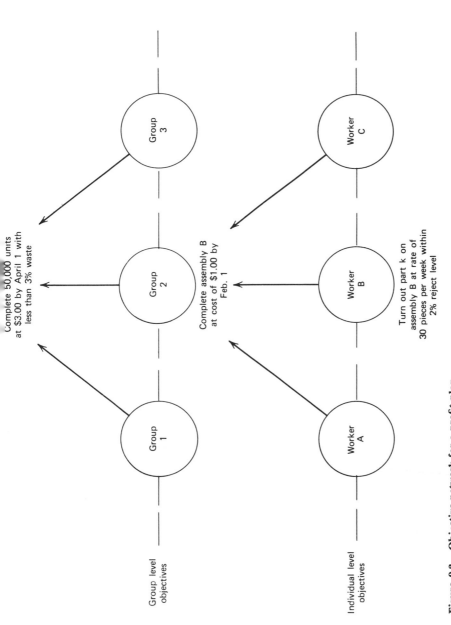

Figure 9-3. Objective network for a profit plan.

chases, and the frequency of their purchases. Sales improvement is another way of saying that the company plans to increase the number of customers, the size of orders, and the frequency of orders placed with the firm. With this in mind, the M.B.O. practitioner needs to focus on customer needs and wants. He needs to understand how these needs change and what competitors offer. A *company that has its sales effort highly centered around customers is a company properly directed toward sales improvement*. This seems to be a simple and naive statement. The fact is that companies give only lip service to the principle of customer orientation. Robert Ferrell develops the basic necessity for customer orientation fully and clearly in the following statement:

> Customer orientation should be a way of business life—a state of being common to the business as a whole. Customer orientation is the awareness of and the fullfilment of the concept that a business enterprises' profitable growth depends upon its future ability to serve selected customer needs rather than sell particular products or services.[4]

The function of marketing planning includes activities and processes for generating strategies through which to achieve the objectives of creating new markets or enlarging existing markets. A major difficulty in developing these marketing plans lies in laying cohesive plans of action throughout the entire enterprise. Preoccupation with obtaining this cohesiveness often inhibits the plan's polarization toward customers. The following are some guidelines for getting sales improvements through customer orientation.

1. *Treat customers as investment.* All businesses have made moves in the way of capital investment. Equipment, facilities, land, materials, furniture, inventory, trained workers, and leasing have been set up for serving the needs of customers. The fact remains that investment does not stop here. It goes right to the customers themselves.

Customers themselves represent assets built up over time if a company regards them as investments.

Orientation toward customers means the following:

(a) Customers represent valuable investments of money, time, effort, and care and should be treated as more valuable than equipment, furniture, and materials.

(b) Customers are the ultimate investments of a company, thereby making them the most valuable. All other forms of investments are in-process steps to this ultimate point.

(c) Customers should be considered in the long run as well as in the short run. In servicing a customer, the service should be considered as a deposit for a continued and repeated return in the future.

(d) Repeat orders from customers can be viewed as a variable, that is, they can reorder many or few times or can buy very much or very little. What the customer does depends directly on his degree of satisfaction with previous orders filled.

(e) Since customers are assets, depreciation, obsolescence, and deterioration are factors a company must guard against. The principal tools the practitioner has are customer satisfaction and competitive edge. Competitive edge was described earlier as the customer favor one company enjoys that its competitors do not.

2. Develop a customer-oriented company. The conflict between cost and price continues. Under our form of economy it will always continue. Does this mean that the only way we can attract and hold customers is with low prices and low costs? The answer is an emphatic no. Obviously, prices are most important and should be kept competitive. There are, however, other approaches to get and hold customers. One such technique is called *sales sensitivity and customer treatment.* Sales sensitivity requires that all employees of an enterprise be sensitive to the importance and value of a customer and conduct themselves accordingly. Employees behave and perform their normal duties in such a way as to elicit customer satisfaction; they project a quality image that affects sales favorably. According to this concept, the waitress in a restaurant is first a saleswoman and then a waitress. The guard in a bank is first a salesman and then a security officer. The telephone operator is first a saleswoman and then an operator. Sales sensitivity is the awareness by all employees that their actions and performance in a company have a great influence on what, how, or when a customer will buy. Everyone in the enterprise is a salesman selling the company in some way. They take the attitude that the customer is important in the enterprise and they do whatever possible to please him. Company response to his order should serve to meet his expectation.

3. Use customer improvement planning. As cited earlier, sales improvement planning is nothing more than planning to increase the number of customers and the frequency of their orders. There must be a plan. The first step toward this plan is to set sales improvement quotas or objectives in terms of customers. An evaluation and review of past and present performance form the basis for the sales volume improvement to be achieved. These measures or guideposts help in appraising progress as plans are implemented. They indicate where deficiencies occur and where opportunity exists. These measures are incorporated in the sales im-

Customer-oriented Plan

Sales Improvement Objectives	Last Year	This Year	First Year of Plan		Second Year of Plan	
			Amount	% Improvement	Amount	% Improvement
Total sales volume in market Sales volume by districts Sales volume by products Sales volume by customers						
Total customers in market Customers by districts Customers by products Customers by sales						

Company's share of market
Percentage sales volume
Percentage customers
Customers per product
Customers per district
Customers per buyer category
Customers per salesmen
Customer profit ratio
Customer turnover per
   district
   product
   salesmen						

Figure 9-4. Customer-oriented sales improvement planning.

provement chart illustrated in Figure 9-4. Customer orientation is an approach taken by an enterprise based on the awareness that profitable growth and improved sales volume depend on the ability to serve customer needs and wants rather than on selling particular products or services. It begins with knowledge of what these needs are proceeds by orienting, developing, and utilizing the resources of the firm to serve these needs. Therefore sales improvement objectives should be specified in the following areas:

(a) Increase competitive edge
(b) Open new territories and broaden customer base
(c) Increase depth of market penetration
(d) Focus and concentrate on sales increase of key accounts
(e) Increase market occupancy factor
(f) Reduce misdirected and wasteful advertising
(g) Increase service to meet or better customer expectations
(h) Reduce quality or price to fit market demands
(i) Increase inquiries through product awareness strategies
(j) Increase service time to meet discretionary buying power
(k) Increase market segmentation where indicated
(l) Make greater number of specific proposals to potential key accounts

(m) Reduce interest-arousing effort in favor of increased contact-making effort

(n) Maintain present level of customers to assure reorders

4. *Sales improvement checklist*

(a) Have you evaluated your situation to find areas for sales improvement?

(b) What is the percentage of depth of market penetration?

(c) What is the number of total potential customers in the market?

(d) Are you competitive in your area with respect to price?

(e) Are you competitive in your area with respect to type, quality, and delivery of service or products?

(f) Are your sales (customers) increasing? decreasing? leveling?

(g) Do you need new services or products to increase sales?

(h) Have you established a plan with objectives for sales improvement?

(i) Where are your greatest sales and customer opportunities?

(j) Do you have an on-going sales improvement training program?

(k) Why do customers buy from you rather than from your competitors?

(l) Why do customers buy from your competitors rather than from you?

(m) How effective are your promotion and advertising?

(n) Do you feel promotions are giving you the depth of penetration you need?

(o) Are you using the right media for reaching customers?

(p) Is your promotional budget related to objectives for improving sales volume?

(q) Do you coordinate promotion outside the enterprise with sales sensitivity within the enterprise?

(r) Do you treat customers as an investment for repeat visitations and orders?

(s) Is the service rendered equal to or greater than customer expectations?

(t) Are production and distribution facilities geared to meet the demand resulting from promotional efforts?

(u) Is there a follow-up procedure for handling inquiries?

(v) Is there a sufficient intensity of persistence in follow-up work?

(w) What is the competitive edge of products and services?

(x) Is the sales staff trained in time-saving techniques and work planning for sales results?

(y) Are product and sales promotions realigned to meet changing market and economic conditions?

(z) Have all sources been utilized for suggesting sales leads?

COST IMPROVEMENT

Profit improvement is the focal point for the practitioner of managing by objectives. The greatest contribution toward this improvement lies in cost control and reduction. To be organized around a profit center, as Staley[5] puts it, is to be organized around cost centers, their identification, control, and reduction. This effort is not just a directive, an order, or a program; it is more nearly a way of life, an attitude. Its core is acceptance of the idea that whatever a firm does to establish quality, service, and efficient operations, it does with minimal costs. This attitude is often ignored because costs are usually thought of in terms of figures and accountants. Costs are primarily a matter of people. *Every move an employee makes has an effect on costs!* It is people who generate and control costs. Consequently, the practitioner cannot afford to overlook his greatest prospect for keeping costs down: the way he deals directly with his employees and the way his employees do their work.

Cost reduction and cost control have always been important, but today, in the face of rising prices, spiraling costs, profit squeezes, and lower productivity, they are more important than ever. The days of automatic price increases to recover costs are gone. A seller's market has for some time been a buyer's market. However, discount practices, growing competition, and expanding franchise chains have become so entrenched that the only solution to rising costs is not increasing prices but planning and organizing activities and efforts aimed at accomplishing reduction and control of costs. Inflation is the rule today, rather than the exception, and the pressure it exerts on company profits is obvious. When revenues remain steady or decline while costs escalate, profits are squeezed out. It appears that the prevailing world-wide inflation trend is here to stay for some time to come. Substantial increases in wage payments are expected to keep pushing prices up since labor is being affected by the rising cost of living. Overcompetition or even wasteful competition has created tight markets in which price margins are very narrow. It is not unusual for companies to become desperate to salvage what they can in order to present to their boards of directors a respectable profit year. These companies have not paid close attention to keeping operating costs at rock-bottom levels. Cost-cutting slashes may indicate a failure to meet long- or short-range targets. It may also mean lack of a consistent cost control program or failure to keep cost management as a way of business life.

Cost improvement is an on-going significant function of the practitioner of managing by objectives. It implies that cost improvement is deliberate, systematic, and planned with year-in and year-out consistency. Cost-cutting and last-ditch slashing by panicked management are desperate one-shot cost improvement attempts made because of a lack of foresight and planning. Cost improvement is planning cost control into the job itself.[6] The cost-cutting pattern is built into the work plan in such a way that the practitioner controls and reduces costs as he moves about completing the technical and functional aspects of his job. Cost improvement is natural to managing by objectives since the strategy's focus capability can lend the cost effort a precision, concentration, and direction not normally offered by other managerial strategies. Cost improvement with the management by objectives approach becomes an organized method to improve cost management systematically in the following areas:

1. *Cost avoidance.* The removal or elimination of a cost item anticipated and budgeted but not expended.

2. *Cost variability.* The use of cost standards to provide guidelines for keeping and holding cost performance to maximum levels.

3. *Cost reduction.* The performance of work in such an efficient way as to keep the incurred costs under and below the allowable standards.

4. *Cost effectiveness.* The expenditure of funds not budgeted or anticipated which, when incurred, reduces considerable costs in other areas.

Managing by objectives is a useful tool with which practitioners can cope with and improve their cost management ability in each of the four areas cited above. Cost improvement is a series of targeted objectives designed to effect a favorable change for an enterprise. The following are some areas in which a practitioner can set objectives for cost improvement.

1. *Labor use improvement.* The use of labor is a cost in itself but, more significantly, it also influences the total cost picture greatly. The practitioner would do well to begin his improvement by using his employees to better advantage. Productivity is the term used for measuring the output of an employee toward meeting performance standards while minimizing the resources consumed in the process. Obviously, any increase in the productivity of substandard performers will raise the average productivity of the entire group or department. Unquestionably, it is better to improve the productivity of substandard performers than to raise the productivity of those who are already meeting the standard. Improving substandard performers starts at the time of hiring and placement. Careful selection, screening, and orientation of new employ-

ees begins the process of better labor use. This is where the proper attitude toward costs should begin to be instilled in the employee. The practitioner must accept the idea that employees should be trained not only to meet a job performance standard wherever they are assigned, but also to meet it at lower cost and on time. Most employees at the time of hire are not cost conscious. Therefore, the practitioner must make them cost conscious through training and retraining. This is not a one-shot operation. He starts at the time he hires them to tell them about his costs concerns. And he must proceed continually with his efforts, which often include daily coaching, urging, and helping toward this end.

Motivation for cost reduction is a little like taking vitamins. Once in a while the illness requires a massive dose, but usually the effectiveness in the cure is the systematic planning and day-to-day taking of the pills.

P. Einstein Mali

The practitioner must train and coach employees to do the job on time, to use the right amount of materials, and to avoid waste in the process.

2. *Repeat work improvement.* To repeat an entire work activity is to double labor costs. Every time a recycling of work occurs because of human error, labor costs automatically go up proportionately. Material costs also double. There are six basic sources of human error that cause repeat work, and they can be controlled: carelessness, indifference, ignorance, incompetence, confusion, and pressure. The following are guidelines to overcoming these sources of human error.

(a) Errors committed must be fed back to the individual so that he knows he has committed the error.

(b) Indicate cost of error to the individual in addition to giving him correctional instruction.

(c) Original training may never have taken hold. Provide retraining.

(d) Get people to focus attention on details. Generally speaking, humans commit these errors because of their inattention to details. When an employee sees that the boss expects attention to detail, he will strive for it. The boss should set a good example.

(e) Watch and evaluate attitudes at the time of hire. Look for indications of sloppiness or carelessness, such as poor appearance and tardiness in keeping appointments. A person will reflect on the job what he is in his personal life.

3. *Waste prevention and reduction.* The best way to avoid waste of materials, tools, and man-hours is to prevent waste from occurring in the first place. Wasted material, idle people, and broken equipment are fundamentally caused by sloppy or imprecise planning. They are the results of the failure to anticipate with greater exactness what is needed and the failure to have a contingency plan to handle the overruns or overages. Waste prevention and control are not accomplished in one shot. They must be dealt with as a continuing day-to-day task within the work itself. Consider and use the following improvement guidelines:

(a) Reduce idle time during slack periods. Develop a checklist of extra work with priorities and set down in advance who will do what.

(b) Practice and encourage conservation of resources such as water, lights, cutting oils, paper, tools, and pencils.

(c) Establish waste prevention and elimination projects. Schedule these projects and assign members of the group to implement them.

(d) Reclaim scrap that can be reused. The reclamation process can be a valuable source of savings provided the cost of reclamation is below the cost of new material.

(e) Plan for greatest material utilization possible. Design a contingency scheme to carry out when all materials are not utilized.

4. Reduced stealing and pilfering. Statistical research[7] has shown that out of every three people who work for companies, one will never steal, a second will always steal every chance he can get, and a third will steal if the opportunity arises and he feels he can get away with it. Thus two out of every three employees are potential problems in security. American industry pays 6.5 percent of their gross sales in pilferage annually. The practitioner must accept the fact that internal security is an absolute must. A person's reasons for stealing from his company vary from a need to support extravagant living or pay unforeseen expenses to a feeling that he must make up for insufficient compensation by the company. The practitioner must set up a system of internal checks that will stop this practice. For this purpose, he may use the following guidelines:

(a) Treat the cash register and the handling of cash with greater respect. Follow an operating manual's procedure for cash control, deposits, tapes, safe control, and reports.

(b) Set up a system of spread control where one person checks the work, deposits, inventory, and so forth, of another.

(c) Keep accurate records as described in operating manuals. Money or stock should be checked by a senior employee.

(d) Practice the surprise audit and be sure everyone knows it. Plan frequent surprise audits of various critical areas where opportunity for defalcation may be high. A changing schedule of surprise audits will keep the potential thief in line.

(e) Leaks of cash, costs, supplies, materials, and tools can be identified by looking at recorded percentages. The more locked doors, the less leakage.

5. Overhead improvement. Overhead costs in most companies, if not in all, are usually too high. The excessive load of overhead costs can determine the make-or-break point for a company. Parkinson[8] in his famous observation of the elasticity of work shows mathematically that the number of overhead staff people will increase each year between 5.17 percent and 6.56 percent, irrespective of any variation in the amount of work to be done. Basic to overhead improvement is overhead control as a percentage of material and labor. There will always be a proportion of fixed expenses that are not avoidable. The practitioner, however, sets a target to maintain or reduce the following overhead expenses on a percentage basis:

(a) Staff departments
(b) Maintenance and repair of equipment, tools, and buildings
(c) Telephone, telegram, and TWX expense
(d) Office equipment and supplies
(e) Employee benefits and indirect compensation
(f) Paper procedures and records retention
(g) Utilities and resources
(h) Data processing and electronic computers
(i) Personnel processing procedures
(j) Communications media and newspapers
(k) Unused space and housekeeping

6. Cost-reduction practices for the M.B.O. practitioner

(1) Plan to keep workers productive between jobs.
(2) Give instructions and orders clearly and understandably.
(3) Provide a full day's work for each employee.
(4) Understand and know operating procedures.
(5) Keep tools and equipment in their proper places.
(6) Avoid overtime.
(7) Do not allow workers to do less than they can.
(8) Get from workers advance notice of termination.
(9) Notify early call-in resources when personnel are needed.
(10) Write records, requisitions, and orders accurately.
(11) Do not allow workers to get the habit of talking, visiting, and killing time.
(12) Get workers started on time.
(13) Do not delay in making decisions.
(14) Investigate immediately when repairs are needed.

(15) Avoid unnecessary visiting and conversations on the job.

(16) Organize yourself in both time and work.

(17) Inadequate training and managing indicate the following conditions:

    (a) New workers not thoroughly instructed.

    (b) Old workers not instructed on new work.

    (c) Failure to follow through with corrections.

(18) Explain the money value of tools, material, and supplies and the costs of waste.

(19) Watch worker's eyesight and health as possible causes of spoiled work

(20) Discourage carelessness and off-quality work.

(21) Do not take a worker's ability for granted. Make sure he can do the job.

(22) Listen to what workers are trying to say.

(23) Encourage workers to offer suggestions.

(24) Ask advice and opinions of workers on mutual problems.

(25) Study business methods for efficiency.

(26) Get from new employees helpful ideas that they may bring from previous employment.

(27) Take an interest in the troublesome areas of the unit.

(28) Guard against failure to control turnover of capable workers because of the following:

    (a) Not appreciating the direct and indirect costs of labor turnover.

    (b) Too much "bossing" and not enough intelligent direction.

    (c) Too strict or too lax enforcement of discipline.

    (d) Not keeping promises that could be kept.

    (e) Making promises that cannot be kept in regard to wages, promotion, and so on.

    (f) Discharging employees without sufficient cause; improper use of the discharge slip as a penalty.

    (g) Keeping a worker on a job for which he has a violent dislike.

(29) Know the right kind of supplies to order.

(30) Do not order more materials and supplies than necessary.

(31) See that materials and supplies are stored properly.

(32) Inspect equipment, machinery, and tools to keep them in good working condition.

(33) Protect idle equipment from heat, dust, or dirt.

(34) Provide instruction on the proper use of equipment.

(35) Do not abuse small equipment by using it for large work.

(36) Avoid treating one person better or worse than others, that is, avoid favorites.

(37) Never take sides in workers' arguments.

(38) Never criticize one worker to another.

(39) Always question employees who leave of their own accord.

(40) Be sure to interpret management's real aims and policies correctly to workers.

(41) Do all you can to adjust wages and working conditions fairly.

(42) Receive new workers in a kindly, helpful manner.

(43) Provide complete job instruction for new workers.

(44) Impress upon new workers the necessity for a full day's work and what it consists of.

(45) Be sure to select new employees with proper qualifications for the work to be done.

(46) Avoid showing impatience with new employees who learn slowly.

(47) Get other workers to show a friendly, helpful attitude to new employees.

(48) Be sure to contact a new worker as often as may be required.

(49) Inform new worker as to conditions and regulations, such as those safety, pay days, lavatories, drinking water, lockers, and washrooms.

(50) Inform the new worker about unpleasant or dangerous parts of his work.

(51) Commend employees for doing good work.

(52) Explain as much about the work as possible in order to make it interesting.

(53) Show interest in workers' progress and personal affairs.

(54) Be ready to admit a mistake to a worker.

(55) Pay attention to a worker's ability and temperament in assigning work to him.

(56) Study employees as individuals in order to get their best efforts.

(57) Do not approve the formation of cliques or groups among workers.

(58) Do not rate employees on any grounds but competence; avoid such grounds as race and religion.

(59) Do not keep an employee in a job for which he is physically or mentally unsuited.

(60) Do not permit an employee to remain at work when he is sick.

(61) Give employees all the help they need.

(62) Always promote workers when it is possible and advisable.

(63) Give due consideration to problems affecting wages and working conditions.

(64) Cooperate with other workers and departments as well as with customers.

(65) Understand company policies thoroughly and explain them to workers.

(66) Deal sensibly with gossip and tale-bearing.

(67) Never pass the buck to other workers.

(68) Be sure to represent the workers adequately to management.

(69) Do not permit disgruntled employees to agitate against the company.

(70) Give full support to unpopular company regulations.

(71) Promote friendliness and cooperation among workers.

(72) Avoid thoughtless criticism of any company policy or of any individual in the organization.

(73) Cooperate wholeheartedly with top management.

MANAGEMENT TIME IMPROVEMENT[9]

Probably, the most basic mistake management people everywhere make about time is in thinking of time as having a single dimension and a single value—hours. Time to many is only a procession of hours and minutes measured by the clock or the stream of days marked off by the calendar. It is more than this. Time has three dimensions and these dimensions are interrelated. As Updegraff stated, "Time has three dimensions— hours, energy, and money. If we waste one we waste others. If we use one wisely, we enhance the value of the others."[10]

1. *Time is hours.* The clock or the calendar gives us a sense of progression, sequence, and pace. It is rhythmic, consistent, reliable, and never-ending. It stops for no one. One cannot delay it or hasten it. One cannot buy it or give it away. One can only collect its output and adjust to it. *Hence, since time yields to no one, we can use it only to gauge and pace our activities. Since we cannot delay the clock, we must play the clock.*

2. *Time is energy.* Time has use value. Since time is rhythmic and a pacesetter, it can coerce individuals to work at an energy production level based on some expected time point. In other words, time can release stored energy within the individual through creating tension about completing a work assignment within a time interval. Setting a schedule and working toward it produce a tension that releases more and more

energy as we drive toward a due date. Of course, this assumes a commitment to a due date. Since tension time or scheduled time can release far more energy than normal, *an M.B.O. practitioner should go into the scheduling business. Play the clock and get greater use value.*

3. *Time is money.* Time costs money. We know this because we have made long-term commitments such as weekly wages, annual vacations, and long-term leases. Whether we do much or little, we must pay for these fixed costs. Additionally, time costs money in terms of lost sales, lost customers, lost opportunities, wasted materials, and lost trained and skilled employees. When we invest our efforts, resources, and energies in facilities and people, unless we get an expected rate of return within a time interval, time has cost us money. The time is now to do what we have to do. The pacesetting nature of time is the same whether we accomplish or not. If we do, we get our money's worth. *If we do not, time has cost us money. Play the clock. Every tick is a drain in operations.*

Time Robbers

We often think that time robbers are external to us and that we have little control over them. Careful analysis will show, however, that basically we steal our own time. We allow and engage in activities without regard to managing time. Following is a list of time robbers that, if stopped, can release more time, energy, and money into an operation.

1. *Job poorly completed.* A job done in haste and so carelessly that it must be done over is a monstrous thief of time. Inefficiency probably ranks first among all time robbers. If a job must be done over, the time required for its completion is doubled. Working fast is never the answer if it results in rework. *Work accurately and completely first. Work speedily second.* To do it right the first time is the first rule for time improvement.

2. *Work not completed.* The necessity of retracing footsteps or re-working something previously begun but not completed has a magnitude of time waste that affects everyone. Review of the records, restudy of the same material, and reanalysis of what has been analyzed are time robbers. The managing by objectives practitioner knows that procrastination can set up a backlog that costs heavily in money. *When work is started, finish it. Do it now!*

3. *Delayed decisions.* Failure to make timely decisions can result in significant long-run waste of effort and loss of time. Making decisions requires a sense of timing. Early decisions can cause some difficulty, but

it is well known that delayed decisions can provide serious time-robbing opportunities. Prompt action, when action is needed, often provides the right risk of time for getting results.

4. *Tranquility and contentment.* There is a notion that tension and quickened pace should be avoided wherever possible, a notion that if tension exists, the organization should be viewed with alarm. This notion has now been discarded, since successful enterprises are those whose managers and executives find tension a way to release energy to get things done. It is the tranquil and contented organization that is alarming. Intelligent dissatisfaction with one's own result and quickening the pace to get things done is harnessing the use value of time. Positive tension, that which avoids stress and distress, is not only acceptable but also desirable. Many managers admit to working better under pressure. Tension, understood and utilized, can be a very constructive factor in effectiveness. Setting objectives and a schedule for their accomplishment is placing the organization under a productive tension.

5. *The excessive communications "orgy."* In response to the great call for more and improved communications, there has been an orgy of excessive communications that have sapped valuable time. Written reports and memoranda too widely distributed, reading material not relevant to the job, correspondence delays, unnecessary outgoing correspondence, and excessively long letters are some of the time robbers contributing to this orgy. Meetings and conferences that ramble for lack of planning are terrific time wasters. Many avoidable meetings are made unavoidable for the purpose of participation and involvement. Subordinates should participate only in those things that directly affect them; otherwise management wastes their time. Conferences and meetings should be planned and prepared. The following are aspects of good conferences:

(a) Held only with persons necessary for the discussion
(b) Agenda and purpose stated and facts ready
(c) Effective conference leadership provided to keep discussion to the point
(d) Responsibility affixed for follow-through

6. *Uncontrolled telephone calls.* The telephone is a devastating time waster when uncontrolled. The manager who has clearly thought through his best procedure for maintaining control of both incoming and outgoing calls is hard to find. Here are some hints:

(a) *Outgoing calls.* Group them. Get them out at one time, as on a production line. Calling others makes it at a time of your choosing. When you say "give me a call," you invite interruptions.

(b) *Incoming calls.* Begin by authorizing your secretary or switchboard operator to screen your calls. Make a list of people to whom you will always speak. List circumstances in which you will always wish to be called. Set up a procedure to determine the name of the caller and the purpose of the call, and establish a system for referral to the appropriate person.

Beyond a doubt, the random ringing of the telephone, uncontrolled, can ruin the best planned day of a manager and drain away his time. This major time waster can cause havoc to an objective strategy for achieving results within a time period.

7. *Casual visitor.* No one is immune to this type of time robber. The casual drop-in visitor may be a fellow manager, a friend, a relative, or an unexpected inquirer. What is your philosophy about such interruptions? They consume time. When an unexpected visitor drops in, it can disrupt an entire day's planning, particularly when there is no time limit set on his visit. The following are possible ways to avoid this:

   (a) Give a friendly word or two suggesting that you get together sometime and indicate that a schedule has been arranged.
   (b) Screen with a secretary or assistant the floaters and drop-ins.
   (c) Close doors if you are in an office.
   (d) Continue your work while the visitor is there. He will get the hint.

8. *Other time robbers*
   (a) Waiting for people
   (b) Failure to delegate responsibilities
   (c) Mediocre personnel who require training and retraining
   (d) Misplaced items and a poor retrieval system

All of us are subject to time robbers of some sort. Find out which ones sap your use value. Most are deeply rooted in habit and cannot be easily discovered and controlled. Before a unit operator can make better use of his time, he must first find what is draining it.

Ways To Improve the Management of Time

The pressures on the practitioner of managing by objectives and the countless details he must attend to in a practical way to implement his objective program increase daily. It is no longer possible to survive by "flying by the seat of your pants." The practitioner must acquire some time tools if he is to get his planned results. The following are some practical ways to improve.

1. *Discover your time robbers.* The first step in getting more time for yourself is to find out what is stealing your time. Make a checklist of those areas you suspect and carefully evaluate whether any time can be salvaged if they are controlled or eliminated. This evaluation should be carefully set down with a simple time and motion study of your daily activities or a cursory but accurate survey of deviations of planned activities from actual activities. Use a systematic approach to do this, as suggested by the form illustrated in Figure 9-5.

Time Analysis

Name _____ Dept. _____ Date _____

Time Robbers	Expected Time	Actual Time	Wasted Time (Difference)	Corrective Actions	Improved Time
Repeat work					
Incomplete work					
Delayed decisions					
Telephone calls					
Overcommunications					
Drop-in visitors					
Waiting for people					
Failure to delegate					
Family interruptions					
Retraining					
Misplaced items					
Poor retrieval system					
Coffee breaks					
Reading					
etc.					
etc.					

Total time wasted _____   Total time improved _____

Figure 9-5. Time analysis for improving management time.

2. *Play the daily clock schedule.* Set a schedule for yourself in daily activities. When you come to your place of work, take 5 minutes to write down what you intend to accomplish during the day. This is managing by objectives in miniature. Do not play it by ear. If you do, you will get only half as far as you want to get. Writing down a schedule forces you to set a timetable for yourself. At the end of the day you will be able to say to yourself, "I accomplished what I was after today." Additionally, this method sets up the productive tension that releases the vital energy to derive use value from time. In writing down your intended accomplishments, compress your time—make it count. Force yourself to do larger projects in shorter periods of time. Tackle the tough problems first thing in the morning, when you are fresh and can think clearly. Do not save the tough problems until the end of the day. Your mind simply will not work as clearly and you will be apt to put difficulties off until another time. A problem never gets easier to solve by waiting. It becomes a time robber. If you take on the tough problems in the morning, you will get the work out more quickly and more effectively than if you wait until the end of the day.

Use the scheduling tools developed in the status reporting phase of your objective program. Scheduling of employees takes time and effort if maximum results are to be expected from each dollar expended. Each scheduling guide must always be adjusted to assure that a minimum crew is working during slow times and an adequate crew during the busiest hours. Analyze your work commitments and schedules.

Keep a record of your scheduling in the past and determine where improvements can be made. Just because a schedule has been used does not mean it cannot be improved upon. Work on maximizing results from your existing schedules.

3. *Set priorities and delegate trivia.* In listing the problems you must tackle, set up a system that separates the critical items you must do from the trivia that others can do. Do not dilute your effort with trivia. A practitioner can avoid diluting his effort, time, and resources by focusing all his concentration on the critical day-to-day activities that meet his daily, weekly, or annual objective plan. He avoids the trivia, which only sap his resources. He organizes his activities to meet his profit plan. For example, some managers spend many hours scheduling employees only to find in the end that the payroll is too high. Instead of trying to fit the schedule to the employees, the manager should attempt to fit the employees to the schedule. He can do this as follows:

(a) Set sales quota.

(b) Establish a payroll budget as a percentage of the sales quota.

(c) Set up a realistic master schedule, using hourly readings as a guide, to meet the payroll budget.

(d) Plan employee staffing to meet the predetermined master schedule.

(e) Stick to the schedule as closely as you can. Overruns must be made up with underruns.

Your system of priorities should help you get rid of detail that consumes your time. Force yourself to become organized. For example, all management jobs require a certain amount of record keeping. To many managers, this is not only a chore but a bore. Purchase records, personnel records, and the like are usually set aside to be done later. Usually the manager falls behind and later finds he has an even greater problem as the paper work mounts. If he had forced himself to be organized and had made these a part of a morning priority plan, he would be much happier, make fewer errors, and cooperate easily with those waiting for the information.

Those items that must be done but do not require your personal attention should be delegated completely to someone else. When delegating, give your subordinate the freedom to do things in your name, following your instructions and guidelines, of course. Choose the individual assuming responsibility for delegated work with care.

4. *Other ways to save time*

(a) *Learn to say no.* Get into the habit of using the greatest time-saving word in the English language, the two letter word "no." Do not listen to the trivia, or spend time on irrelevant commitments and unwanted activities that only serve to drain your time.

(b) *Carry on two activities simultaneously.* Wherever possible gain time by doing two things at once. We are already practiced in making time serve a dual purpose. For example, we read the newspaper while eating breakfast; we drive a car while listening to the radio.

(c) *Know when to stop.* Countless hours, days, and weeks are wasted because we pursue a target or execute a plan that is faulty to begin with or elusive or unattainable. Know when to stop going in a direction if you have made an initial mistake and take a different direction.

(d) *Develop retrieval procedures.* Organize your activities, records, and materials in such a way that they can be efficiently retrieved. Organize now for banking information, data, records, materials, equipment, forms, letters, telephone numbers, names, addresses, inventories, supplies, and so on in such a way that *there is no time lost in retrieving what was deposited. Do not store unless you know how to retrieve quickly.*

(e) *Listening to a great time saver.* Much time is spent, resources are wasted, and employees are lost because a manager has failed to listen to what really happened. Develop your listening skills so that you are alert for factors that affect the operation of a unit. Listen for relevant and pertinent details. You will avoid later rethinking, redigging, and reworking.

Can a practitioner of managing by objectives master time and make it his servant? Sometimes! But he gets greater and greater control over time as he becomes more and more skillful in pinpointing results to be accomplished on a time spectrum. He comes to realize the importance of daily accomplishments as contributions to the larger and more significant programs that affect the enterprise.

COMMUNICATIONS IMPROVEMENT

Ever since the Tower of Babel, man has been struggling with a confusion of languages. And, unfortunately, the confusion remains even where everyone speaks the same language.

Recently, the processes of human relations have added to the confusion and the difficulty of achieving understanding among people. We have noted that the real problem of communications lies in both language and human relationships. In trying to get ideas across, directives understood, or facts collected, interferences or blocks occur, causing conflicts, confusion, misunderstandings, or serious omissions. Two people must be "tuned in" to each other before they can communicate. The classic example is the manager who wants to talk to his employee about improving his work, only to discover that the employee wants to talk to him to find out when he can get his raise. The face-to-face meeting of these two with their two different sets of expectations seriously disrupts communications.

It is impossible for the practitioner to implement objective programs efficiently and smoothly without communicating effectively.

Meaning of Communications

Communication is the means by which we get other people to understand us. Historically, speaking and writing have only been considered the major ways to communicate. Recently, we have discovered other means that are more significant. The average time,[11] in percentage, devoted to these means by a manager or supervisor in the course of a day is as follows:

1. Listing   32%
2. Body language (Physical gestures)   30%
3. Speaking and telling   21%
4. Reading   11%
5. Writing   6%

How well we listen forms an important basis for communicating. Body language, physical actions, gestures, and behavior communicate to employees without a word being spoken. How well we speak and tell is the crux of communications. Reading and writing, important as they are, play minor roles in the communications process between the M.B.O. practitioner and his staff.

Barriers to Communications[12]

1. *Defensive listening.* When we listen defensively, we do not listen at all. When the other person is speaking, we are taking that time to compose our rebuttal. In other words, we have already decided he is wrong, confused, misinformed, or at least stupid.

Avoid defensive listening. Listen actively for meanings and do not always be thinking how you are going to answer!

2. *Boss consciousness.* Employees tend to tell the boss what he likes to hear: that things are going well. As a consequence, information flowing up through the organization often does not reflect the true state of affairs. A subordinate will sometimes avoid asking for important information because he feels he may be criticized for not knowing already. In somewhat the same fashion, a manager is reluctant to admit to his subordinates that everything is not going well, because it might be seen by them as an admission of weakness.

Develop a climate of confidence so that employees can ask questions, communicate, and give truthful information without being criticized.

3. *Inability to express clearly and concisely.* It is important to use the right word or expression in terms of the receiver of communications. Brevity is also a key consideration. The Gettysburg Address contains 266 words, the Ten Commandments, 297 words, but the government's O.P.S. regulation on pricing contains 26,911 words.

Avoid words or expressions that cannot be understood by the receiver of the communication and be brief.

4. *Feelings of insecurity.* A manager is sometimes unwilling to pass on his skills and technical know-how to others. He feels that he ceases to be important as soon as there are others who can do his job. He feels insecure if his subordinates are as well-informed on some important subject as he is.

Give employees all the information and know-how they need to do their jobs. You will get in return respect, high performance, and a feeling of security.

5. Failure to select the proper medium. There are many ways to communicate with people: face-to-face dialogues; body movements; telephone calls; memos; letters; reports; conferences; posters; visual aids; facial expressions; physical gestures and actions; grapevine; and so on. How well you can convey understanding to your subordinates depends on the method you choose.

Use the medium that will best serve the message and the receiver. Telephone for short, quick exchanges of information. Use face-to-face dialogue for correcting and disciplining, and so on.

6. Preoccupation with other parts of the job. There is poor reception when a supervisor gives an order that an employee has not been conditioned to expect. Subordinates preoccupied with and committed to other tasks are not good receptors.

Get an employee "tuned in" to you before you communicate. If you interrupt a subordinate to tell him something, be sure you first get his attention. Take time to communicate.

7. Inability to remember. The average individual remembers 50 percent of a message directly after receiving it and only 25 percent after 2 weeks. All human beings are "leaky vessels." Recognize the fact that subordinates will forget.

Set up a system of reminders and use repetition to highlight what you want remembered. Do not trust memories; use notes!

8. Listening to the grapevine. One way to get an inkling of what is going on is to listen to the grapevine system that exists among employees. Listen to it but never use it to spread information. The grapevine always exists in the absence of good communications. If your company does not have a grapevine, the chances are that it has good communications. The grapevine usually carries rumors, half-truths, speculations, and outright lies.

Spike rumors and half-truths by giving reliable, timely, and needed information to subordinates.

9. *Misinforming with facts.* Statistics, data, and facts are often used by people to distort, misinform, or oversimplify. Statistics have a mathematical base, hence suggest accuracy and truth. Hanging a sign out stating all meat is "government inspected" does not assure that it is.

Be careful in using facts and data. Avoid poor use of known facts and information.

Improve your Communications Skills

The practitioner's problems of communication are not far-flung. They are related to the many in-house groups and individuals that he needs to implement his objective programs to achieve results. Since these groups are many and varied (Figure 9-6), the practitioner should develop the

Figure 9-6. Practitioner communicates with many groups.

skills to handle them effectively. The practitioner will find that using these skills in his organization will cause definite improvement in the progress toward both long- and short-range objectives.

1. **Tell it right.** The "tell it right" skill ranks high in getting ideas, directives, and information over to people. Following are some practical guidelines to using the skill of telling well:

(a) *Tell enough.* Individuals require information in varying amounts. Under the pressure of time, a manager may forget that there are individual differences in know-how and experience. His tendency is to give one message to everyone. A new worker, however, must be told more than a seasoned, senior worker.

(b) *Tell soon enough.* Do not surprise your subordinates by telling them at the last minute. Foretelling and forethought help reduce resistance to change. Telling in advance helps the subordinate to respond to and to accept what you are trying to say.

(c) *Tell often enough.* New workers must be continually reminded. Older workers must also be reminded because they forget. Constant repetition to new and old workers alike in important matters will eventually pay off.

(d) *Tell everyone concerned.* The often-quoted expression, "Why doesn't anyone tell me?" is very definitely true. Someone was left out. The practitioner must tell all those subordinates who are concerned with the message to be communicated.

(e) *Tell it in the right tone.* The tone of the communication is fully as important as its content. People see and interpret behavior, tone, and facial expressions as well as the content itself. Use tones and body language that fit the content.

(f) *Tell it in writing.* The chance of confusion or failure to remember is minimized when you give your information in writing. There is always a place for verbal orders but there is also a place for written orders.

2. **Listen for meanings.** In the words of Epictetus, "Nature has given men one tongue but two ears that we may hear from others twice as much as we speak." This bit of philosophy suggests that we need to listen more than we tell, since people generally prefer to talk more than to listen. Listening can be developed as a skill with which to collect information about what others are thinking and doing. Listening for meanings means listening beyond words, or listening for intent. You are stuck in a snow bank and a passer-by finds you looking over the situation. "Having trouble?" he asks. If you were listening beyond words, you would hear, "Can I help?" The situation, the person, and the context

should be taken into consideration to discover the underlying meanings of the words uttered. Listening for meanings also means listening for feelings. Communication is face-to-face eye contact with people. The emotional component is bound to be tied up in the message content. Be on the alert to detect feelings and handle them accordingly. An outburst over a small issue may mean that the individual is loaded with emotional dynamite. Be on guard for bad listening habits, such as the following:

(a) *Assuming the communications to be uninteresting.* The good listener is a sifter or a screener, always hunting for something worthwhile that he can store away. People are always trying to say something even though it may seem uninteresting.

(b) *Listening only for facts.* When you listen only for facts, you miss how the facts hang together. When you listen, try to get the gist of it—the main idea.

(c) *Faking attention.* Subordinates may fake attention to their boss when he is telling them something because he is their boss, but actually they are inattentive to the content. The unit operator must get the attention of his receiver first before telling. Usually, a short dialogue is a good means to do this.

(d) *Tolerating distractions.* The two ears of humans are built to receive all sounds, wanted or not. It is the brain that separates, accepts, or rejects. The more there are of these distractive sounds, the more complicated and difficult the separation.

(e) *Evading the difficult.* People tend to avoid tough, technical, and complicated communications. They prefer to listen to the easy, light, simple, and known sources. Break down a difficult communication into easier component parts.

(f) *Using emotional words.* Emotion-laden words throw the listener out of tune with the teller. Use these words carefully and sparingly. Watch out when you are listening to them.

3. *Plan for communications*

(a) *Plan the media you will use.* Telephone calls, written notes, face-to-face dialogues, body language, group conferences, time cards or schedules, memos, statements of policy, posters, and blueprints are some of the many media that can be used. Select the one most appropriate for conveying the message to people so that they will understand. Avoid the grapevine, channel jumping, hearsay, rumors, and gripes. In the absence of planned media, employees will use their own.

(b) *Keep the number of go-betweens to a minimum.* Each person through which a message must pass to get from the teller to the receiver is a layer of insulation carrying the potential to multiply the barriers, blocks, or omissions. Effective communications allows the teller to go directly to the receiver.

(c) *Plan intershift communications.* Two shifts must pull in the same direction if there is to be a smooth transition between the two. Allow shift overlap; managers of both shifts should be on friendly terms; keep shift notes or a log book of items to be done; reserve a time to communicate and do not trust memory.

(d) *Plan what to pass along.* Decide in advance what information to pass along, how will it be passed along, and to whom. Subordinates who must have certain information must be identified in advance.

(e) *Develop the skill of questioning.* Raising good questions at the right time will facilitate communications.

WHY is it necessary?
WHAT is its purpose?
WHERE should it be done?
WHEN should it be done?
WHO is best qualified to do it?
HOW will it be done?

(f) *Watch carefully the giving of orders.* Every person has a zone of acceptance of an order from his supervisor (Figure 9-7). Each individual's zone will vary as to what he will or will not do for his boss.[13] This zone is conditioned by needs, desires, experiences, and relationships. Do not assume that a subordinate will do whatever the supervisor asks.

The zone of acceptance can be enlarged under the following conditions:

1. Subordinate understands order without false implications
2. Subordinate takes positive and constructive view of order
3. Subordinate sees that order consistent with his needs and values
4. Subordinate can physically and mentally carry out order
5. Subordinate sees that order compatible with his interest
6. Subordinate understands order will not violate prior conditions of agreement

(g) *Set up the conditions for easy communications.* A practitioner must create an atmosphere in which a subordinate can and will go to him and

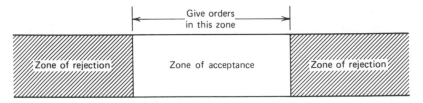

Figure 9-7.   Each subordinate has an order zone of acceptance.

communicate. A subordinate is generally reluctant and will communicate under the following conditions:

1. When it occurs to him
2. When he decides to
3. When the boss has time
4. When the boss will listen
5. When the boss takes action on what was communicated

A climate in which there is free flow of information, ideas, problems, solutions, and so on develops when status and bossism are not obstructions, time and media are available, the prevalent policy is to expect communications, personality factors are not allowed to interfere, and listening is regarded as an important human right.

(h) *Communicate to subordinates in terms of the jobs they occupy.* Know what your employees want from their jobs and give them specific information about the following:

1. What is expected of them and how they measure up to expectation.
2. How their job fits into the business and their chances for advancement.
3. Outlook for the business and prospects for steady work.
4. Policies of the company and how they affect the employee.
5. Background and organization of the company.
6. Reasons for changes in methods or procedures.

4. *Communicate using good human relations*
   (a) Let each person know where he stands. Do not fail to discuss his performance toward objectives with him periodically.
   (b) Give credit where credit is due, that is, give credit commensurate with accomplishments.
   (c) Inform people of changes in advance. Information makes people effective.
   (d) Let others participate in plans and decisions affecting them.
   (e) Gain your associates' confidence. Earn their loyalty and trust.
   (f) If a person's behavior is unusual, find out why. There is always a reason.
   (g) Try to make your wishes known by suggestion or request whenever possible. People generally do not like to be pushed. But do not use innuendo, hint, or implication.
   (h) When you make a mistake, admit it and apologize. Others will resent your blaming someone else.
   (i) Explain the *why* of things that are to be done. Workers do a better job then.
   (j) Know all your workers personally. Find out their interests,

habits, and touchy points and capitalize on your knowledge of them.

(k) Listen to your subordinates' proposals. They have good ideas, too.

(l) Show workers the importance of every job, thus satisfying their need for security.

(m) Criticize constructively. Give reasons for your criticism and suggest ways in which performance can be improved.

(n) Precede criticisms with mention of a man's good points. Show him you are trying to help him.

(o) Do as you would have your people do. The supervisor sets the style.

(p) Be consistent in your actions. Let your workers be in no doubt as to what is expected of them.

(q) Take every opportunity to demonstrate pride in the group. This will bring out the best in them.

(r) If one man gripes, find out his grievance. One man's gripe may be the gripe of many.

(s) Settle every grievance, if at all possible; otherwise, the whole group will be affected.

(t) Set short- and long-range goals by which people can measure their progress.

(u) Back up your workers. Responsibility must be supported by authority.

METHODS IMPROVEMENT[14]

Methods improvement is the systematic study and analysis of existing work methods and procedures by management to discover new or easier ways of accomplishing work. Its greatest benefit lies in improving the firm's operating efficiency or productivity, which is generally measured in output units per time or costs per unit. The interest in methods improvement to gain greater productivity has recently become more pronounced as a result of several causes: increased size and complexity of firms; increased worker specialization; increased work and quality standards; increased influence of government; and increased availability of scientific approaches to productivity. Individual productivity depends upon several factors: intelligence, experience, skills, facilities, methods, time, supervisor, and situation. Here we will be concerned primarily with methods since methods have one of the greatest effects on worker productivity. In an earlier chapter, the performance stretch concept was discussed in some detail. Targeting and getting performance stretches is targeting and getting greater productivity. It is possible with good methods improvement to increase individual productivity from 10 to 20 percent. This increase is obtained through an organized approach to methods improvement. The complexities of modern companies are so great that best results are attained when an organized procedure is set down and teamwork is behind it. Three basic steps are involved: objectives and areas for improvement; investigation and analysis; approval and implementation.

Objectives and Areas for Improvement

The overall objectives of methods improvement are increased productivity and lower operating costs. The degree to which these are met will depend upon successfully meeting the following specific objectives:

1. Reduce handling time of equipment, tools, and materials.
2. Eliminate all unnecessary or nonessential activity.
3. Decrease time completion of an operational activity.
4. Eliminate duplication of effort.
5. Make work safer and less fatiguing.
6. Eliminate waste of time, energy, and materials.
7. Increase deliveries to customer.
8. Decrease clerical and paper work.

These specific objectives of methods improvement parallel objectives sought by management, generally, as described in earlier chapters. These objectives are usually sought in work areas that contain symptoms or indications of the need of action toward improvement. For example, idle time and job delays are productivity robbers. Waiting for materials, tools, and equipment raises the question, Why the wait? Can the existing methods and procedures be altered or changed in some way to reduce the wait? Excessive handling and backtracking are other examples of productivity reduction. The methods analyst attempts to identify flow processes to see if there is smooth flow of material from job to job through the department without backtracking and extra handling. Bottlenecks create another obstacle to productivity improvement. A single element in a series of elements in a job process that delays the whole process can rob the entire department or company of a higher level of productivity. Still another area that suggests productivity improvement are those jobs or situations in which repetitive volume is greatest. A small savings in time, cost, or material on an operation repeated many times a day can amount to large overall savings during the course of the year. High-cost items often indicate obvious areas for which reduction analysis can lead to savings. These high-cost items are not just materials, equipment, or labor rates; they include equipment set-ups, job changeovers, schedule changes, low production speeds, and poor housekeeping.

Most companies are engaged in the effort to improve work. Unfortunately, most of their effort is informal and based on happenstance. Work improvement must be formalized since it requires a series of techniques and procedures as well as a philosophy of work. Setting objectives for work improvement is the first step in this formal approach. The degree to which a company is successful in reaching these objectives will depend for the most part on how carefully the objectives are selected and decided upon. The three basic processes of relating, involvement, and commitment described in earlier chapters apply here.

Investigation and Analysis

The practitioner who has selected an area for improvement should go through a work improvement analysis. This analysis will give him data on cost and estimates of the costs or time that might be saved by his efforts if the situation is improved. The work or methods improvement analysis compares old method values with new method values when it is complete and installed. The time and money required to put the improvement into operation are estimated and recorded. The proposal for improvement, once approved, can be the basis for finding the objective, as described in Chapter 3. To ensure that the results of the analysis are obtained and recorded, it is advisable to set up the analysis in logical steps, using a form similar to that shown in Figure 9-8. Data collected for improving the situation are tabulated so that top management can see the situation at a glance, thus participating in the procedure. This participation is important for the ultimate implementation of the improved procedure. Several techniques are available for assisting the analyst to collect information to make his proposal for a method improvement.

1. *Process analysis.* The process chart is a visual tool for recording and observing an operation or process in the sequence in which it occurs. It organizes the operational steps in a logical system from start to finish. This arrangement allows the operations to be analyzed systematically and critically. It is helpful for analyzing facts and relationships to develop an improved method. It can assist in communicating to others an understanding of the overall problem or overall picture. The five basic activities used in flow process charts are operations, transportation, inspection,

Methods Improvement Analysis

By_____ Dept._____ Date_____

Dwg. No._____ Item No._____

Areas of improvement:

- ☐ Fewer man-hours
- ☐ Lower material costs
- ☐ Increase mach. prod.
- ☐ Safer operation
- ☐ Less scrap
- ☐ Less downtime
- ☐ Lower overhead
- ☐ Less turnover

Old Method

Description:

Operations	Standard Time	Direct Labor Costs	Materials	Material Costs

New Method

Description of change:

Operations	Standard Time	Direct Labor Costs	Materials	Material Costs

Summary

	Material Costs	Direct Labor Costs	Overhead	Total
Old method				
New method				
Savings				
Total savings				

Figure 9-8. **Methods improvement analysis.**

delay, and storage. These are illustrated in Figure 9-9 for a proposed method of assembling pencil slabs. By totaling the types of activities, the distances traveled, and the time consumed, a summary of facts about a situation can be grasped. Improvement is attempted through reducing the number of activities, the distances traveled, or the travel time from station to station. In the summary table of Figure 9-9, the difference column suggests the improvements possible if the old flow processs layout is replaced by the proposed new one.

2. *Systems flow chart.* A flow chart is another useful tool for breaking down a total situation into areas targeted for improvement. The systems flow chart, using flow-charting symbols, shows the direction of flow of information, data, decisions, work, materials, or personnel. Here the flow is analyzed to see how it is processed, what is processed, where it is processed, and when it is processed. Processing refers to handling or manipulation. The analyst checks to see if it is skillful handling and purposeful manipulation. He checks the system to see if the results accomplished are meaningful and efficient. There are many levels of flow charts depicting total systems and many types of flow charts depicting different applications. The art of flow charting is individualistic. Two skillful flow-charters will not set up a flow chart system in the same way although dealing with the same problem. This suggests that there is no absolutely right or wrong way but rather several good ways to depict a system. Computer programming is an application of systems flow charting, and the reader need not be reminded about the many and varied ways of programming a problem as instructions to a computer. Examples of systems flow charts are given in several earlier chapters.

3. *Work simplification.* Work simplification is defined as setting out in an organized manner to find a better and easier way of doing a job. It requires an attitude of mind that always seeks to find a smaller number of simpler motions to execute a job task. It has one vital principle: every detail of a job should be challenged for the purpose of spotting wasted or excessive time, energy, materials, or motion. The questioning attitude and the skills described in an earlier chapter are most important in work simplification. The complacent individual with a closed mind is a major obstacle to simplifying work. These self-imposed limitations on thinking prevent the emergence of alternatives or possible solutions. Work simplification is a systematic way of attacking procedural work layouts for the purpose of increasing the amount of quality work produced in the shortest possible time by making best use of manpower, machines, and material. It deals with the three basic ingredients of a work flow situation: distribution of work; sequence of work; and volume of work.

Flow Process Chart

Job: Assemble slab—wooden pencil

Follow the: ☐ Product ☐ Man ☐ Material ☐ Form

Chart begins: Slabs in storeroom

Chart ends: Assembled and clamped

Chartered by: P.O.E. **Date** 9/29

Summary — 600 Assemblies

	Present No.	Present Time	Proposed No.	Proposed Time	Difference No.	Difference Time
◯ Operations	7	304.8	7	700	–	234.8
⇨ Transportations	10	4.2	4	.5	6	3.7
☐ Inspections	–		1		+1	–
D Delays	–		2		+2	
▽ Storages	3	v	1	v	–2	
Totals	20	309	15	70.5	–5	238.5 (min/lot)
Distance traveled	417 Ft		80 Ft		337 Ft	

No._____ Page_____ Of _____

Details of proposed method

Details of proposed method	Symbols	Distance in feet	Quantity	Est. Time	Notes
1. Stores in storeroom	◯⇨☐D▽				
2. To slotter–groover by hand truck	◯⇨☐D▽	25	1200	.25	Finished stock thinner one box contains 1200 four– stock slabs (2400) (Pencils)
3. Slot cut in bottom and four grooves in top	◉⇨☐D▽		1200	30.00	One pass thru tandem set machines
4. To lead laying machine (one–half lot – see 9)	◯⇨☐D▽	25	600	.13	Hand truck
5. Wait for lead layer	◯⇨☐D▽		600	v	Stock delay between lots all four-grove run be– fore starting next size
6. Loaded in machine magazine	◯⇨☐D▽		600	–	Loaded during machine operation
7. Lead layed in slab	◉⇨☐D▽		600	20.00	Push bar mach. pushes slabs from bottom of mag. under lead hopper
8. Inspected for full leads, moved to topper (see 12)	◯⇨☐D▽				Inspected by machine tender on steel bench slide on way to topper during machine time
9. To glue–topper (one–half lot–see 4)	◯⇨☐D▽	30	600	.15	Hand truck
10. Wait for glue topper	◯⇨☐D▽		600	v	Refer 5
11. Loaded in glue machine magazine	◯⇨☐D▽		600	2.40	Glue-topper loads 25 slabs at time into mag. = 24 loads @ .10 min/load
12. Glued	◉⇨☐D▽		600	–	Push bar mach. pushes slab over glue wheel into topping position
13. Topped and turned	◉⇨☐D▽		600	11.60	Topper places glued slab on leaded slab and turns on edge
14. Assembled slabs clamped by topper	◉⇨☐D▽		600	6.00	Topper clamps unit of 25 assem. slabs = 24 units (Topper paced by layer)
	◯⇨☐D▽				
	◯⇨☐D▽				

Figure 9-9. Flow process chart for assembling pencil slabs.

Methods improvement through work simplification raises questions about job descriptions, job design, and work assignments. Some of these questions are the following:

(a) Are the duties spread too thin?
(b) Is the work load evenly balanced?
(c) Can work operations be reduced? combined?
(d) Are skills of employees used to best advantage?
(e) Is there duplication of duties?
(f) Is too much time being spent on unimportant tasks?
(g) Is the job too complex?

The questions pry loose facts about the work distribution in terms of activities taking the most time, misdirected efforts, too many unrelated tasks, proper utilization of skills, workload on each employee, and conditions that hamper efficiency and enthusiasm. The process chart or systems flow chart can be used as the basis of a work simplification effort. The operation under study is examined step-by-step to reveal ways to make additional improvements. Analysis of time in the operational step-by-step process is a constructive effort toward determining pace and speed of sequence. Simple techniques of time and motion study allow a practitioner to see more clearly the time increments of work distribution. Standard time, normal time, allowed time, lost time, handling time, indirect time, and idle time can be measured in the work distribution for purposes of breaking down the complex into the simple. Motion economy is that part of work improvement concerned with reducing the number of hand motions requiring time and energy. Fundamental consideration of these managerial tools will expand our concept of work simplification and methods improvement.

TRAINING IMPROVEMENT

Most companies of necessity must recruit and hire many employees who do not meet job requirements in many ways. These companies are often forced to place personnel in jobs for which they are only partially qualified. The management of these companies hopes that the individual will acquire the remaining skills necessary to do an outstanding job. Unfortunately, this is a hit and miss proposition that often leads to problems of inefficiency and waste.

The managing by objectives practitioner must accept the fact that training problems not only exist but will always exist if the practice of encouraging performance stretches is followed. Training problems are not to be regarded as extra chores in his many duties. They are part and parcel of his job if he seeks improvements. The practitioner will find his operations running smoothly, his costs low, and new customers coming when he has a well-trained and skillful staff.

1. *Indicators[15] of the need for training within a company*

   (a) Gross sales leveling off or declining
   (b) Material or labor cost percentages rising
   (c) Percentage of overhead expense increasing
   (d) Number and type of customer complaints increasing
   (e) Waste excessive
   (f) Pilferage and stealing high
   (g) Errors in filling orders
   (h) High frequency of bottlenecks and poor storage
   (i) Equipment breakdowns excessive
   (j) Excessive time needed to complete a job
   (k) Excessive absenteeism, tardiness, or resignations
   (l) Repairs continually needed
   (m) Maintenance costs high
   (n) Time to take and fill a customer order high

These indicators should flag the practitioner that something is wrong. Although it might be a number of things, the practitioner will generally find that people are involved and are probably causing these problems. Providing training to employees, if the employees are improvable, can be a solution. The need for training can be discovered through budget and variance reports, operations reports, performance ratings, observations, face-to-face dialogues, and customer complaints.

Once improvement needs have been identified, actions should be planned to correct and meet these needs. Advantages will be gained for both the supervisor and the employee: for the supervisor, sales targets and costs budgets are met; for the employee, feelings of self-respect and confidence are developed.

2. *The training cycle.* Training is not imparting information. This is only one of the steps. It is providing a series of stimulating informative experiences for an employee to adjust his performance toward an objective or goal. The first step is to establish the goal to be reached by training, and subsequent steps are to identify the needs, plan the experiences, conduct the training, evaluate the results, and retrain if need be. These steps are illustrated in the training cycle of Figure 9-10. The training cycle contains steps from beginning to end. It starts with training needs revealed by operational deficiencies and ends with results improvements

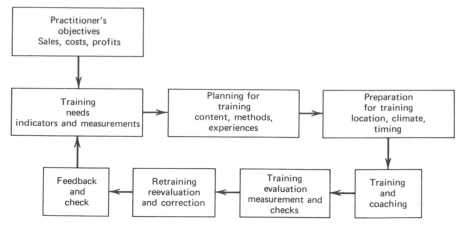

Figure 9-10.   The training cycle.

specified within an objective. The advantages of a systematic and deliberate approach to training over trial-and-error methods are that it shortens learning time, reduces errors, forces a higher level of achievement, and permits the company to have more confidence in the trainee. The managing by objectives practitioner should systemize his training activities to ensure that his training responsibilities are completely and confidently carried out. Figures 9-11, 9-12, and 9-13 are some suggested logical approaches to systemizing the training effort. Homer Rose puts it this way:

A plan of training and instructions should be directed toward requirements of the job. Training methods, approaches, aids and techniques must be coordinated toward eliminating a deficiency within an organization.[16]

3. *On-the-job training.* Probably most of all training in business and industry is man-to-man on-the-job training. This has proved to be the most useful technique in teaching a specific job. Job instruction training (JIT)[17] is a formalization of this technique that can be used at all skill levels. The JIT procedure is the following:

1. Preparation
   (a) Know precisely what training is required (set objectives).
   (b) Set up a training-activity timetable.
   (c) Prepare information, procedures, or skills to be demonstrated.
   (d) Select training aids most useful for the training.
   (e) Decide on where training should take place.
   (f) Decide on who will train and answer questions.

2. Get set
   (a) Put the employees to be trained at ease.

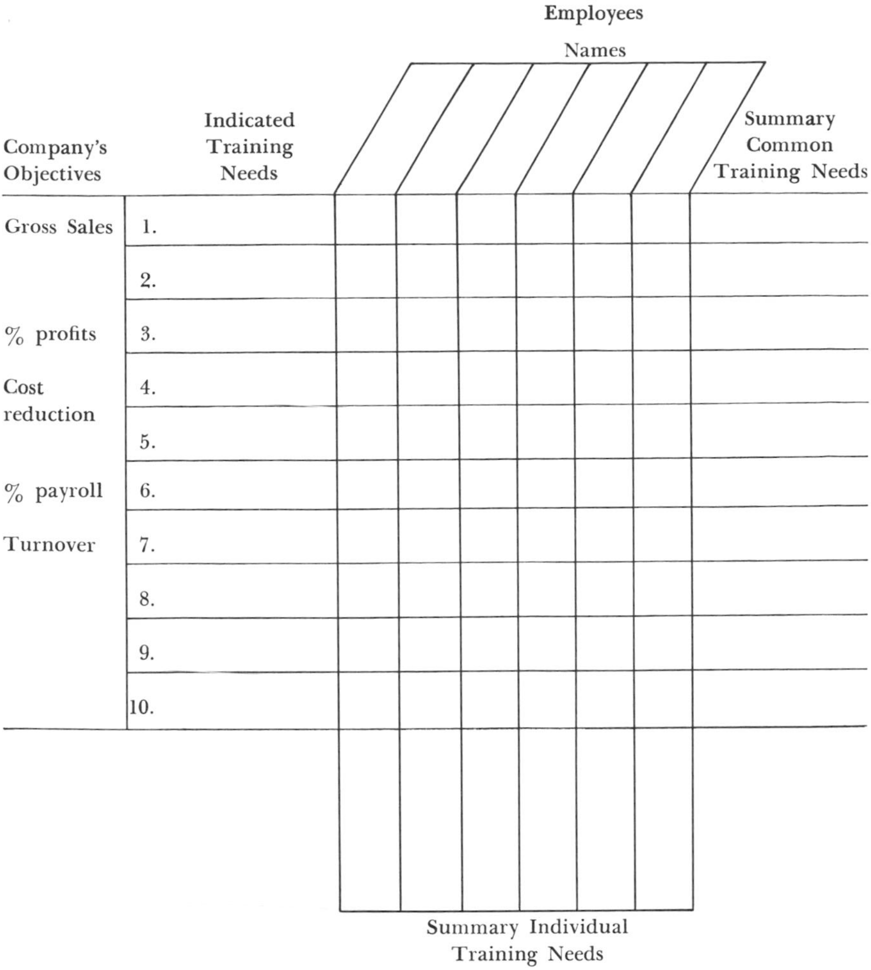

Employees

Names

Company's Objectives	Indicated Training Needs							Summary Common Training Needs
Gross Sales	1.							
	2.							
% profits	3.							
Cost reduction	4.							
	5.							
% payroll	6.							
Turnover	7.							
	8.							
	9.							
	10.							

Summary Individual
Training Needs

Figure 9-11. Determining deficiencies of company as training needs.

(b) Emphasize the importance of doing the job correctly.
(c) Arouse the employees' interest in learning.
(d) Control all environmental factors that may distract or interfere.

3. Instruct
(a) *Manager explains* what is to be done and why. He points out the key points that make the operation easier and faster.
(b) *Manager demonstrates* while workers observe. By questioning, make sure the workers are following you. Repeat points that may not be clear.

Training Project Number	Who Will Be Trained?	What Is Needed?	How Can It Be Achieved?	By What Date? (Completion)	Responsibility Check-off

Figure 9-12. **Plan and act on deficiencies.**

    (c) *Manager lets workers try* while he observes. He points out mistakes and praises what they do well.

    (d) *Manager repeats demonstration* where workers did not do well. Workers observe and are questioned. He repeats points that may not have been clear.

    (e) *Manager lets workers try again.* Avoid proceeding too rapidly. Be patient. Remember, everyone was once a beginner.

    (f) *Manager puts workers on their own.* Let the employees perform at will. Assign a senior fellow worker to help the new employee when the occasion demands.

4. Check and follow-up

    (a) Performance results must meet the objectives set in the unit, such as gross sales, customer satisfaction, costs control, and better time.

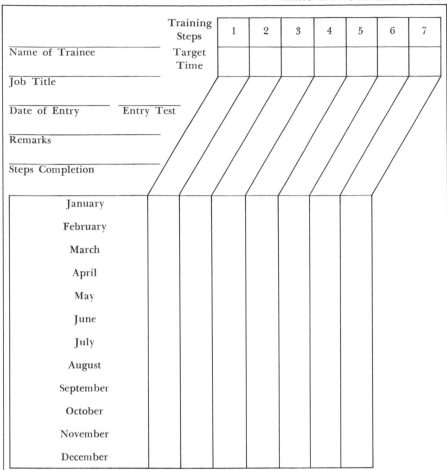

Figure 9-13. **Keep training progress and follow-up on individual.**

(b) Manager from time to time checks objectives of his unit with the performance level of employees.

(c) Frequent follow-up of an employee is a must.

(d) Prepare and schedule improvement training.

The practitioner should never be satisfied with the level of performance he is getting from his employees. If sales are to grow, performance must grow proportionately. Improvement training is not necessarily for correcting employees. Rather, it is designed to increase the number of results and the frequency of reaching new sets of results.

5. Guidelines for effective on-the-job training

(a) The manager is the best choice to conduct training. Workers see him as the boss and regard what he says and does as most important.

(b) To be a good trainer, the manager must first know the content of the job in which the worker is to be trained. Additionally, he must know how to train, as described in the JIT procedure.

(c) The manager must recognize that each individual is different in learning ability. Some will learn fast, some slowly. Learning rates vary with each individual. Give the slow learners time to pick up their training.

(d) The manager should recognize that learning rates vary with the type of tasks involved. Single-skill motor abilities can be acquired with fast learning time. Complex skills, both mental and motor, will be acquired at a slower rate.

(e) The manager must recognize the value of motivation in the learning process. When employees understand how and why training will benefit them personally, interest will develop and they will want to learn.

(f) The manager must space the training. Workers will learn more rapidly if their instruction is spaced over several short periods rather than concentrated in one.

(g) The manager will find the worker more ready to learn if the worker feels and understands the need for training.

(h) The manager will find training in one thing at a time best for learning concentration. Stick to a principal training objective until the trainee has learned how to do it.

(i) The manager should let the trainee correct himself. Do not overdo correction. Correction is like seasoning, a little goes a long way and too much spoils the dish.

(j) The manager must train so as to encourage the worker. Do not correct him in front of others. Do not be quick to blame the trainee. Compliment the worker after a performance step has been properly executed.

SUMMARY

The mission of improvement is generic to the managerial function. Managers should never be content with the state of affairs. They should never rest on their laurels; rather, they should search for new plateaus of accomplishment. The mission of improvement must be the very foundation for any planning effort. It must recognize a simple truth: even though the future of a company is uncertain, the company must act and react to make itself better than it has been in the past.

There are many approaches to improvement. Some are primarily concerned with obtaining improvement in the efficiency of using direct labor. Some are primarily concerned with the application of a new technology. Still others are concerned with material utilization and cost. The possibilities for improvement are endless in an enterprise. The principal move on management's part is to reach and achieve improvement where it is needed. Repetitive thrusting can be achieved by continually planning and making improvements.

This chapter dealt with a selected few of the many areas of an enterprise that a practitioner of managing by objectives may pursue: profit improvement; sales improvement; cost improvement; management time improvement; communications improvement; methods improvement; and training improvement. A unified approach to improvement within an organization is possible with the conceptual strategy of managing by objectives.

REFERENCES AND NOTES

1. The Peter Principle is an alternate view of this same condition. See Laurence J. Peter and Raymond Hull, *Peter Principle*, Bantam Books, 1969.

2. Phil Carroll, *Profit Control: How To Plug Profit Leaks*, McGraw-Hill Book Co., New York, 1962, pp. 1–17.

3. Edward C. Bursk and John F. Chapman, *Modern Marketing Strategy*, New American Library, New York, 1964, pp. 1–69.

4. Robert W. Ferrell, *Customer-Oriented Planning*, American Management Association, New York, 1964, p. 28.

5. John D. Staley, *The Cost-Minded Manager*, American Management Association, New York, 1961, pp. 17–20.

6. Murphy W. Bradhurst, "Cutting Costs: Get Everyone in the Act," *Cost Control and the Supervisor*, American Management Association, New York, 1956, p. 30.

7. Saul D. Astor, "Plant Security," *Handbook of Business Administration*, McGraw-Hill Book Co., New York, 1967, pp. 7; 185–195.

8. Northcote C. Parkinson, *op. cit.*, p. 12.

9. James T. McCay, *The Management of Time*, Prentice-Hall, Englewood Cliffs, N.J., 1959, pp. 157–168.

10. Robert R. Updegraff, *All the Time You Need*, Prentice-Hall, Englewood Cliffs, N.J., 1958, p. 6.

11. Ralph G. Nichols and Leonard A. Stevens, *Are You Listening?* McGraw-Hill Book Co., New York, 1957, p. 6.

12. A more detailed discussion of barriers to communications is given in *Are You Listening? op. cit.*

13. The idea of zone of acceptance and rejection has been borrowed from probability and statistical inferences of the normal curve. The range of these zones varies with each individual. In large aggregates 68, 95, and 99 percent will fall in different standard deviations. See Hanson and Brabb, *Managerial Statistics,* Prentice-Hall, Englewood Cliffs, N.J., 1955, p. 87.

14. Ralph M. Barnes, *Motion and Time Study,* John Wiley, New York, 1966.

15. Needs for training are as individualistic as the organizations themselves. The list suggested is a sample.

16. Homer C. Rose, *The Development and Supervision of Training Programs,* American Technical Society, New York, 1964, pp. 5; 9; 74.

17. Homer C. Rose, *op. cit.,* p. 253.

Index